The Best Canadian Essays 2010

THE BEST CANADIAN ESSAYS 2010

Edited by ALEX BOYD & KAMAL AL-SOLAYLEE

Tightrope Books

Tightrope Books
602 Markham Street
Toronto, Ontario
M6G 2L8 Canada
www.TightropeBooks.com

ONTARIO ARTS COUNCIL
CONSEIL DES ARTS DE L'ONTARIO

Canada Council
for the Arts

Conseil des Arts
du Canada

COPYEDITOR: Alanna Lipson
COVER DESIGN: Karen Correia Da Silva
TYPESETTING: Shirarose Wilensky

Produced with the support of the Canada Council for the Arts and the Ontario Arts Council.

Printed in Canada.

LIBRARY AND ARCHIVES CANADA CATALOGUING IN PUBLICATION

The best Canadian essays, 2010 / editors: Kamal Al-Solaylee and Alex Boyd.

ISBN 978-1-926639-17-8

1. Canadian essays (English)—21st century. I. Al-Solaylee, Kamal II. Boyd, Alex, 1969-

PS8373.I.B48 2009   C814'.608   C2009-903915-X

CONTENTS

INTRODUCTION

WHEN 2009 WAS ONLY a few weeks old, the world was still reel-
ing from the worst financial crisis since the Great Depression. The
word "recovery"—the theme of the latter half of 2009—seemed
more like wishful thinking than a reality. Still, some economists
and business journalists seem to think that Canada was spared
the banking meltdowns and real-estate collapse that brought the
American economy—and the British, the Irish, Icelandic, you
name it—to its knees. Our conservative banking system, we were
told, saved us from the financial meltdown.

Out-of-work Canadians and cultural workers who've seen their
already-meagre funding disappear before their eyes may disagree

with this rosy picture, but as editors of *The Best Canadian Essays 2010*, we have ample evidence to suggest that as the world turned, ushering in a cycle of penny-pinching and overspending (a.k.a. stimulus), Canadian magazine writers managed to invest their capital in a range of timely and timeless stories. The economy may have dictated newspaper headlines, but introspection and social and environmental concerns gave our writers a chance to examine a bigger picture—one that transcends the ups and downs of trading indexes, banking scandals, and the increasing popularity of the frugality cult.

The anthology you're about to read captures a year in the life of Canada through the eyes of some of its best essayists. For a few, the word "essay" conjures up images of returning to school and being forced to write about your summer vacation, but we're out to prove it isn't a dirty word. These essays cover everything from dogsled racing up north to urban attempts to beat the aging process. Our writers contemplate subjects as personal as faith and as large as environmental Armageddon. This is writing loaded with good observations and ideas.

Still, it's a tricky thing to put together an anthology like the one you hold in your hands. Canada has a handful of general-interest magazines such as *The Walrus* and *Maisonneuve*, and beyond these a couple of editors can only take a sincere, laboured, and flawed stab at covering as many special-interest titles as they can. Despite our best attempts to represent a cross-section of Canada's diverse ethnicities and cultures, we still ended up with a largely white and mostly male selection. Many Canadian magazines remain—as has been pointed out of dailies in the past—as white as the paper they're printed on, and there are undoubtedly more men writing (or at least publishing) feature articles. Why did a culture that nurtured the talents of writers such as Vassanji, Brand, and Ondaatje in the literary world fail to spot, nurture, and give a platform to their feature-writing counterparts? We think this diversity gap is a reflection of the general media landscape in Canada, which remains predominately white and, outside of fashion and design titles, male-centric. Still, as evidenced by stories about illegal immigration, Nunavut, and the Iranian Revolution in this volume, there's considerable interest in stories about the full range of our communities, and giving some of them a second appearance is another goal of a book like *The Best Canadian Essays*.

At what may prove to be a critical time in history, Canada stands at something of a crossroads, looking one way and then the other. For decades we've formally embraced cultural diversity and a social support system, but more conservative politicians now seem to have enough momentum to continually stalemate those who'd support more progressive policies. As we've edited an anthology of 2009 material, 2010 has started to unfold and we've already seen unprecedented environmental disaster and the biggest mass arrests in Canadian history sharing the headlines with continued speculation about economic recovery. When and if it comes, that recovery will make life possible, but a compassionate society will make life worth living. Just as support for clean energy and sustainable living needs to be paid more than lip service, so does our support for diversity, which—despite conservative hints to the contrary—is a unifying experience. It encourages readers and writers to look for the unique in a community but brings the commonality to the fore. Canadians often speak of solitudes and massive landmass that make connections physically and psychologically difficult, if not impossible. This isolation has led to scattered regional magazines and has left a gap when it comes to truly national general-interest publications.

We have precious few magazines acting as our nation's intellectual conscience. As the once-venerable *Maclean's* continues to cater to an ultraconservative agenda, Canadians are looking to American publications (*The New Yorker*, *Harper's*, *Vanity Fair*) for mental inspiration and social aspiration. Advocates of citizen journalism and the democratization of media (see Ira Basen's "Citizen Uprising" for a sobering account) may see the general-interest magazine going the same way as the morning paper or bottled milk delivered to your door, but we prefer to resist this trend. As the federal government tinkers with arts funding so that magazines must have an arbitrary circulation number to be deemed worthy of support, we're forced to wonder what effect this will have on various magazines, and the possibilities when it comes to producing a book like this. If the federal government is going to assume quantity means quality (and some Canadian magazines have been described as having the print run of a "well-edited church newsletter"), perhaps they'll invest in a new general-interest magazine that helps pick up some of the slack.

Aside from supporting books like this one, Canadians need to support our magazines, even as hardworking and stressed editors need to struggle for gender balance and diversity of opinion. If most Canadian households subscribed to even one magazine, it would make a tremendous difference. There are, no doubt, some very articulate bloggers in Canada, but as they're somewhat lost in a daily avalanche of online material, it's doubtful that blogging can be the only answer or the best solution in terms of nuanced accounts of issues that are important but aren't frequently picked up by the mainstream media. Essays like the ones in this anthology can only see the light of day in a magazine structure where ideas are pitched and developed, and stories are written, rewritten, edited, and re-edited to create a narrative that may take minutes to read but leaves an impact that can't be measured in time or influence.

Kamal Al-Solaylee & Alex Boyd
TORONTO
2010

The Best Canadian Essays 2010

SKIN DEEP

KATHERINE ASHENBURG
Vancouver Magazine

DR. ALASTAIR CARRUTHERS, NAMED by the *Observer* as one of the "50 men who really understand women," is sitting in a room papered with his diplomas, certificates, and publications. He calls it—wryly—the Credibility Room, and credibility is important to him. He explains that he's had his vertical frown lines removed so as not to look threatening, but the horizontal lines in his forehead are okay for a man, as they suggest curiosity and involvement. Maybe there's something to this; he certainly looks trustworthy when he says, "There's no putting the genie back in the bottle." The genie is Botox, whose wrinkle-busting talents he and his wife, Jean, discovered in 1987. Since then, it's become a billion-dollar

industry, North America's number one cosmetic procedure, and
the inspiration behind a crowded new generation of fillers, intense
pulsed light and radio-frequency therapies, and other age-fighting
products. This husband-and-wife team, you could argue, has
played a major role in reshaping our notion of beauty.

Given all that, one might expect the Carruthers' Broadway
offices in Vancouver to be rather grand, with wide hallways and,
perhaps, lashings of granite. They are far from that. They're located
in a stocky, no-nonsense 1970s building between Oak and Laurel.
Jean's office, on the seventh floor, is a feminine warren of small
rooms, with creamy brocade wing chairs and a framed thank-you
note from the Queen in the waiting room. (The Carruthers guard
their patients' confidentiality religiously, and the note refers to
congratulations sent on the Queen's eightieth birthday.) Alastair's
eighth-floor suite is roomier and more masculine, with grey and
brown chairs that would suit a boardroom, and a framed note
from Katharine Hepburn. (He met her when Jean treated her
for an ophthalmological condition and she wrote Jean, "Very
handsome husband!") Everything is immaculate and comfortable,
but designed to be reassuring rather than impressive.

Somehow that fits with the whole Botox founding legend,
which is low-key, even familial. In 1987, Alastair was a dermatolo-
gist who divided his practice between surgery for skin cancer and
cosmetic dermatology. He shared his office with Jean, an ophthalmologist who treated pediatric disorders as well as adult conditions
such as blepharospasm. An uncontrollable blinking and spasming
of the eye and surrounding area, blepharospasm was treated with
injections of a dilute solution of a botulinum toxin, which tem-
porarily paralyzes the relevant muscles. (Although botulinum, the
source of botulism, is the most acutely toxic substance known, its
ophthalmological use, in minute quantities, had been established

several years before.) One day, in Jean's account, one of her blepharospasm patients became irate that her forehead was not being
injected. "But your forehead isn't spasming," Jean responded, and
asked why she cared. "Because when you inject my forehead," the
patient said, "my wrinkles go away."

At dinner that night, Jean mentioned the woman's reaction
to Alastair. He and his dermatology patients were frustrated in
their attempt to erase vertical frown lines between the eyebrows,
known to doctors as glabellar lines—the fillers available at the
time didn't last long and could be painful. But dinner in those
days— their sons were then aged six, eight, and nine—was not
conducive to concentration, and Alastair remembers, "The comment went straight over my head." Next day, Jean talked their
receptionist, Cathy Bickerton, into being the first guinea pig for
the cosmetic use of botulinum toxin. Once Alastair saw the frown-
less Bickerton, he needed no persuasion. "I had the patients," he
says, summing up what would become one of the most successful
symbioses in late-twentieth-century cosmetic medicine, "and Jean
had the toxin."

Both expected the world to embrace their discovery. Instead,
says Jean, the typical reaction was "You want to inject what into my
wrinkles?" At this point, Jean injected herself, whence her famous
boast that she hasn't frowned since 1987. When they presented
their results at the American Society for Dermatologic Surgery
meeting in Orlando in 1991, she remembers, medical friends told
them it was "a crazy idea that's going nowhere." They continued
conducting clinical trials, although it was difficult to find willing
patients, and presenting their findings at dermatology meetings,
watching their audience size grow from small to medium.

The snowball effect started in 1993, when three doctors in the
audience at the American Academy of Dermatology had actually

used Botox, as it was now called. As Botox swept the world, Jean qualified as a cosmetic surgeon; she now does mostly head and neck procedures, and treats very few ophthalmological patients. Her husband says her transformation has been so complete that, in a group of dermatologists, "they forget she's not one of us." He stopped doing cancer surgery, and now does full-body liposuction as well as head and neck cosmetic procedures. Botox was, as Jean says, "a three-year overnight success story."

Wearing slim black pants and a tiered purple vest over a black blouse, Dr. Jean Carruthers has mildly spiky hair and perfect red nails. She leads me into her bright corner office. I study the pictures of her three sons—an architect in New York City, a neurology resident in Boston, and a business student in Toronto—while she calls a restaurant and arranges for "a bottle of Dom" to be delivered to a birthday celebration that weekend that she and Alastair can't attend. As she dictates warm wishes, I remember the last time I saw her, about thirty years ago.

My daughter, then six, had an optical problem, and we were referred to a young pediatric ophthalmologist in a dowdy office on Commercial Drive. I remember Carruthers as taller and bigger than she is now, English (or so I thought), and not a woman who paid much attention to fashion. I would never have recognized her in this petite, chic woman, although I do recognize the light, rapid voice and the mid-Atlantic accent. I also recall that she had a nice, uncondescending way with my daughter, and that her explanations to me were models of clarity.

No doubt she was already a rather unusual combination: a maternal superachiever. She traces her "deep desire to nurture," as she puts it, to her childhood dog, to the family's horses, and to the caring environment her parents produced. Whatever its source, it's still in evidence: she hugs her staff hello and goodbye daily, sends her patients birthday cards, brings bagels for medical students who shadow her, loves to cook and entertain, hosts a Thanksgiving dinner for "waifs and strays."

The achiever part is not hard to explain. She was born Jean Elliott in Brandon, Manitoba, to two English doctors who had emigrated after World War Two. When her mother, a GP, decided to do a year's training in England to become a radiologist, she took her two young daughters with her. Jean found school in England so demanding that when she returned to Canada, she was advanced a year into Grade 4. The English sojourn, she says, was a turning point, giving her a taste for striving that has stayed with her. At sixteen she went into honours chemistry at UBC, and she remained there for medical school.

After graduation in 1971, she wanted to stay at UBC for an ophthalmology residency, but female surgeons were rare and she was given the distinct impression that her application would not be particularly welcome. In any case, by then she had met an English medical student who was doing an internship at Vancouver General. Both Carruthers agree that Jean is the decisive one in the couple; Alastair tends to ruminate. She demonstrated this the night they met at a UBC mixer and spent two hours talking. At the end of the evening, Alastair said they should have dinner sometime. Jean answered immediately, "That would be nice. When?" That was the moment, he says, that captured him.

Born in Cheshire in 1945, Alastair was also the child of a doctor father; his mother was a teacher. He and Jean went to England for their residencies and married in the chapel of Brasenose, Alastair's Oxford college, in 1973. Jean became one of the first women to work at Moorfields, England's premier eye hospital, and Alastair had a prestigious appointment at Hammersmith Hospital. They might have stayed in London's stimulating medical atmosphere

permanently, but consultants there worked until nine or ten at
night. They wanted children, and Vancouver promised a more bal-
anced life. "We gave up the academic excellence of London for the
whole family thing," Alastair says, "and yet I think we've managed
to do quite a lot."

An understatement. Before Botox, the Carruthers had each
already accumulated a career's worth of laurels. Since their concentration on cosmetic medicine, their hefty résumés now include
more than 100 new articles in peer-reviewed medical journals,
sixty book chapters, and five textbooks. Travelling the world, they
give about thirty talks a year, to dermatologists and cosmetic and
plastic surgeons. The Carruthers' kingdom includes a research in-
stitute (in the same building as their offices) that coordinates their
studies on new products and procedures. (A recent one, funded by
the pharmaceutical company Allergan, investigated the eyelash-
growing potential of the eyedrops used to treat glaucoma.) All
told, they employ about ten people—nurses, researchers, admin-
istrators, patient-care coordinators. People often ask them why
they maintain separate offices, and Jean says, "Because we prefer
to stay married." It goes back to their differing styles and speeds—
Jean full of drive and Alastair more reflective. "It works out fine at
home," Jean says, "but not in the office."

Cosmetic medicine demands a personal touch. Sydney, one of
Alastair's few male patients, praises his literal touch: "He's not fuss-
ing—it's precise and confident and quick and it's over. As a makeup artist, I know what it feels like when someone is insecure—you
can feel it in their hands. You don't get that from Alastair."

Making the procedures as painless as possible is another part of
the job, and the Carruthers use topical anaesthetics, dental blocks,
or needles inside the mouth to dull the nerves, and a medical
massager designed to prevent the brain from feeling pain. Jean

plays classical music and talks nonstop to distract the patient; her nurses, two of whom worked in obstetrics, are available for hand-holding.

It all helps to ensure return visits. If you've kept a patient comfortable while fixing one thing, Jean says, "something else starts to bother them." On the follow-up visit after a procedure, she hears new comments about lips or neck or cheeks that need attention. The doctor-patient bond in the cosmetic world, she says, lasts thirty to forty years: "We're talking about family." It's such an intimate relationship that getting a locum in is impossible. And when a patient absents herself for a while, the doctor is sympathetic: some patients are struggling with aging parents and have no time for themselves, Jean says, while others are spacing out some of the larger procedures because of the recession. The Carruthers' staff are crucial to this bond, and each has a coordinator of patient care. Jean's is Barbara Kelly, Miss Canada of 1967; when workaholic patients have an early-morning procedure, Kelly covers any bruises with professional makeup, and the women are at their desks by the start of the business day.

Jean says admiringly that the staff all look like "after pictures," a reference to the before-and-after photos they take for their records. Does that mean the young beauties at the clinic, all helpful and efficient—? She answers my question before I finish it: "It's important that all of us in the office are . . . I'm going to say 'users.' " When she interviews a job applicant, she's careful to get a sense of how open the person is to the idea, asking if she's ever had cosmetic work or considered it. "What message does it give if Christa [Campsall, the clinic coordinator] can say, 'Oh, I've done crow's feet and frowns'?" Staff are treated for free, since it's to the Carruthers' benefit if everyone in the office not only looks good but is a source of reassurance.

Campsall, a friendly, statuesque brunette, agrees that it's much easier for her to put a patient at ease now that she's had Botox and Restylane tissue fillers. When she started managing the clinic seven years ago she was only thirty-two, and the other staff would tease her, reminding Jean, "Christa's still a Botox virgin." She hadn't been there long before she volunteered to be injected, to soften her "really strong frown," her crow's feet, and her smile lines. She's had her lips puffed up a few times, too. A Botox virgin myself, I'm surprised—outside of Los Angeles, Miami, pockets of Manhattan, and the middle-class suburbs of Latin America, I thought you waited until you were middle-aged before starting these procedures. Campsall shrugs. Her husband was a little disapproving when she began treatments, she says, but he's gotten used to his unlined wife and now occasionally asks her if it isn't time for another round. "There is a certain look" about the staff, she admits, adding that free work is a perk—"I've had thousands of dollars of treatments."

Jean Carruthers is too canny not to understand that she herself is the main poster girl for their office. She's matter-of-fact about the procedures she's had: a complete face-lift ten years ago, lid lifts, Botox, fillers ("I lost thirty pounds five years ago"), Thermage, and intense-pulse light treatments. Most cosmetic procedures aren't permanent: gradually, gravity will relax or undermine (depending on your point of view) a face-lift; Botox and fillers eventually dissolve. So perhaps I saw her at the tail end of some procedures, but I liked her face. True, it has the very slightly masked or veiled effect that cosmetic work can produce, but it has enough subtle creases that it looks appropriately lived-in for an attractive woman of sixty-one.

She's also matter-of-fact about costs. Botox runs $16 a unit and most people require 30 units, close to $500. Restylane, one of the best-known fillers, used for lip augmentation and for injection into wrinkles and facial folds, costs $600 a syringe (one millilitre); most patients use three or four syringes. Botox and the fillers, as well as the newer thermal treatments, all need to be repeated, sometimes every three or six months. Jean tells her patients, "Think of a nice handbag or several manicures."

When I ask her if she thinks of Botox as a watershed in her career, or if she sees the last thirty-five years as a continuum, her answer is typically savvy. It's a continuum, she says, because it's all about the patients. In pediatric ophthalmology, she learned how to win the child's trust and how to explain things to a child's parents, so that they could make decisions. Now, the mothers and aunts of her pediatric patients come to her for cosmetic work.

Not surprisingly, she has ready answers for the hard questions about her practice. She sees herself as being in the business of restoring self-esteem, and "there's no higher calling." Like it or not, she says, we're hard-wired to be attracted to beauty. Beautiful people earn more money, and people who look after their appearance have better cardiovascular health and live longer. She's not interested in transcending the wish to look as good as possible: "Freud used to take people with baggy eyelids and send them to therapy. That's so negative." Better to use Botox, which she has called "penicillin for self-esteem."

Asked if she feels part of a climate that makes people unhappy about aging naturally, she answers, "What is aging naturally?" Then she adds, "It's a choice. In 2005, I sold my car and I ride a hybrid bike and take the bus and walk—that was a choice. There's always going to be a spectrum." She likes the story of a young woman who excoriated her aunt, one of Jean's patients, for having had Botox. The aunt listened to the lengthy scolding, and responded with two words: "Just wait."

Cassandra, a patient of Jean's, equates the procedures she's had with exercising and taking her vitamins: "They are part of my wellness package, and psychological wellness is not to be underestimated." She agrees there may be too much pressure to look young, but on the other hand it's better for a woman who's gotten "kicked to the curb in a divorce" to be able to feel good about herself. When I ask if she thinks cosmetic work could help that woman, she widens her eyes in a "Duh!" look. A "workaholic professional," Cassandra has a pleasant, unlined face and sunny blond hair cut in a pageboy. Had she not told me that she's fifty-six, I would have taken her to be in her late twenties.

Sydney, Alastair's patient, also in his fifties, rattles off the fillers he's used. Unlike the unblinkingly descriptive Botox—a contraction of "botulinum toxin"—these newer names shimmer with promise: Radiesse, Evolence, Juvéderm, Dermalive. "I'm plastic from the neck up!" he jokes, but adds, "I just want to maintain the way I was at thirty-five, and I started in time to make that believable. These lips aren't new; they're what I had in my thirties." A professional in what he calls a "youth-obsessed industry," Sydney is a discriminating user, keeping his horizontal forehead lines because he wants to look expressive. He praises Alastair's conservative approach: "You'll never leave his office with dolphin lips." Last year, to mark their ten-year anniversary, Alastair sent him a bottle of wine.

Most people assume that the Carruthers' discovery of Botox made them rich. Jean was interested in patenting their idea, but Alastair was not. When he trained in the UK, he says, "we learned that if you have an idea you give it away." Jean prevailed, and they consulted a Toronto patent lawyer. He advised them, incorrectly, that it wasn't patentable. Allergan marketed Botox, and today no one holds the patent, as it's in the public domain.

These days, Alastair has changed his mind about patenting discoveries, but neither Carruthers seems to spend much time regretting a lost fortune. True, their income has risen significantly now that they are concentrating on cosmetic medicine: they live in Shaughnessy and travel widely, to visit their sons, to bicycle in the Basque country, to see the ruins in Turkey. Alastair says that after thirty years of doing what he calls "straight medicine," he's paid his dues: "I gave society back what it gave me in education. If I'd started out doing cosmetic medicine right after medical school, I'd feel less proud."

Are some non-cosmetic doctors critical of his career shift? "That I used to save lives, and now I get rid of wrinkles?" He nods. Apparently he's made his peace with that. He prefers thinking about all the research he and Jean have done to make cosmetic medicine "academically respectable." When I ask him about being part of a sensibility that pushes people to try to stay young forever, he pauses. Finally, he says, "I think my job is to help people to be themselves." He tells a story of a psychologist, in the early days of Botox, who accused the Carruthers of giving everyone the same expressionless McLook. "I felt bad for about two weeks until I realized that he was totally wrong—we were allowing people to express themselves." Patients do come in with pictures of film stars' lips, he says, but he refuses to turn them into someone else.

Musing about people's negative attitudes to cosmetic medicine, he says, "Where do you draw the line between wanting to look your best and something that's too extreme? Right now, for example, I'm looking at Katherine . . ." For a split second, I wonder if he's going to point out the many ways his procedures could improve me. But he's far too smart—and probably too much a gentleman. "I'm looking at Katherine," he goes on, "and I notice that she has highlights in her hair. Where do you draw the line between normal grooming and something else?"

It's a good question. For me, a potent but unstable brew of warmed-over feminism (why are 90 percent of the Carruthers' patients women, while we admire men's seamed and furrowed faces?), egalitarianism (why should the well-off be able to buy the semblance of youth when the poor cannot?), nostalgia (can't we turn the clock back to the days when people believed there was beauty at every age?), and—maybe most of all—needlephobia has me drawing the line well before anything that involves injections. As for Alastair himself, he's had his frown lines and underarms Botoxed, and that's it. Although "it hurts like hell," having his underarms done means that he doesn't sweat while speaking in public. He injects the armpits of about 10 percent of his patients, including many teenagers, for that purpose.

Where's all this leading? "The Holy Grail," says Alastair, "is skin tightening and in a simple, safe, effective manner." He expects to see a Botox cream before too long, and is bullish about the long, thick eyelashes produced by the drops for glaucoma. Jean also sees good things on the horizon—new neurotoxins will give Botox a run for its money, she believes, and fillers will be developed that don't just fill in cracks but encourage skin tightening. Also, Thermage will get better at shrinking skin.

In their sixties, the Carruthers remain awesomely vigorous. They're up by 5 a.m. to exercise in their home gym, and they've taken up golf and bicycling. Alastair is an enophile who relishes his post as the Grand Pilier of the Canadian Confrérie des Chevaliers du Tastevin, a French organization that promotes the wines of Burgundy. But the promise of new developments entices them more than retirement. Jean compares her vantage point on cosmetic medicine to that of Cosimo de' Medici, the Renaissance founder of a political dynasty. She can't imagine retiring: "I'm having too much fun." Her patient Cassandra shakes her head, disbelieving and even alarmed at the thought of the Carruthers closing up shop: "The good work they do for their patients, they should work until they're 110."

CITIZEN UPRISING

IRA BASEN
Maisonneuve

THIRTY-SEVEN SECONDS LONG, it opens with the cameraphone swooping in on a man trying to stanch a young woman's chest wound. She's lying on her back, wearing jeans, blood streaming from her nose and mouth. In her last moments, she seems to stare straight at the viewer.

Filmed on a Tehran street on Saturday, June 20, 2009, and posted to the Internet within minutes, the grisly video quickly spread from site to site. Seven days earlier, President Mahmoud Ahmadinejadhad had been re-elected in "the most free election in the world." But his opponents were still marching in the streets to protest the result. Events were not unfolding the way the country's regime anticipated. So it did what governments, both authoritarian and democratic, have done for over a century: it kicked out the press. If there's something you'd rather keep hidden, then deny access to anyone who has the power to expose it.

Well, not so fast. The government could bar foreign reporters from working inside the country, confine them to their hotel rooms, even put them on a plane back home. But it proved to be much more difficult extending the same control over Iranian citizens, many of whom were using cellphones to take pictures, shoot videos, and text-message directly from the front lines, then uploading the results to Facebook, YouTube, and Twitter.

Back in the US, the talking head on CNN was excited. Working at breakneck speed and in run-on sentences, he realized the technology that allowed the images he was seeing—fires in the street, stones hurled at helmeted police, tear gas—was a very big deal, almost as big as the story itself.

> *. . . and we're going to keep following these things and pretty much before I pop on air we grab things that have come on literally within seconds, grab them, put them into a format that you can see them and share them with you on air because the Twitter universe I'll tell you, is playing an historic and amazing role in what's been going on . . .*

If that anchor had gone to journalism school, he probably would have read a textbook called *The Elements of Journalism*, by Bill Kovach and Tom Rosenstiel. And he probably would have been told to pay special attention to this sentence: "In the end, the discipline of verification is what separates journalism from entertainment, propaganda, fiction, or art."

But that day, the "discipline of verification" was breaking down throughout the mainstream media. Journalism has always been a hyper-competitive business. Editors and reporters have been known to go to great lengths to beat the competition to a scoop. But with more than a billion video-equipped mobile devices in circulation around the world, the first news and images of disaster—riots, plane crashes, bombings, nasty weather—now almost always come from citizens. In 2008, CNN even created a website called iReport where viewers could post their unfiltered, unedited and unverified "news" stories.

And if journalists happen to be first on the scene, exercising the "discipline of verification" usually doesn't happen quickly. It takes time to make sure you are, to quote again from *The Elements of Journalism*, "getting what happened down right." So even the nimblest, most resourceful newsrooms can appear old and plodding when measured against upload speeds.

Which is why, when confronted with amateur video of the apparent death of an innocent protester, and with CNN correspondents nowhere to be found, verification took a back seat:

> . . . *and on Facebook along with this there is posted a story that she had been a bystander at a protest and that a member of the Basij, which is the paramilitary that answer to the government, had shot her. We, as we have been emphasizing here, cannot confirm the situation, nor her name. However she is known as Neda on Twitter, many people saying that was her name . . .*

But for hundreds of others elsewhere throughout the mainstream media, old habits kicked in. It was fine for people in Iran to post their stories and pictures online. That's what was expected on the Web. But viewers didn't need to turn on their TV to watch Twitter and YouTube feeds. Networks didn't need to employ high-priced anchors and hundreds of producers for that.

"There was a lot of discussion about using those videos," recalls David Millan, the senior producer at CBC Newsworld that Saturday. "We knew that some kind of turning point was being reached."

In the end, Newsworld chose to hold off running the now-iconic clip of Neda (later identified as Neda Agha-Soltan, a twenty-seven-year-old student). "We didn't know enough about it to put it on air," Millan now says. "We couldn't confirm or verify it and we were using our normal journalistic standards. We were trying to be fairly cautious, but we knew something was changing, and our thinking about how we were going to use pictures like those was evolving."

But CNN was a lot less cautious. "Newsgathering," another anchor raved, "is becoming a collective pursuit, and we welcome that." What he also welcomed on that Saturday was another watershed moment in the relentless, unstoppable democratization of the news.

Neda's death might very well have been missed by the mainstream media if not for a profound transformation that has up-ended the old relationship between journalists and their readers, viewers, and listeners. Technology—in the form of blogs, video-sharing sites, and social networks that allow users to create their own content and distribute it to the world—has helped shift the balance of power into the hands of what media critic Jay Rosen calls "the people formerly known as the audience." It's a revolution that's been gathering momentum for much longer than Twitter has been on the scene.

Owning a newspaper used to mean having a licence to print money. But in Canada, shares of media giant CanWest Global—the country's largest newspaper publisher—are now trading for pennies on the TSX. The *Halifax Daily News* folded in 2008, and over the past year every major newspaper company, including the *Globe and Mail,* announced significant layoffs. In June, Gesca—which owns *La Presse, Cyberpresse,* and *Le Soleil*—put out a call among its employees for volunteers interested in taking early retirement with a buyout. In the US, long-established newspapers in major markets like Denver's *Rocky Mountain News* and Seattle's *Post-Intelligencer* have ceased publication altogether, or now only appear in digital editions. Both dailies in Chicago are hovering near bankruptcy, and the *New York Times* is struggling to deal with a billion-dollar debt.

The age of newspapers is drawing to a close because their economic model appears to be irrevocably broken. Newspapers thrived in an age of scarcity, and one of the most precious resources was space. With only a limited number of pages available for content, editors hustled to find the right mix of sports, business, entertainment, and commentary to attract the readers that advertisers were looking for. Newsstand sales and subscription fees covered only a small percentage of the publication's cost. The rest of the tab—reporters, ink, paper, printing press, distribution—was picked up by advertisers. Newspapers also benefited because competition was slim. Confined to what was available in their local market, readers didn't have many options if they weren't happy with what they were getting. Newspapers spoke to them; journalism was lecture, not conversation, and it worked splendidly for publishers for a long time.

No more. Scarcity has been replaced by abundance. Readers don't need to rely on the local paper to get their news fix.

Satellite dishes now provide access to twenty-four-hour news
channels from Canada, the US, and Europe. Readers can also scan
their newspaper online, choose from thousands of other papers
from around the world, or select one of millions of other news
sites, radio stations, and blogs—all for the price of an Internet
connection.

As a result, paid circulation—what advertisers study when
agreeing to rates—is dropping. At the industry's peak in 1984,
sixty-three million newspapers were sold daily in the US. Today
that number is closer to thirty-three million.

As circulation continues to fall, more advertisers will seek
other ways to get their message across to potential customers.
The impact of this on newspapers, which still shoulder the cost
of maintaining traditional structures and editorial processes, has
been devastating. This year, American ad revenues fell 30 percent, the largest annual decline since the industry started keeping
track in 1950. Hardest hit were classifieds, typically a cash cow
for newspapers. The result was billions of dollars in lost profits
as readers took their unwanted stereos, apartment rentals, and
used cars to free sites like Craigslist. Without advertising, newspapers lose a core revenue generator. So severe is the threat that in
July, the *Toronto Star* outsourced its classified ads department to a
Buffalo-based company, cutting twenty-seven jobs.

Making the situation grimmer is the fact that young readers
are increasingly only interested in getting their news online. In the
US, in 1972, nearly half of those aged eighteen to twenty-two read
a newspaper; by 2005, less than a quarter did. A recent Canadian
survey on attitudes towards the media found that among those
eighteen to twenty-four years old, only 7 percent considered newspapers "very important," compared to 46 percent for the Internet.
And there's little reason to believe that today's youth will suddenly

embrace paper once they get older. In 1972, three-quarters of Americans aged thirty-four to thirty-seven read newspapers; by 2005, only one-third did.

And so newspapers have been spending money they don't have beefing up their digital content, adding new websites, and introducing audio and video to give readers a richer experience. But on average, online advertising accounts for only about 10 percent of a newspaper's total ad revenue, and though that percentage will undoubtedly rise over time, online ads will never be as valuable a source of revenue as the print ads they are replacing.

To add insult to injury, the majority of online readers never actually see the newspapers' carefully designed front-page portal. They arrive at their desired story through search engines or news aggregators or links provided by blogs, tweets, Facebook or online friends. Those readers could come from anywhere—further reducing the appeal for local advertisers—and they're often drawn by their curiosity for a particular story, not loyalty to the newspaper's brand. Many may not even know the name of the paper they're reading.

The good news for reporters—those of them left—is that many of their stories now have a worldwide audience. Their readership has never been bigger. That's why the US-based Project for Excellence in Journalism declared last year that the "crisis in journalism" is not strictly a loss of audience, but "the decoupling of news and advertising" caused by "the emerging reality that advertising isn't migrating online with the consumer."

But the "crisis in journalism" runs much deeper than the industry's shaky economics. Only a cockeyed optimist would think that selling more banner ads or "monetizing" more online content could solve the woes currently besetting the mainstream media in general, and newspapers in particular. That's because the fundamental "crisis in journalism" is not really economic or technological; it is existential. The assumptions that governed journalism for more than a century, assumptions that elevated it to the heights of the democratic pantheon, are now being questioned.

In a 2008 Angus Reid poll, only 49 percent of Canadians said they had a great deal or fair amount of respect for journalists; down from 73 percent in a similar 1994 poll. Back then, journalists ranked slightly behind members of the clergy; now, they are struggling to stay ahead of lawyers. The reason for the disrepute can be found in a survey conducted for the first Future of News Summit in Toronto last spring. A bare majority believe news organizations get their facts straight; nearly two-thirds believe the media cover up their mistakes.

An American poll taken in 2007 revealed similar bad news. Only 19 percent believed all or most news reporting. The Project for Excellence in Journalism reports that between 1985 and 2002, the number of Americans who thought news organizations were "highly professional" went from 72 percent to 49. Those who thought the press was "moral" dropped from 54 percent to 39. And those who thought it "got the facts straight" fell from 20 percent to 35.

This is clearly problematic for an institution whose credibility is its only real currency, though these wounds are self-inflicted. We live in an age that is more fractious, less deferential, more skeptical, and more eager to be entertained than informed. The press, particularly TV, has fostered these trends and has profited handsomely from them. But there was always going to be a price to be paid, and it now appears the bill has come due.

Then there are the high-profile plagiarism scandals; the unwillingness to stand up to the rich and powerful; the failure to ask the right questions in the lead-up to the Iraq War; the eagerness with which standards and ethics are sacrificed for profits; the pandering to the lowest common denominator. And then add to that an arrogance and misplaced sense of privilege that has further eroded the connection between the press and its audience.

Consider a 2006 book by Glenn Reynolds, who publishes a leading US political blog called Instapundit. It's called *An Army of Davids: How Markets and Technology Empower Ordinary People to Beat Big Media, Big Government and Other Goliaths*. The inclusion of "big media" in that list of "goliaths" begging to be slain is clearly not a good sign.

Or consider the blogosphere's barely suppressed *schadenfreude* over the way journalists were sidelined during the political upheaval in Iran. The fact that breaking news had occurred without the filter of a media institution was, for many, something to be celebrated ("While Twitter provided updates to the world," one user sneered, "Larry King gave us Jeff Foxworthy.").

But it's one thing to believe that mainstream media has shot itself in the foot and deserves some kind of comeuppance, and quite another to argue that the solution lies in using an army of untrained, unpaid giant-slayers called "citizen journalists."

Now that audiences are no longer content to be passive consumers of news, how do they intend to separate the wheat from the chaff? In the old scarcity model, readers relied on editors to synthesize mountains of information and point them towards the truth. Today, the argument goes, people peruse a dozen news sources a day, so they are already exposed to several different perspectives on a story, and therefore don't need editors to tell them what to think. According to the new abundance model, the accuracy of each individual source becomes less important because it is one among many. At least, that's the theory.

To which, Kirk LaPointe, managing editor of the *Vancouver Sun*, responds: "Special interest groups, businesses, all kinds of players are profoundly good at cultivating information in such a way and disseminating it in such a way that we can be wildly misled." For LaPointe, gatekeepers—full-time, paid, professional journalists, disinterested and unattached to any political or commercial sponsor—are necessary to keep the misleaders at bay.

The problem is that those gatekeepers have too often kept everyone else at bay too. Take, for example, the controversy that erupted in 2008 when the Canadian Islamic Congress (CIC) complained to various human rights commissions about an article that Mark Steyn published in *Maclean's*. The CIC considered the piece hateful to Muslims, and was angry over the magazine's refusal to provide a forum for their grievances. Ignore for now the issue of whether the complaint was legitimate, or whether human rights commissions should have jurisdiction over such issues, and focus on the mainstream Canadian media response: near-universal outrage.

The *Globe and Mail* described the CIC as "grievance-mongers." The *National Post* called the investigation "an insult to free speech," and proclaimed that "freedom of the press [does not] carry with it an obligation to give space to views opposed to those held by the press's owners or their editors." The editors then helpfully pointed out that no one was stopping the complainants from starting their own newspaper or magazine, thereby confirming A. J. Liebling's observation that "freedom of the press is guaranteed only to those that own one."

Looking back at the behaviour of the mainstream press over the past two decades, it's hard to conclude that the decline in public trust is anything but justified. But right on cue, an alternative has emerged that allows frustrated audiences to take news reporting and distribution into their own hands. When *Time* magazine in 2006 named "you" as its Person of the Year, thereby recognizing the growing power of social networks, it declared, "this is a story about community and collaboration on a scale never seen before." One of the characteristics of those online communities is that their members are consistently more inclined to trust each other than anyone who wears the mantle of "expert"—and that includes reporters and editors. With growing speed, the professional filter is giving way to the social filter. In its 2006 "Trust Survey," Edelman Public Relations discovered that the answer to the question, "Who do you trust?" is, increasingly "People like me." "We have reached an important juncture," concluded company CEO Richard Edelman, "where the lack of trust in established institutions and figures of authority has motivated people to trust their peers as the best sources of information."

This means that, economic troubles aside, the "crisis in journalism" won't be solved until the Fourth Estate and the public come to some agreement about how their relationship will be re-invented in the twenty-first century: why journalism matters, and who has the right to deliver it.

In August of 2008, I attended the 77th annual Couchiching Conference at Geneva Park, an hour's drive north of Toronto. The topic of the three-day retreat was "The Power of Knowledge: The New Global Currency." But it was the debate on the second evening that created the most buzz. The question posed was "Citizen Journalism or Amateur Hour?" and it featured a couple of heavyweights. Speaking for citizen journalism was Paul Sullivan, who was then editor-in-chief of Orato.com (Latin for "I speak"), a Vancouver-based citizen journalism site whose motto at the time was "citizen news: your story, your words."

Sullivan was the host of the CBC radio morning show in Vancouver in the mid-1990s. He had also been the western editor of the *Globe and Mail*, managing editor of the *Vancouver Sun*, editor-in-chief of the *Winnipeg Sun*, and senior news editor at *The Journal* on CBC TV. In other words, he was as mainstream a journalist as you could get in Canada.

But in much the same way that former smokers become the most militant anti-smokers, Paul Sullivan has morphed into a passionate defender of citizen journalism, and a sharp critic of the mainstream outlets that kept him so well fed for so many years. "I think there are no more free rides, no more entitlement," he told me when I asked him about his barely disguised contempt for mainstream media. "Let's have openness, let's have information exchange, let's have intelligence, but let's not have entitlement, and if that's what the mainstream media want to keep bringing to the table, then enough of them already."

Sullivan was especially regretful of the gatekeeping role he had played for so many years as a print and broadcast journalist. His central argument was that the concentration of power in the hands of the traditional media had caused people to feel alienated because they had legitimate stories to tell, but no opportunity to tell them. And when they were given the opportunity, their stories were appropriated by journalists acting as "gatekeepers." At Orato, he said, "editors work for the correspondents instead of the other way around."

Sullivan's sparring partner was just as unlikely an advocate for his own side. Andrew Keen made his money during Silicon Valley's first Internet boom in the 1990s. But in 2007, he decided, like Sullivan, to bite the hand that once fed him, and wrote a highly provocative book called *The Cult of the Amateur: How Today's Internet is Killing our Culture*. It was an attack on what he considered the mythologies of Web 2.0, including the idea that amateurs had a role in the world of journalism. Since then, Keen has travelled the world, embracing every opportunity to stick pins into the Web 2.0 bubble, which is precisely what had brought him to the shores of Lake Couchiching on a muggy August night.

Sparks flew almost immediately. "What's a citizen journalist?" Sullivan asked rhetorically. "Turn to the person next to you. That's a citizen journalist." No it's not, Keen responded. "When you turned to each other, you didn't see a citizen journalist, you saw a citizen. There's a difference," he said. "A citizen is someone who votes. A journalist is someone who reports on the world, particularly who reports on the world outside themselves. Paul's definition of a citizen journalist is someone who has an opinion."

Unsurprisingly, they also clashed over the role of the editorial gatekeeper. "In mainstream media," Sullivan argued, "what we call the news has been a one-way conversation for too long. We finally have the technology to talk back and we don't have to put up with some gatekeeper making decisions for us in a newsroom, about what we can and cannot have access to."

When Sullivan was running Orato.com, he sent two former sex workers to cover the trial of serial killer Robert Pickton, a Port Coquitlam, BC, pig farmer who preyed on Downtown East Side prostitutes. He ran their observations unedited. "At some level," he told the audience, "you have to give people the opportunity to say it without being mediated. That's what freedom of expression is all about, right? It's your story, you get to tell it."

Keen wasn't buying it. Verification, for him, was a collaborative process between editor and reporter. If no one is asking the writer, "How do you know this is true?" how can we be sure it is? "My point generally," he declared, "is that the more people, the more layers that exist between the author and the reader, the more reliable it is, the better quality, the more value it brings to media. If you care about quality, honesty, veracity, and credibility, then mainstream media is superior."

Sullivan countered that the effectiveness of such gatekeeping was vastly overblown, pointing to, among other examples, the *New York Times* plagiarist Jayson Blair, who cooked up fictitious stories and managed to escape detection for years. Calling the verification argument "the last resort of a desperate mainstream media community," Sullivan insisted that it's a "blatant over-simplification" to suggest that professional journalists adhere to standards of accuracy and citizen journalists do not.

At the core of Sullivan's answer to the verification question is the notion of "the wisdom of crowds." "Citizen journalism may not be bound by some sort of professional ethic," he pointed out, "but they're bound by ethics, they're bound by the comment gallery, and the peanut gallery is quite vociferous when anybody spots a problem." Make a mistake at sites like Allvoices ("where anyone can report from anywhere") or Thisisdiversity ("Your World, Your Voice") or try to pull a fast one, and you will be quickly exposed, your credibility will be shot, and you will lose the rewards that come with online success: seeing your work linked up and spread around the Web. This self-correcting mechanism is critical to the citizen journalism model. There is an editorial filter in place, but the collaborators have changed.

That the burden of determining truth no longer lies in the hands of a reporter and editor means that journalists and their audiences can interact in ways impossible before. Some, like California newspaper columnist Dan Gillmor, have adapted. "I take it for granted," he writes in his book *We The Media* (2004), "that my readers know more than I do, and this is a liberating not threatening fact of journalistic life. Every reporter on every beat should embrace this. We will use the tools of grassroots journalism or be consigned to history."

For other old media journalists, it will take some getting used to. It's the difference between seeing journalism as a process or as a product. Newspaper reporters work hard to make their stories as good and as accurate as possible given the limitations of time, access and other variables, because once those stories reach their audience, there is—as Sullivan is quick to remind us—a notorious, and often infuriating, reluctance to admit errors.

A few years ago, Scott Maier, a journalism professor at the University of Oregon, conducted a survey of 3,600 people who had been named as primary news sources in stories from ten major market American newspapers. His researchers asked these sources whether the stories that appeared in the paper were accurate. It turns out that more than 60 percent of the stories contained errors of fact. More damning still, fewer than 2 percent of those errors were ever corrected in print. Maier found that 130 of the sources had asked that the mistakes be corrected, but their complaints resulted in only four corrections. Maier's study didn't look at error and correction rates in broadcast media, but when was the last time you heard a correction offered on a radio or television news story?

If mainstream journalists see the stories they publish as products completed upon delivery, citizen journalists see their stories as works in progress. They engage readers in an interactive exercise that is never really finished as long as there is information to be added, or, in some cases, subtracted. So while citizen journalism sites may contain more errors, they will likely be corrected more quickly, and with fewer hassles, than on mainstream sites.

That's partly because the legal stakes for getting something wrong are much higher for traditional news. Media companies employ teams of high-priced lawyers because anyone who feels they have been libelled can sue both the person who uttered the libel, and the outlet that broadcast or printed it.

But those rules don't apply to sites that allow their content to appear unfiltered. Using a legal defence still untested in Canadian courts, they argue that because they do not see material before it is posted online, they are not legally responsible for it. They regard themselves as distributors of content, not publishers, much in the way a telephone company can't be blamed for any slanderous content transmitted through their phone lines onto the radio.

To date, nobody has challenged this interpretation, but Kirk LaPointe believes it's only a matter of time. As the managing editor of the *Vancouver Sun*, LaPointe spends lots of time and money keeping his paper out of court. He describes the current situation online as "the wild west," but he thinks the sheriff will soon be coming to town. "The people who are offended and defamed and are treated cavalierly by people who just think that they can go online and say whatever they want are going to have their way awfully soon," he argues. "Hosting a portal where everybody can say what they want doesn't mean that the guy in his pyjamas in his basement isn't one day going to be hauled into court."

If LaPointe is right, and the courts ultimately decide that these sites are indeed publishers and not strictly distributors, the entire model of citizen journalism could come crashing down. Gatekeepers would be back in business, at least as far as determining whether a story passes the legal smell test.

Those are worries for the future. For now, stories continue to be posted directly onto the sites. Readers—i.e., "the community"— vote for stories they want to see featured, weigh in with their comments, and correct errors. But there's another important role gatekeepers play that is undermined in a world where content is published directly to the web. Gatekeepers have historically been the custodians of standards. It is an article of faith amongst editors and producers that long hours spent re-writing and re-structuring stories results in a better product. They've always believed audiences appreciated the effort. But maybe not.

Now that audiences can have it all, what do they really want? What does journalism without gatekeepers look like?

There was a time when the massive shrines that housed newspapers reflected their dominant position in society. The New York Times skyscraper in midtown Manhattan. Chicago's majestic Tribune Tower. The Toronto Star tower at the foot of Yonge Street. That's why when I set out to find the newspapers of the future, it seemed odd to be walking up a seedy block of Seymour Street in downtown Vancouver, between Pender and Dunsmuir.

This area, however, happens to be home to one of the most closely watched experiments in citizen journalism. On the second floor of the turn-of-the-century Arts and Crafts building, right next to Casanova Jewellers, you'll find the headquarters of Now-Public.com. It's just a few blocks away from Granville Square, the thirty-storey tower that houses both the *Vancouver Sun* and the *Province*. More than a hundred reporters and editors are needed to ready the stories for those daily publications, and hundreds more employees run the presses, sell the ads and deliver the paper to newsstands and doorsteps.

By contrast, only a couple of dozen people work at NowPublic. None of them are reporters. It looks more like an Internet start-up than a newsroom. And yet, the company—which was founded in 2005 and has raised more than $11 million in private venture capital—has a big dream: to become the world's largest newsgathering organization, "the new Reuters."

That's somewhat surprising, since neither of the site's co-founders have any background in journalism. Both are Van-couver-based, thirty-something, veteran Internet entrepreneurs. Michael Tippett, the company's chief marketing officer, created one of Canada's first Internet companies back in 1995, while CEO Leonard Brody has several start-ups under his belt, and is an internationally known technology consultant and author. In 2007, *Time* magazine named their news site one of the top fifty websites of the year. "Nowhere are the merits of citizen journalism more apparent than at NowPublic," the magazine proclaimed.

Tippett and Brody, however, refuse to use the term "citizen journalism" to describe what they do. "We are part of the user-generated news business," Brody insists. "I think the term 'citizen journalism' is ridiculous. I think it's like telling someone they're going to be a citizen dentist."

Like most people who try to get rich dreaming up new ways to harness the potential of the Internet, Brody and Tippett saw an opening. With hundreds of millions of camera-equipped cell-phones, video recorders, and other devices in the hands of people around the world, Tippett says they anticipated "an explosion of content from unconventional sources." If they could "build a platform" to take advantage of that content, one that ordinary people could participate in, they could "create what we think is the largest news organization in the world, because anyone is a potential reporter."

Of course, there are several important differences between the "old" Reuters (now Thomson Reuters) and the "new" Reuters. Calling itself "crowd-powered media," and with a stable of more than 170,000 "correspondents" in 160 countries, NowPublic already dwarfs the roughly two thousand people on the editor-ial staff at Reuters. The difference is that Reuters reporters and editors are trained journalists, while NowPublic correspondents are, well, citizens.

At Reuters, people get paid for producing content. At Now-Public they do not. Reuters correspondents covering breaking news frequently use eyewitnesses, but they filter and attempt to verify that eyewitness testimony before incorporating it into their stories. At NowPublic, eyewitness testimony is posted directly to the Web, unfiltered and unverified.

The NowPublic front page is arranged in much the same way as any other news site. The big stories of the day are prominently featured. And there are sections that cover health news, the arts, the environment, and all the rest. On a conventional news site, the top stories are chosen by editors, who generally rely on their years of experience and "nose for news" to help them determine what stories are new, interesting, and important. At NowPublic, the editors are more accurately described as enablers. "We don't make decisions about what is or is not newsworthy," explains Rachel Nixon, a former BBC online producer and editor, who, until leaving to become director of digital media at the CBC in June, was NowPublic's news director. "Those decisions are primarily decided by members of community who can flag materials. If other people think it's interesting then that story will graduate up the ranks. What the community decides is important floats to the top."

So on a day last summer when most mainstream news sites were focused on the worsening war in Afghanistan and the fortieth anniversary of the moon landing, the NowPublic community had voted for "Migaloo, World's Only White Humpback Whale, Could be Hunted" as its top story. That story, which was posted by a member of the NowPublic staff, was typical of most of the news content on the site. For all its talk about eyewitness reporting and "explosions of content from unconventional sources," NowPublic generates very little original reporting. The whale story came from the website of the British newspaper the Telegraph. Most stories are cut and pasted from a mainstream site, with a few lines written by the contributor. And since real names aren't required, top Now-Public correspondents include "albertacowpoke," "LotusFlower," and "Babel-Fish."

So what's the appeal? In the absence of major breaking stories like the Iran election, why would anyone look to NowPublic as a source of news? Yes, you can get stories from a wider range of sources than you can on a mainstream site, but you can do the same thing by using search engines and aggregators like Google News. What you can't do there, or on a conventional news site, is join a social network. In the age of social media, journalism has become a social tool. Think of NowPublic as Facebook for news junkies.

One of those news junkies is Margi Blamey, a Vancouver grandmother who started writing for NowPublic last fall. Her daughter and granddaughter were both contributors, and she wanted to see what all the fuss was about. Before long, she was spending at least an hour a day searching the Web for stories to post, and commenting on and recommending stories posted by others. She's written and commented on a wide range of topics, from labour and social justice issues, to stories about food, gardening, and even sea creatures.

Blamey confesses to loving CBC Radio, but admits her enthusiasm for most mainstream media has waned since she discovered NowPublic. And the reason is that NowPublic offers something better: friends. "I bump into people on NowPublic, and it is clear that we share a common interest," she tells me over the phone. "And as that's come about, we built a community that isn't based on geography, it's based on issues and interest, and in a lot of cases, on wanting to talk on a variety of points of view on an issue."

NowPublic is currently "pre-revenue," which is Internet-speak for losing money. It hopes to turn that around in the next year through a combination of revenue generators. One is charging people to advertise and post promotional content on the site; another is licensing and selling the technology that NowPublic has developed to other user-generated content sites. Potentially the most important source of revenue will come from syndicating stories to mainstream outlets like the Associated Press, with whom they have already signed an agreement to provide content.

Co-founder Brody argues that breaking news has always been a loss leader for newspapers and broadcasters, and the eyewitness reporting provided by NowPublic correspondents can allow mainstream outlets to focus on what they do best, namely analysis and context. Jim Kennedy, AP's vice president and director of strategic planning, heralded the partnership in 2007 as a great fit. "In a world where people have the tools at their disposal to contribute on a regular basis you'd be foolish not to tap into that."

Of course, Kennedy was quick to point out at the time that NowPublic material would only get the AP stamp of approval after it had been authenticated and verified. That doesn't happen now on the NowPublic site. But the question remains: how are the AP authenticators going to corroborate stories by frequently anonymous correspondents? Furthermore, it fundamentally changes the nature of reporting to ask a journalist sitting at a desk in Toronto to do the "analytical part" of a terrorist attack in Pakistan—who's doing it and why—by relying on reports from eyewitnesses whose reliability cannot really be vouched for. There is no doubt that NowPublic is a useful social network for news junkies like Blamey, but it is not the "new Reuters." Nor is it likely to be the future of news.

But there is another Canadian citizen journalism site, newer and smaller than NowPublic, that may be closer to what news will look like. It's called DigitalJournal.com, and it operates out of a trendy New York-style loft on the fifth floor of a restored Sears mail-order warehouse in downtown Toronto. When you enter, you're asked to remove your shoes for fear of scuffing the floor. The office is located almost directly across the street from the School of Journalism at Ryerson University. Both the CEO and managing editor of DigitalJournal are recent graduates, and perhaps because of that, they seem to understand some important truths about the strengths and weaknesses of citizen journalism.

"The biggest knock against citizen journalism is that you can't trust it," acknowledges Chris Hogg, the twenty-seven-year-old CEO. "People put their faith in the mainstream media because you can verify and fact-check it. So when you can integrate that with citizen media, we see a real future there."

Both Hogg and his twenty-nine-year-old managing editor David Silverberg act as real editors, carefully vetting the seventy-five to one hundred stories that get filed every day by the site's seventeen thousand correspondents worldwide. They proudly wear the title of gatekeeper. Give a quote to a DigitalJournal reporter, and don't be surprised if you get a call from Hogg or Silverberg checking up on whether you've been quoted accurately. There's no relying on the wisdom of the crowd or the Web's self-correcting mechanism.

This is definitely not Paul Sullivan's idea of citizen journalism. "We don't want to open the floodgates," says Silverberg. "That can lead to sloppily written articles, inaccuracy, bias, and spam." So if you're going to write for DigitalJournal, you'd better be prepared to use your real name. And you'll have to submit a bio, a sample of your writing, and some indication that you know what a news story is before the duo will give you their stamp of approval. They believe in quality rather than quantity, and have no interest in creating a social network.

And if you are picked to write for the site, you'll actually have to write. Cutting and pasting articles from other sources is not allowed. If you're having difficulty, you can join Hogg and Silverberg in one of their monthly live blogs, where they offer instruction on different aspects of news writing.

It sounds daunting, but at least you won't be asked to work for free. Unlike most citizen journalism sites, DigitalJournal believes contributors should get paid for what they write. Your compensation is based on the number of pageviews your story attracts, and how many votes it gets from readers. News stories pay more than opinion pieces. You won't get rich doing this. At the moment, the most active contributors can earn between $200 and $500 a month, but as a principle, paying writers for their work is a step in the right direction.

Where that money comes from is unclear. Hogg says DigitalJournal is "privately financed" but he won't say by whom, or how much money has been invested. He does concede that it, too, is currently "pre-revenue." The site does make some money from advertising, but probably not enough to pay writers, the five employees, and the rent on the downtown loft.

DigitalJournal began in 1998 as a traditional online technology site, but in 2006, it broadened its focus and started accepting contributions from outsiders, with the lofty goal of "democratizing the media." Like NowPublic, it eventually hopes to be able to syndicate material to mainstream news outlets. "We want to be seen as a credible news source with citizen correspondents all over the world," Hogg asserts. "We see ourselves as complementary to mainstream media, not competitive with them. They're looking for other places to find content, and we're cost effective and fact checked and well written, so we have an extreme competitive advantage over other citizen journalism sites."

One day that may be true, but at the moment DigitalJournal's reach still exceeds its grasp. The attempt to inject quality into citizen journalism is to be applauded, but despite Hogg and Silverberg's best efforts, much of the writing is still journalism-school quality, and there is still a lot of reporting about places the writer has never visited, and possesses no obvious expertise. An article about the then-upcoming Afghan election was written by a correspondent in Minnesota who had never been to Afghanistan, but had obviously read accounts from various media sources. That same day, CBC Radio ran an election story on its newscast by a correspondent who had spent several months on the ground in Afghanistan. Is there any doubt which journalist brought greater value to that story?

But if present trends continue, the day is approaching when the CBC, the *Globe and Mail* and others in the traditional press will no longer be able to afford to fly their correspondents around the world, or even send them to cover city hall, the provincial legislature, or Parliament Hill. Mainstream media has historically relied on freelancers and "stringers" to fill gaps in their own reporting. As those gaps get bigger, they will need to be filled somehow.

What Hogg and Silverberg are attempting to do is create a worldwide network of trained and trusted freelancers whose first loyalty would be to DigitalJournal, but could ultimately serve the mainstream as well. Whether they can pull it off remains to be seen, but DigitalJournal, with its rather old-fashioned commitment to the discipline of verification, seems a more likely complement to traditional media than NowPublic ever will be.

Another promising glimpse into the future came during last year's US presidential campaign. Off the Bus was an experiment run by the popular news site the Huffington Post. It brought together a small group of professional editors and about 3,000 "amateurs" who filed stories on how the campaign was unfolding in their communities. The stories were reviewed by the Huffington Post editors and posted on the site.

Off the Bus produced the first "star" of the citizen journalism age, a sixty-one-year-old woman from California named Mayhill Fowler, who used her own money to follow the candidates around the country. She broke two important stories during the campaign: Bill Clinton describing *Vanity Fair* journalist Todd Purdham as a "slime ball" for his report on Clinton's post-presidental years, and Barack Obama calling working class people in Pennsylvania "bitter" at an event that was closed to reporters covering the campaign.

The secret to her success, she told me when I interviewed her at a political blogger conference in New York, was that she kept herself at a "middle distance"—not as close and cozy as the accredited mainstream reporters, but closer than the bloggers who wrote about the campaign without ever leaving their apartments.

The most encouraging thing about Off the Bus is that it joined together the expertise of pros, and the enthusiasm and originality of amateurs in a way that brought added value to the campaign coverage. You often learned something new by going to the site. DigitalJournal is trying to develop a similar kind of sustainable pro-amateur model for news reporting. It seems clear that the future lies somewhere along that road: Goliath and David playing on the same team.

But there will be many bumps along the way. Many perceptive critics continue to doubt that there is any significant role for amateurs in journalism. David Simon is one of them. He's a former *Baltimore Sun* reporter, and the creator of the gritty police drama *The Wire*. At a US Senate hearing last spring, Simon argued that high-end journalism "requires daily full-time commitment by trained men and women who return to the same beats day in and day out until the best of them know everything with which a given institution is contending." It was "absurd," he said, to think that city officials and chief executives could be held to account "by amateurs who pursue the task without compensation, training, or, for that matter, without sufficient standing to make public officials even care to whom it is they are lying or from whom they are withholding information." The next few years, he concluded, are shaping up to be good for corrupt politicians.

David Simon is undoubtedly correct that the role professional journalists have historically played—agents of the public engaged in battle against corruption and wrong-doing by governments and big business—will never be completely filled by self-styled reporters, journo-hobbyists, and well-intentioned amateurs. Given the amount of information we're exposed to every day, the wisdom of crowds can only carry us so far. There will likely be a growing need for gatekeepers who have the knowledge and experience to help make sense of it all. And those people will have to be paid for their labour.

But the future of news will clearly not look like the past. There will not be a small group of professional truth-tellers whom we call journalists, with everyone else looking on, hungry for instruction. Those days are gone. If we didn't know that before, we learned it when broadcasters reached out to those Twitter feeds and YouTube videos from the streets of Tehran.

And while it may be legitimate to raise concerns about the breakdown in the "discipline of verification," it is hard not to be impressed by the way pros and amateurs together helped thwart the best laid plans of the Iranian regime. It was a real-time dramatization of what can happen when the editorial gates are stormed: a chance to bring the public back into traditional journalism— not as just another interest group that needs to be placated, or as "real people" to whom lip service must be paid, but as genuine participants. That's what the mainstream can learn from citizen journalism. Let's call it a good idea, and get on with it.

THE CASE OF THE CUSTOMIZED CHRIST

WILL BRAUN
Geez

"IF GOD CREATED US in his image, we have more than reciprocated." That's what French philosopher Voltaire said of the human tendency to mould God into our own likeness. Similarly, God's son has been adapted to a great variety of human-created roles. To capitalist Christians, Jesus was a model entrepreneur. To socialist Christians, he was a hardcore socialist. To eco-Christians, he was a lily-loving environmentalist. To self-help Christians, he was a motivational guru. And to Christian activists, he was a revolutionary.

I used to fall into this last category. For much of the past decade

I have been involved in social justice advocacy for marginalized people, and for many of those years I put my stock in the Jesus-as-activist characterization. But there was always some uneasiness about such a specific and selective interpretation of Jesus's life. This discomfort has steadily increased. How can the story of Jesus shape me if I am so busy shaping it? While I see a link between social justice and the life of Jesus, it just feels too convenient to customize Jesus into an idealized version of my activist self.

This leaves me at odds with fellow Christian activists who eagerly talk about Jesus as an activist. One of the favoured cases for Jesus as a revolutionary is Ched Myers's 1988 book, *Binding the Strong Man: A Political Reading of Mark's Story of Jesus*. The 500-page commentary on the Gospel of Mark finds revolutionary politics at the heart of Jesus's life. According to Myers, the "good news" in Mark is "a declaration of war upon the political culture of the empire." The gospel is an activist manifesto that promises "to overthrow the structures of domination in our world."

Myers uses literary and cultural analysis to draw out the political and revolutionary meanings of Mark. For instance, he argues that Jesus's call to be "fishers of men" is not a call to save souls but to "join [Jesus] in his struggle to overturn the existing order of power and privilege." And when Jesus casts an evil spirit named "Legion" out of a man and then drives it into a herd of pigs that stampedes down a steep bank into the sea, Myers argues that the pigs represent the occupying Roman forces being driven out of Palestine. It's all part of Jesus's "war of myths." Similarly, the concept of forgiveness is interpreted as an alternative to the temple sacrifices which required the poor to buy offerings they couldn't afford. As for the many stories of healing, Myers explains them as "an essential part of [Jesus's] struggle to bring concrete liberation to the oppressed."

Myers's scholarship is helpful in highlighting the complex political significance of the Gospel of Mark. It leaves little doubt that Mark viewed Jesus as someone who boldly spoke out against exploitation, fought a battle of political myths, and engaged in "civil disobedience" (for example, openly violating Sabbath laws). But this is only one reading of one gospel. It is helpful and useful, but not if we take it as the exclusive lens through which to see Jesus. While I find much of what Myers writes affirming for me in my own activist efforts, instinct tells me that it's more valuable to focus not on what I want to see but on what I may *not* want to see. It is the latter that can stretch me.

When I look at those parts of Jesus's story to which I am less drawn, I see two main things that expand my sense of activist vocation: the caring, pastoral side of Jesus, and a conspicuous absence of success. First, the pastoral dimension. Jesus was a compassionate and dedicated shepherd. Even if the healings and forgiveness had political significance, surely they were also about simply caring for the immediate physical and spiritual needs of people. He was present to needy people and he created a community in which the neglected people of society found a place of belonging and inner wholeness. Task-oriented activists like myself don't tend to talk much about belonging, pastoral care, and being present to people. Efforts at structural change tend to trump, rather than accompany, efforts to create loving community centered on marginalized people.

The second aspect of Jesus's life that pushes me in new directions is the fact that he quietly submits to an entirely unjust death and then leaves the earth before accomplishing a revolution or achieving activist success of any sort. If Jesus were the archetypal activist, I would have expected him to accomplish successful land reform, remove the Roman occupiers from Palestine, or make poverty history. While he did many kind things for exploited people (as well as for some exploiters), and while he offered an incisive critique of the oppressive structures of his day, at the climax of the story he does not play what would have been his ultimate activist trump card: to appear to the authorities in his risen form to lobby, convert, or depose them. Instead, Jesus quickly exits the scene and the Romans, along with the corrupt ruling class, remain intact. If Jesus is a model for activism, he seems to be a model for failed activism.

Consider Jesus's so-called triumphant entry into Jerusalem. Commentators suggest that anti-Roman rebel movements were common in Jesus's time and the crowds who cheered for him as he rode into Jerusalem likely hoped Jesus would lead a successful political revolution. They projected their activist aspirations onto him. But those expectations quickly proved entirely misguided. Jesus ended up slouched on a cross, not leading a victorious revolt.

Though the resurrection—with its layers of meaning—was a victory of sorts, it did not achieve the type of ends most of us activists work toward. The meekness of Jesus as he is condemned and crucified is hardly the posture that activists usually emulate.

I should note that Myers also considers the cross a "failure" by revolutionary standards. For him, this failure leaves room for us to continue the story in communities of "radical discipleship" and inclusion. And he concludes that Jesus's submission to death on the cross teaches that the powers can only be countered with symbolically charged non-violence.

When I look at Jesus's track record as an activist, and the rather non-activisty pastoral dimension of his life, I am led to a somewhat different (though not entirely contradictory) conclusion. My conclusion, tentative though it may be, is that Jesus's primary focus was not activism or revolution as we commonly understand those terms. It was broader, more nuanced, more mystical perhaps. In my own efforts to live into a vocation broader than standard goal-oriented activism, I find helpful examples in the lives and writings of Caryll Houselander and Óscar Romero.

Caryll Houselander—a Catholic mystic, writer, and companion of the needy in England—demonstrated pastoral presence and holy failure in the midst of oppression. While working as a nurse during the chaotic violence and suffering of the World War II bombing raids in London, she wrote the following:

> *It came to me like a blinding flash of light that Christ did not resist evil, that he allowed himself to be violently done to death, that when he gave himself to be crucified, he knew that the exquisite delicacy and loveliness of the merest detail of Christian life would survive the Passion, that indeed . . . it depended on it. And so it is now: that which is holy, tender, and beautiful will not be swept away or destroyed by war.*

The story of Jesus did not hold for her the promise that the bad guys would be overthrown but that there were certain things that live on beyond the reach of the destructive powers. The poetry of life itself will be resurrected no matter what.

Romero was another example of a response to oppression that went deeper than activism. He was Archbishop of El Salvador in the late 1970s, a period during which peasants and priests who opposed the oppressive powers were being disappeared and murdered. While he spoke with great conviction and eloquence against the injustices of his time—to the extent that he too was assassinated— he remained more of a pastor than an activist. While legitimizing the concrete needs of the peasants, he warned the more activist-minded in his flock that an ideal "political and social order" would not be complete unless people's hearts were converted to "deep joy of spirit" and peace with God and each other.

Despite giving his life, he failed to stop the repression or prevent civil war. But he both named the essence of the powers and fostered a spirit that no bullet could hit, famously declaring shortly before his death: "If they kill me, I will rise again in the Salvadoran people."

As I look beyond the Christian activist model, I ask myself three questions that for me arise from the story of Jesus. First, what is the incisive word and the symbolic sacrifice required in the present-day battle of political myths? Second, how can I contribute to a community of physical and spiritual caring? And finally, in all my efforts, how can I best nurture the holiness, tenderness, and beauty that will live on even when the powers prevail?

THE THINGS INK MAY DO

TYEE BRIDGE
Swerve

I.

IT'S A FAIR BET that in North America we consume more stories per day than any culture in history. Every year, a quarter of a million new books are printed in Canada and the US; one month's shipment of magazines could sink an aircraft carrier. The multiplex cinema features ten fresh movies a week, and cable TV will, if it hasn't already, mainline 200 channels of crime-scene dramas, "reality" programs, and talk shows into your living room. My DVD rental store down the street, and it's a small one, carries

28,000 titles: new releases, classic films, TV-series box sets, spe-
cial-edition box sets, documentaries about the making of the spe-
cial-edition box set. All this before even mentioning the billion
stories on the Internet, that paragon of instant gratification—the
digital blob that will soon subsume all books, magazines, television shows, and movies.

This could be good news. We've filled our silos with such a vast
hoard of stories no seven-year famine could deplete it. The irony—
and it is a mythic one, the curse of Midas—is that amidst all this
wealth, we're starving to death. We eat far too many stories that
are packaged by corporate minds to hit the widest demographic
and reap the largest profit margin. They have the nutrient value
of potato chips, and we consume them accordingly. The twenty-
two-minute sitcom, the chick-lit paperback at the airport, the
tongue-in-cheek heist flick. There are plenty of nourishing meals
out there, a smaller but still nearly endless number of books and
films rich with literary and spiritual content. But when we're lucky
enough to read or see them, we usually don't have the time to digest them. By the next day we're on to the next thing, while their
symbols and meaning pass through us like watermelon seeds.

I'm addicted to the fast-food story as much as anyone. If I had
the chance to take three months off to watch every episode of *Dex-
ter*, *The Amazing Race*, the new *Battlestar Galactica*, and any British
murder mystery starring Helen Mirren, I'd jump at it. But I don't
know that I'd be better off. Occasionally fast food is fine, but when
it's all you eat you're in trouble. This is the fix: we're constantly
entertained by stories, but rarely, if ever, nourished by them. This
may lead to heart disease, figuratively at least, along with other
subtle ailments. As a child I used to watch a cheaply animated
series from the late sixties called *Rocket Robin Hood*. There was
one oft-repeated sequence in which a wide-eyed and very plump

Friar Tuck sat at a well-laid feast table, taking a single bite out of an apple, a drumstick, a bunch of grapes, and a giant bratwurst before tossing the remains over his shoulder. This is a pretty good metaphor for the way most of us consume stories these days.

We not only need less potato-chip entertainment and more real meals, we also need the hearth, the lodge, the pub fireplace to sit around with friends and talk them over. We need to let them linger, give ourselves some unbuttoned time to digest them. At the end of a 1968 book called *The Mixed-Up Files of Mrs. Basil E. Frankweiler*, the eponymous Mrs. F. gives some advice to two children on the lam from their parents and holed up in the Metropolitan Museum of Art.

> *I think you should learn, of course, and some days you should learn a great deal. But you should also have days when you allow what is already in you to swell up inside of you until it touches everything. And you can feel it inside you. If you never take time out to let that happen, then you just accumulate facts, and they begin to rattle around inside of you. You can make noise with them, but never really feel anything with them. It's hollow.*

With so little time to linger over the stories we read—not to mention the story we're living in our relationships and careers, which have their symbolic side— most of us rattle these days. But the good news is that we've reached an age of reconsideration. Naiveté is at a low ebb and more people than ever are savvy about what they consume. Organic and local foods are on the rise; factory-made food and unpronounceable ingredients are on the way out. Instead of bolting our food down for fuel en route to the next scheduled diversion, we're starting to actually taste what we're eating, even to spend time talking about where it came from and who grew it. After some thirty years of countercultural plodding, the slow-food revolution is well underway. The slow-story movement, however, is just beginning

In the mid-nineties, a certain talk show host encouraged millions of women to start hosting book clubs. This may have been the kickoff to the slow-story movement in North America at the mass level. It has a long way to go yet. I've never been in anything resembling a book club, at least since my last university seminar, but Oprah deserves credit for using her power well. Getting people to unplug from cellphones, laptops, and TV screens in favour of reading and talking about books is a minor miracle.

I haven't joined or started a book club, partly out of embarrassment, as it does have the imprint of girls-night-in—and partly because I've just started to figure out the kind of slow stories I want to sit around and discuss (in someone else's living room, since mine is about the size of a coffee table). Namely, fairy tales. Or rather, mythic tales—the stories of the soul that appear as fantasy, legends, and folklore.

II.

"Legends and myth are largely made of truth, and indeed present aspects of it that can only be perceived in this mode; and long ago certain truths and modes of this kind were discovered and must always reappear."
—J.R.R. Tolkien

ONE OF MY FAVOURITE places to spend an afternoon is a used bookstore called Macleod's. A hoard of mercantile chaos, it smells of old books—a dusty and comforting smell of disintegrating pages and powdery binding glue. It's the kind of bookstore that

was boarded up in most cities decades ago. The owner sits at a
desk at the back, peering out from behind chin-high stacks of
unshelved books. Everything imaginable is in these erratic piles,
from sci-fi pulps and poetry anthologies to lip-gloss romances and
leather-bound Rubaiyats. Antiquarian volumes enter the store by
the barrow-load, though they seem to exit much more slowly. I'm
not sure where they put all the new arrivals. I picture catacombs
under the shop, lamp-lit chambers with middens of books piled
to the ceiling, slowly being sorted by indentured gremlins or children who didn't eat their greens. If the modern world of stories is
a dashboard screen in a minivan hurtling down the info-super-
highway, then Macleod's is located down a potholed off-ramp that
doesn't see much traffic.

Last year, tucked into a low shelf in the mythology section,
I found a book called *The King and the Corpse: Tales of the Soul's
Conquest of Evil*. A collection of essays by Heinrich Zimmer, a
professor of Indian culture and folklore, the book is a freewheeling, depth-psychology exploration of the images and symbols in
various stories—from the Arabian tale of Abu Kasem's slippers
to the epic *Sir Gawain and the Green Knight*. (The title story is
a thousand-year-old Kashmiri tale, about a king who must answer twenty-five riddles posed to him by the corpse on his back,
which, for complicated reasons, he has cut down from a tree and
must deliver to a magician.) Downplaying his own expertise,
Zimmer encourages readers to take off their socks and step into
the grape barrel of interpretation, turning stories into wine with
their own wits.

Images and symbols are always newly alive to the eyes that
read them, Zimmer tells us, brushed in with the fresh oil paints
of personal experience. "It is because they are alive, potent to re-
vive themselves, and capable of an ever-renewed, unpredictable

yet self-consistent effectiveness in the range of human destiny, that the images of folklore and myth defy every attempt we make at systematization," Zimmer wrote. "With a sudden laugh and a quick shift of place they mock the specialist who imagines he has got them pinned to his chart. What they demand of us is not the monologue of a coroner's report, but the dialogue of a living conversation."

Zimmer was a contemporary and friend of Carl Jung, and like Jung was mostly interested in a *certain* kind of story. The catch-all term might be mythic. It's not a great word, since it has taken on the connotation of "false" in our dutifully rational culture, but it's better than "fairy tales," which is too specific. Mythic stories might include not only fairy tales but Greek drama, Goethe's *Faust*, epic poems, some of Shakespeare's plays (*Hamlet* and *The Tempest*, to name two), even religious scripture. "Myth is what we call someone else's religion," someone once wrote. That's a good jab at parochialism, but doesn't explain what myth means, or why it grabs us. As Tolkien points out, myth is truth. Truth in this sense is a subjective affair. In myth, truth is always found in the relationship between the reader and the story. One man reads Hans Christian Andersen's *The Snow Queen* and knows that the fairy tale describes the glass splinter in his own eye, the one disposing him to see the ugliness rather than the beauty in everything. The story speaks directly to him. He feels himself hailed—or nailed—by it, and he senses that the way to wash the splinter out is revealed, somehow, by the story's ending. Exactly how to enact the clue left by the story is not spelled out, but the hint is in there, waiting to be lived.

This is not to say that non-mythic stories, literary or otherwise, have less value. Good stories of any kind sideswipe us: historical dramas like *Schindler's List*, or gorgeous, sensualist fictions like

Oscar Hijuelos' *The Mambo Kings Play Songs of Love*. Well-crafted literature draws us into other lives, other losses, so convincingly that we lose track of time, cringe, get angry, weep. This is a minor miracle of the human imagination. How can we enter stories so deeply that we forget where we're actually sitting—in bed eating crackers, or in a sticky-floored multiplex with 200 other people— and feel so much for people we know aren't real? "Story is what human beings do. It's where we live, it's what we are, and we live in a web of it constantly," said the husband of a friend of mine, an actor who's been performing on stage and teaching for over forty years. "Everything we are not experiencing physically in the moment is story. Maybe whales do tell stories at the bottom of the sea, but as far as we know we are the only animals on the planet who can conceive of *what is not*."

When you tune a guitar relatively, you know you've hit the right note when you pluck the adjacent string and the one you're tuning vibrates. This is how it is with mythic stories. Hearing something from the other world, our inner world responds and resonates. "The mythic world is the world behind this world," says Seattle storyteller Michael Meade. Myth may point us not only to personal revelations and relative truths about the particular splinter in our eye, but even begin to draw the shade for a glimpse of some ultimate truth beyond the veil. But myth never offers the easy lessons of Sunday school or Aesop's fables; its paradoxes can't be reduced to a pat moral or resolved by the clap of a gavel. Instead, mythic tales give us archetypal images and situations: a deformed boy who grows up behind the stove, or a brow-beaten girl who, if she wants to go to the ball, must pick out of the fireplace coals all the lentils her jealous stepmother threw into them.

Despite the ranting of the latest round of pop atheists, it is more than cultism that keeps people reading the Torah and the

New Testament. It must be more than academic canons and literary pretension that keeps Greek tragedy, Arthurian legends, and Shakespeare alive. But what is it? Why have *Grimm's Fairy Tales* been popular for 200 years, or the tales of King Arthur for almost a thousand? Why has *The Hobbit*, written in 1937, sold more than 90 million copies?

One first and fairly obvious guess is magic. This again is not the perfect word, because I don't mean it only in the wizard-wand sense, or in the sense of the kind of scintillant, otherworldly glow of a Maxfield Parrish painting. Magic appears in scripture as much as myth; it means the rules get bent, that a light or a presence pops up in the story that places it outside the everyday. Realistic literature might have a mythic structure, like James Joyce's *Ulysses*, which is based on *The Odyssey*; but unlike *The Odyssey*, no one in Joyce's version gets turned into a pig by an island sorceress. This is what puts Harry Potter in the same rowboat with Odysseus, Cinderella, and Prospero. The word "magic" has appropriately mysterious origins in Greek and Persian, and is likely related to the ancient Indo-European word for power—sharing, ironically, the same root as the word "machine." Machines depend on Newton's laws for power, but the magic in mythic stories means the power to make a rose out of ashes, or spin straw into gold.

Something inside us relaxes and takes a deep breath when we read about the impossible, or what our rational minds take to be impossible. Like the phrase "Once upon a time," magic in literature lets us set aside the left brain and listen with a different, less acidic part of our intelligence. North Americans need to be refreshed by the presence of what is not possible, by the miraculous that exists outside our daily grind. And who knows: if we spent more time bridging our everyday lives with the world of myth, those rules we good rationalists believe are so fixed might relax a bit.

"The Western reader . . . has to be roused from his old in-grained way of thinking in order to awaken him to another order of things," Henry Corbin said four decades ago. Corbin was a theologian and scholar of Persian and Arabic literature who coined a new term for the inner terrain where we experience dreams, visions and mythic symbols: the *mundus imaginalis*. He was careful to distinguish between what is imaginary (i.e., unreal), and the realm of the imaginal, which he believed was an experience of a different reality—one with as much claim to authenticity as the world of freeways and coffee tables. "We must make a real effort to overcome what one might call Western man's 'agnostic reflex,' since it is responsible for the divorce between thinking and being," he wrote. "We try to run from this reality, even when we are secretly attracted by it." If tuned to meaningful symbols, imagination allows us to enter a threshold world—"the country of non-where," in the phrase of 12th-century Persian philosopher Sohrawardi—which bridges the conscious world with the inner world of the psyche, and the spiritual reality beyond.

Psyche: that creaky-floored house with high-windowed rooms, a garden courtyard, a dark basement, and several padlocked closets that is fully furnished with the images of our personal and cultural symbology. Psyche is our persona, with all its shadows, influences, desires, fears, and hopes relating to an image. A ripe pear, a wild fox, a Grail, a salmon, a mother, a father, a raven, a kitchen, a locked box, a key, a fireplace. Through these symbols, mythic tales speak to us about growing up, about transformation, about living well. In scripture, the descent of magic is called a miracle. In myth, it reflects inner reality—our psychological life, conscious and unconscious. There are apparently worthless qualities in us that, seen with a new eye, turn out to be beautiful. Ashes to roses, straw to gold. "The aim is to awaken in ourselves the old ability to read with intuitive understanding this pictorial script, that at one time was the bearer of the spiritual sustenance of our own ancestors," Zimmer wrote. "The answers to the riddles of existence that the tales incorporate—whether we are aware of the fact or not—are still shaping our lives."

III.

"Stories make us more alive, more human, more courageous, more loving. Why does anybody tell a story? It does indeed have something to do with faith, faith that the universe has meaning, that our little human lives are not irrelevant, that what we choose or say or do matters, matters cosmically."
—Madeleine L'Engle

IN HINDSIGHT THE PLACE where I grew up—abandoned dairy farms, hayfields slowly being overtaken by forests of alder—was pastoral. It felt that way on summer vacation, when my cousin and I would ride to the store to buy snow cones, or stay home and pelt each other with windfall apples. But in autumn the days turned ominous with wind and drizzle, giving my favourite books an appropriately solemn backdrop. I was drawn to fantasies of the Great Quest variety, usually ones in which a youthful misfit (or someone merely childlike—like a hobbit) is called on to assist in some cosmic struggle between good and evil. The number of books that fit this description is surprisingly large, though there are few really good ones. *The Lord of the Rings* is one, as is L'Engle's *A Wrinkle in Time* quartet, and Ursula K. Le Guin's *Earthsea* series, from which J.K. Rowling likely poached her idea of a school for young wizards. I read them all greedily, feet up on our family's couch, gobbling baked beans and grilled-cheese sandwiches.

I was equal-parts insecure and arrogant as a boy, not much different from how I am thirty years later, and I didn't settle well into the American small town we'd moved to when I was seven. I was, no doubt, a little tetched. By the time we moved to rural Washington state, we'd lived in BC, Australia, Singapore, and Malaysia. I had strange and vivid memories of Southeast Asia: giant bats silhouetted over the palm trees at dusk, monsoon storms on the South China Sea. I recall a motorcycle ride into the Malaysian jungle, where the local kids led me to peer into a deep well in the middle of the village. They dropped cabbage leaves into it, and when they hit the water—as I gaped, the villagers giggling at my reaction—I swear I saw some kind of giant beast, maybe a snake or crocodile, thrash around in the reflecting black water at the bottom. These experiences didn't dispose me well to Little League baseball. I once told my classmates that we lived in Malaysia because we'd washed up on shore after a shipwreck, and since I didn't know the real reason, I believed it. Unlike many square-peg children who get crushed by their sense of displacement, I took it as an indication that I was exceptional.

The ideals in mythic stories temper egotism and channel it toward higher purposes. I probably needed such stories more than most. In his book *The Uses of Enchantment*, Bruno Bettelheim argued that fairy tales and fantasies help children to discover who they are and to deal with the daily suffering of being newly human. In such myths young people hear, when the time is right, the call of something beyond homework and soccer games, something beyond the hopes and fears of their parents. (Then a tidal wave of adolescent hormones floods the system, smashing this fragile castle to matchsticks. But if we've built it once, a mythic structure for conscience and identity will reassemble itself later in life—often around the mortal forties, sometimes sooner.) Consider the plot of the Great Quest: a weak and unlikely character is thrust into a struggle he or she doesn't understand, against complex forces he or she can't hope to defeat, and is required to endure all kinds of hardships to serve the long struggle against the forces of darkness. This is a pretty good metaphor for childhood. Later, adults realize it's a spiritual sketch of life in general.

Mythic stories often tell us that there is some treasure hidden in the dark forest or in the underworld—an abandoned mine or an overgrown cave—and that the ugly or the outcast usually have inside information we should listen to. They point us, in general, to where we don't want to go. This is invaluable spiritual advice. In the Great Quest, human ignorance and greed throw the world out of balance, and it teeters on oblivion's edge. Reluctant heroes are called to make great sacrifices in order to turn things around and dispel the gathered clot of darkness. It's an honoured theme in Jewish and Christian scripture: selfish and heedless mortals open the door to the ruin of their people, and the fur-footed hero or unlikely prophet—never recognized as such by family and friends, who know his imperfections all too well—must come to set things right. "And God looked upon the Earth, and, behold, it was corrupt; for all flesh had corrupted his way upon the Earth."

Lidded under the rain-clouds that would last until April, the world outside the window all black branches and dead field grass, I would lose myself in imaginal landscapes that to me were more real, if less immediate, than long division and baseball practice. It was escapism, of course, and also compensation, as like many bookish kids I was short, underweight, and clueless in a fight. (Fortunately the Great Quest is encoded with the comforting message that weakness is, in the end, an asset: the weak, sensitive, and jumpy as they are, tend to look for solutions missed by stronger and more capable folk.) In the evening the burn-off flare of the oil refinery a mile away would cast a fire-glow onto the fields and low clouds, and the air smelled of waste sulphur—the very whiff of Mordor, or some other end-of-days purgatory. When you're a child the next world is close, especially at night. You can almost open the door and stride right out into it.

Life is monstrous. Horror, darkness, and suffering are part of the deal. Children sense this as keenly as adults, if not more so. Facing this reality, the protagonist of such mythic adventures— whether Ged of Earthsea, Harry Potter of Hogwarts, or Meg Murry of *A Wrinkle in Time*—often asks, "But what am I sup-posed to *do*?" The answer from the wizened elder is generally along the lines of, "We can't tell you, but we know you've got it in you. You'll have to make it up as you go along." Eleven-year-olds can reframe a lot of the bullying, injustice, and frustrations they en-dure every day, as well as their overall sense of lostness, by reading this kind of message.

For adults, there's a social cost to talking about the hidden light in all things. Most of us spend our days thrice-denying that other world, but there comes a time—again, around age forty—when we hear the accusatory crowing. Some parents are lucky to be drawn back into that world by their children. That's harder to do these days, when most fairy tales are encountered onscreen and in picture books, and have been Disneyfied and pixelized out of their archetypal substance.

Children know that the rational adult world is a fragile one, and until we train it out of them they understand the dif-ference between fast-food corporate myths and real ones. They are drawn, as the fairy tales tell them, to the light in the shad-ows. Those magic places they love, like the ones from our own childhoods, are usually forgotten zones—abandoned houses and ravines, bramble-grown lots lorded over by scavenging crows. The absence of landscape grown chaotic, the absence of a place where kids can sense the gathered darkness of the woods or be frightened by a rushing river, poses a spiritual danger to childhood. In grade two my cousin and I created an entire alternate world—which we gravely called "the desert," and knew to be a numinous landscape where anything could happen—out of a suburban gravel pit. Now it's a soccer field.

Humans are not creatures born of science. We are made of stories before we are concerned with information: creation stories, quest stories, love stories, end-of-the-world stories. Entering mystery is the heart of all great tales. The infotext-hyperlink-turbotech marketplace grows exponentially, but the human psyche does not. It remains childlike, stubborn, clinging to the places in memory where we've known magic. "Between two worlds life hovers like a star," wrote Byron, and American poet and essayist Kate Farrell, commenting on Byron's words, writes: "This sums up what countless poems, myths, teachings and traditions, in one way or another, assume or hint or say. That we belong to two worlds: the invisible, hard-to-know eternal one we come from and the noisy, obvious, temporal one all around us."

IV.

> "And little he knew of the things that ink may do, how it can mark a dead man's thought for the wonder of later years, and tell of happenings that are gone clean away, and be a voice for us out of the dark of time, and save many a fragile thing from the pounding of heavy ages; or carry to us, over the rolling centuries, even a song from lips long dead."
> —Lord Dunsany

AS I WRITE THIS, IT'S been grey and rainy for days. We have no field views here in Vancouver, but there's a wind in the door of our basement apartment. It makes the same forlorn sound— an eerie whistle, with an undertone of kazoo—that used to seep through the windowpanes of my family's old farmhouse. Autumn is here, and even in the city it's a season of introspection. Mostly. Childless for the moment, my wife and I are drawn more than we should be to the DVD store, food-show television, and pricey restaurants. Willa Cather, in her novella *The Song of the Lark*, summed up the dominant mood of the metropolis, where elder wisdom and youth's idealism are replaced with something called urban culture, which amounts mostly to eating out. "The rich, noisy city, fat with food and drink, is a spent thing; its chief concern is its digestion and its little game of hide-and-seek with the undertaker. Money and office and success are the consolations of impotence. Fortune turns kind to such solid people and lets them suck their bone in peace."

Where I walk in the forest near the university, the trees are matted from trunk to trunk with fallen leaves. The alder leaves are small and green, tooth-edged, and the platter-sized maple leaves are either a rusty cinnabar or an absurdly bright banana-yellow that lights the glades from the ground up. These fresh losses overlay the twigs, fir cones, needles, and last year's leaves— not quite soil yet—in a mat about an inch thick. This is the secret of life in the forest: death, or more accurately, the uptake of what was dead into new life. In the places of rot, the bottom-land muck is fertility, the ground of being. How what is lowly and lost allows the top branches to reach for the sky is an autumnal wisdom I've just started to appreciate. It's easy to miss the leaves for the forest, or to forget that the bare trees of late fall mean rich soil for spring.

The forest metaphor may hold for the human psyche. It's the same message delivered by myth. Where death is, where things are dark and left behind and forgotten, lies the soil of renewal. But we are not plants, we say; we are humans, creatures of mind and light and heart and soul, and we don't eat muck for breakfast. True, at least physically. But the psyche is an ecosystem, more like a forest than a kitchen nook, and within it we're bound to the old laws of root and soil. We have to eat our greens, and our browns, if we want to be soil for good seeds and grow up to be a tall tree—or, at least, be more than a patch of weeds.

Myths furnish spiritual nourishment, Zimmer says, and I agree, though I have a hard time defining those terms—"spiritual" is always a suspect word, and "nourishment" is vague. What is nourished? The mind? The soul? And what do those words mean? Pickling such terms in academic formaldehyde for later dissection doesn't work, because they must be alive to be understood, and some part of us that is not purely intellectual must be awake to understand them. Soul, spirit, nourishment: of all the possible adjectives that could be invoked to qualify them, "numinous"—a word favoured by Jung as well as C.S. Lewis—might be the best. Like the word "magic," *numinous* hints at the breaking through of some other reality into this one, suggests that things here are not quite what they seem.

For better or worse, these are the words that limn the Faery realm. I respect their flitty nature. Like quarks or pixies, grab for them and they're gone. But they do have meaning to us, if we sense something beyond the material world, or before it, or infusing it. That something is best left unnamed, because it is, simply, the presence before names. Spiritual nourishment means having that essential part of us—what is nameless and eternal—reflected back to us in art and literature, or in other people. We sense that presence in mythic stories, an echo of longing that we can't quite place.

The intention of myths, if they have one, is to change us, either by inspiring or troubling us. They seed our souls. For a culture to deserve the label, a relationship to land and pleasure like that proposed by the slow-food movement is essential. But if sustainability is what we're after, it won't be enough to load up the back of the electric car with heirloom tomatoes and whole-grain organic bread, cultured oysters and local turnips. A sustainable culture depends not on full bellies, but on longing souls, on people who are reaching within and beyond themselves to bring their tiny portion of light into the world. In this sense the age of reconsideration has a whole other ecology to reconsider, and these stories—fairy tales, legends, myths—are its heritage seeds. They are not processed by entertainment executives and market-tested for maximum profit yield. They contain substances thousands of years old that are essential to the human soul.

There is something suspicious about people who are a little too interested in myth, like the woman with five cats who wears three shades of lavender in one outfit. But this was always the kind of woman—the misfit, thick-spectacled with a walleye—who knew magic. Then there are pallid young goths, or aged poets with compass pendants wandering the halls of small colleges. All of these people want the world to be what they know it is, which is magical. But they appear to be as stuck as the rest of us. Maybe there is a way of story, an approach to myth, that has more to it than comic conventions and crystal shops.

Yes, it might be good for goths and poets to set out into the world and do something tangible rather than dawdle about in archetypal realms. It might mean even more to the world, teetering on the brink as it always is, for those who are out in the offices of the world—doing far more tangible business than the planet can support—to spend some time considering what a Grail is anyway, and what myth they are living. Because if you don't become conscious of what myth you want to live, or have been doomed to live by your history—most of us have had our myth stamped into our souls by the time we're eleven—there is a good chance that somebody else's myth will live you. As Robert Bly pointed out, most people don't even think about this sort of thing until they reach middle age. This is bad news because these other myths foisted on us are usually the blandest sort. They don't acknowledge the existence of the Fisher King wounds described in the Arthurian canon or the sacred words that might, at some level, undo such stubborn curses. Mostly they are myths like "I'm a good father, I earn a good living for my family." Or "I am a faithful wife and a good Christian" (or Jew, or Hindu). You know you're being subsumed by a lesser myth when the most potent word in it is "good." Good is not what fairy tales, scripture or myths try to draw out from us, or get us to embody. They ask more of us than that.

How do we start, as Zimmer suggests, a living conversation with mythic stories? My next move will be to buy some anthologies of folklore, and search the storage locker for that retelling of *The Snow Queen* my parents bought me when I was five. From there, maybe—maybe—a book club. For men, if I can find at least three other guys who want to sit around over tea and discuss fairy tales. Maybe beer would help. We could start with Simon Armitage's new translation of *Sir Gawain and the Green Knight*, the Arthurian tale based on the old Irish Cuchulainn story of a beheading contest. It's an unusual epic poem, a kind of reverse quest that may contain some potent symbols for North Americans in an era of ecological catastrophe.

At the level of the soul, we've been crawling across an apocalyptic wasteland in Western culture for at least a hundred years, which is partly why the outer world is starting to look the same way. As we consume things to fill the hole left by the absence of the sacred—tangibles like gourmet food or intangibles like the nightly TV fix—the world gets used up. And oil refineries do look quite a bit like Mordor from a distance. Either we were born into a pathless culture, or we have tried every door and now our faith in life has been shattered by having seen too much—too much tragedy, too much horror. When this happens the two most obvious paths are to become a hedonist or a devotee of end-times fundamentalism.

We are not living at the end time, but in a between-time, when an old world has been bombed to ruins and the new villages have not been built. We're in the Waste Land of T.S. Eliot, where "the last fingers of leaf / Clutch and sink into the wet bank. The wind / Crosses the brown land, unheard. The nymphs are departed." In this blasted and unmagicked landscape—a kind of permanent autumn, thin black trees and dull rain—we hope for home, but don't know where to find it. Maybe this is why we have a mania for real estate. We all want to feel stable, and we're hoping we can purchase stability from an agent.

Slow stories are part of our journey back from the landscape of apocalypse to the living villages of post-postmodern life—whatever those may look like—where hopefully there is more hearth than high-definition video. Where ordinary things like dinner and myths are sacred because they are allowed the time and space to be so. "The reason why the world lacks unity, and lies broken and in heaps, is because man is disunited with himself," Ralph Waldo Emerson wrote. Myth unites us with other people by showing us our common pain, faults, glory. But a possibly greater value is the inner unity it brings to our souls—collecting our fragments, recognizing our deeper selves in the stories. We're all Midas, but also all prodigal sons, having spent much time in riotous living, getting and spending. Mythic stories, inspiring us to leave behind the troughs of the pig shed for the numinous light of the *mundus imaginalis*, are part of the way home, part of our return to an enduring mystery.

REVOLUTION OF THE TWO AHMADS

ABOU FARMAN
Maisonneuve

AHMAD, THE SON OF our family's gardener, wanted to be a get-away-car driver. Not just any old getaway driver. He wanted to be like those guys we'd seen together one night on the small black-and-white TV in the pantry, the Baader-Meinhof Gang, West German urban guerrillas with a penchant for BMWs and Mercedes.

Images of the Baader-Meinhof Gang were probably among the first accompanied by the caption "terrorism" on television news in Iran. Whatever the word's intended meaning, it has only ever referred to "the bad guys," but in the Iran of the 1970s many had developed a deep sympathy for political outlaws. After all, they were struggling (like so many Iranians) for a world arranged somehow differently, with more justice and more freedom. Ahmad harboured similar dreams, but at age sixteen, he hoped to get in a few joyrides on the way to that better world.

When he was a toddler, Ahmad had stuck his fist inside a wood-burning oven, scorching his left hand down to a charred stub. All he had left were finger stumps, ugly as cigar butts. The grafted, discoloured skin was taut like plastic in some places, wrinkled like an old man's elbow in others. Nothing he could imagine now or in the future could help him fix that—not God, not modern medicine, and certainly not the wealth and influence of his dad's employers. Ahmad didn't like school or work, but most of all he hated being powerless. The only influence he felt came from waving his frightening fist in our faces.

His father, Mr. Nabi, often found himself frantically searching for his son. Ahmad, it would turn out, had taken off on his dad's moped again, and was zipping around Tehran, a feverish city of four million. The moped was not the ideal getaway vehicle: you had to pedal hard to start it up and it could only do about twenty kilometres per hour. The double-sided *khorjeen* draped across its back—a colourful, woven sack traditionally slung over donkeys—smelled of wet lamb's wool, petrol, and cilantro. But it had a motor and wheels, and in Ahmad's imagination, it could take corners like a black Mercedes.

Whenever Ahmad came around to our house, I'd run out to see him. He was four years older than me, and more rebellious. He smelled of danger. He never said anything concrete about where he'd been and what he'd seen but I always got the sense that he'd been somewhere, seen something, or was involved in some big plan. He'd shake his head impatiently, knowingly, and say, "Things are happening."

And they were.

One Friday in September 1978, Ahmad took off again on his dad's moped. The heat of the summer was subsiding, the promise of a long freshness lay ahead and suddenly a million people were marching on downtown Tehran to protest against the Shah, his regime, and society as it had been arranged for them. The revolution was blooming unexpectedly in early fall.

The signs were unmistakable, though no one knew quite how to read them. The religious city of Qom had experienced demonstrations. A few people had been shot. The Shah had declared and lifted and redeclared martial law. Liquor stores, movie theatres, and other "dens of corruption" had been arsoned around the country. The universities were boiling over with leftist ideological passion, and through the year a series of workers' strikes (especially those in the petroleum industry) had frightened the silk pants off the royal state. Strikes by oil workers!? The organization, the unity, and the power they implied struck right at the heart of the state. Then, in the oil-producing southern port of Abadan, Cinema Rex was doused with cheap Iranian petrol and set on fire, killing 400 moviegoers.

Whispers around the schoolyard said the Shah's secret police had set the fire, or maybe the CIA; other rumours fingered the communists, the left, or union organizers. That summed up the two main forces in the world at the time: right against left, West versus East, each projecting images of its own rightful victory in the march of Modern History. It was only years later that everyone began to blame the cinema fire on the mullahs, the ultimate victors of the revolution, who came out of nowhere to blindside History itself.

That September, when the radio announced that martial law had been re-declared, Mr. Nabi changed his boots and rushed to get home before curfew, but his moped was nowhere to be found. Ahmad had got wind of a huge protest in Jaleh Square and driven down there on his getaway moped. That was the place to be on September 8 if you wanted to raise a charred fist against the feudal skies.

The revolution had many peaceful days, days when soldiers refused to open fire and dismounted their tanks to embrace their brethren and have red roses pinned onto their fatigues. But this was not one of those days. The details were never clarified. Troops fired on the protestors and the army's US-made helicopters swooped down, chasing crowds out of the square and into surrounding alleys. Later that night, trucks arrived and carted the corpses away to dumps outside the city. No one is certain whether a couple of hundred died or a few thousand, but during a stand-off in an alley somewhere, a gardener's son got caught in the crossfire and his dreams of freedom, of getting away in a black Mercedes, lay lifeless next to an upended moped with its wheels spinning in the air.

Revolution. On the one hand, it means a dramatic break, a new start; on the other it describes a completed path around a circle, ending up in the same old place, over and over, like a wheel spinning. So in one word we see two opposing senses of time, one open and linear, the other closed and cyclical. History is change; history is repetition.

Unlike uprisings, rebellions, insurrections, or conquests, revolutions are built on grand visions of history and progress, legacy of the Enlightenment's quest to create a rational world of equality, safety, and opportunity for all by breaking the hold of the aristocracy's inherited power and privilege. From each according to his ability and no need for getaway-car drivers. Let us march, then, you and I, with a million others down this path toward a better life, sharing our potential and purpose as one. History moves towards fellowship. Washington, Robespierre, Lenin, Mao, and, yes, Khomeini may be considered equal heirs to this modern vision of society.

By the 1970s, though, the promises of previous revolutions seemed bankrupt. Capitalism thrust people into the world as solitary, unequal individuals ready to put a real or metaphorical gun to each other's heads for a dime of profit. Communism turned people into instruments of the state. Nationalism was an emotional Pavlov's bell ringing people to their feet in large stadiums to hail megalomaniacs. Instead of a humanistic dawn, the global landscape was silhouetted with inglorious pumpkins.

Down into modernity's midnight floated the darkly-robed and white-bearded Ayatollah Khomeini. The Ayatollah—literally meaning "Shadow of God"—first came to us as a blazing image on television. Exiled to Iraq, then to a Parisian suburb with the noble name of Neauphle-le-Chateau, he kept repeating his most important mantra, "Neither East nor West." He spoke of a world beyond money, state, and nation. When he declared, "All as one" or "All together," he reached out to large, forgotten swathes of the world, renewing their sense of communion and significance. And who could ask for anything more than a sense of significance in the world? Islamic activists and ideologues had been around since the nineteenth century, cobbling together a hodgepodge of ideas about self-determination, imperialism, and authenticity. But it was the practical victory of Khomeini's revolution that made Islam available as a viable modern political identity. Hundreds of millions everywhere took it on and the rest, so to speak, is history. Whatever else one might have to say about Allah or Allah's bearded shadow on earth, the fact is that the Ayatollah changed the world. In many ways, we're still living in the world he created.

These days, with religion playing politics everywhere, it is
difficult to recall how improbable a religious revolution seemed
thirty years ago. An Islamic Republic sounded so retrograde, so
outdated that even clerics feared the idea at first; while everyone
else, from the democratic centre to the communist Tudeh Party,
underestimated the political potential of Islam. What could a
soft-spoken, God-fearing seventy-eight-year-old anachron-
ism do? With his bushy eyebrows ending in a sharp point and
those staunch eyes staring out from under all his facial plum-
age, Khomeini looked like an extinct species of owl, not a fear-
some revolutionary leader. The young engineers and architects—
they were the ones to worry about, bursting out of universities
with hot ideas in their heads and blueprints for a better future
rolled tightly under their arms. The paradigm was still the Cold
War and the enemy was communism and Reds like the Baader-
Meinhof Gang.

The Iranian Revolution began, for all intents and purposes, as
a secular, leftist uprising. Throughout the '70s, the unions organized worker strikes, Marxist students distributed leaflets, guer-
rilla groups camped in the woods, and exiles mobilized anti-Shah
sentiment abroad (the Baader-Meinhof Gang itself was formed in
the aftermath of a visit to West Berlin by the Shah of Iran, after
a protestor was shot by German police). It was the left that "educated the masses"—from soldiers to students to shopkeepers—
toward revolution. On weekends, when thousands flocked to the
mountains north of Tehran to hike and picnic, leftist organizations would take turns laying down photocopied pages of banned
books on the trail. By the time hikers reached the top of the trail,
they would have sidestepped their way through a chapter of *Das
Kapital* and gained a different understanding of social class and
surplus value.

There were good reasons for revolutionary sentiment. In 1953, the United States engineered a coup to oust the popular, democratic Prime Minister, Mohamad Mossadegh. That ended the country's slow but sure steps towards political democracy. Backed heavily by the Americans, the Shah took total control of the state and outlawed the Soviet-supported Tudeh Party along with all other dissident voices, including clerical ones. SAVAK, the Shah's notorious secret service, jailed and tortured as many leftists as it could find.

Then, in January of 1979, the Shah kissed the tarmac of Mehrabad airport and flew into wandering exile. Without the Shah's regime and his American imperialist puppeteers, the country experienced a few months of turmoil followed by a raucous year of democratic struggle. Leftist groups broke open the prison gates and released thousands of colleagues. They attacked the army barracks, and their ranks and weapons caches swelled. People of all convictions demonstrated regularly, even as the army held out. On February 1, 1979, the Ayatollah returned from exile. Eleven days later, the army collapsed, its arsenal fell into the hands of the people, and the radio changed its greeting to "This is the voice of the Iranian revolution."

Hundreds of thousands celebrated on the streets. Women with and without veils marched for their rights. Newspapers printed whatever they liked. Other exiled leaders returned as well, including my aunt, Maryam, who was a pioneering feminist. Accompanying Maryam was her husband, Nouredin Kianouri, who was head of the Tudeh Party and whose first name ironically meant "Light of Religion." I remember Kianouri as having merciless eyes. We visited them once in East Berlin where they were being humbly housed in exile by the East German government. We flew to West Berlin and walked across Check Point Charlie at night,

dragging suitcases across the spotlit sliver of no man's land between West and East. It felt like we were in a movie. Maryam
and Kianouri picked us up on the other side and drove us to their
small house outside Berlin. On the highway, the car door swung
open by accident and I almost fell out. As my sister grabbed my
arm, I saw Kianouri looking back at me in the rear-view mirror. He said nothing. His expression did not change. He did not
slow down.

My aunt and Kianouri honestly thought the revolution was
theirs. The Tudeh Party aligned itself with Khomeini and a hybrid
of Islam and Marxism worked its way into the political system.
But the left was basically adrift in unfamiliar waters and the alliance with clerics caused internal schisms. The leftists were not
sure how to manoeuvre politically or build the right institutions.
They were mainly trained in writing manifestos and issuing class
analyses. And in this case, Marxism got it all wrong: religion was
not just an apolitical opiate, it would not simply get kicked aside
like a bad habit.

As the left analyzed, the clergy acted. Khomeini, already a
popular figure, shrewdly built his support structures. In exile, he
had mastered the trick of mixing modern tools with old structures.
He famously sent recorded sermons down the pipeline of mosques
and religious networks to reach millions of semi-literate Iranians.
As provisional governments tried to build coalitions, Khomeini set
up parallel groups of armed men, judicial councils and provincial
representatives. These groups slowly purged the uncooperative.
By the beginning of 1980, Khomeini was writing a new religious
constitution and confidently calling the revolution "Islamic." The
left, like the rest of the world, fell into utter confusion. "Islamic
revolution" was an oxymoron, a historical impossibility. Yet, like
so many impossible things, it became a part of history.

One by one, leftist groups split, were persecuted, and died away. By 1983, even the cooperative ones had been crushed. My aunt and Kianouri were jailed. A little later, Kianouri, visibly bruised and beaten, confessed on television that he had been a puppet of Soviet designs and reneged on all his ideals. He died under government surveillance in 1999.

My aunt was released from prison into house arrest soon after. When she came out, the Soviet Union and East Germany no longer existed, the Berlin Wall and Check Point Charlie had vanished, and everyone was using something called the Internet. She had been imprisoned in one kind of universe, then released into another. My brother who visited her in Tehran said she had trouble reconciling the two. She died under house arrest last year, but lives on at YouTube.

My family left Iran at the end of 1978, two weeks after my thirteenth birthday. I experienced the actual revolution hunched over a small Grundig short wave radio in a foreign kitchen. Through phone calls to friends and family we got the skinny on imprisonments, confiscations, and raids. My father, who was already seven years dead by then, absurdly appeared on the revolution's wanted list. That list (a thousand names of families for some reason or other associated with the old regime) was originally concocted by leftists. Soon, those leftists found themselves on another, much longer list, and had to flee to places like Sweden and Canada.

One of them, a trained architect also called Ahmad, was a student in an English Second Language (ESL) class I taught. The ESL classes were organized by a left-leaning cultural centre that used to operate out of the basement of a warehouse building on Coloniale Street in Montreal. In the back of the Nima Centre—named after a poet—there were fading photocopies of newsletters and broadsheets issued by fragmented and bickering groups in Europe and North America, which nevertheless gave their publications titles like Solidarity and Unity. Moustachioed men hunched over ashtrays and leafed through them, swearing at the long Montreal winter. Inside their coat pockets, they kept their fists clenched. There was still talk of organizing, sending word back to Iran, protesting in front of the embassy. These were men who once directed marches, risked their lives for a better society, escaped prison with fingers missing, had friends hunted down and assassinated. Who could tell them it was all over? Who dared say it was all for nothing?

Clean-shaven, energetic, and a non-smoker, Ahmad stood out. He too had been tortured in prison. He too escaped. It took two arrests and one imprisonment for him to decide to leave in 1984. The night Ahmad took off, for the border of Pakistan, he carried nothing but his architecture licence and a roll of blueprints, which he'd secretly obtained from a friend, for a project near the border. He used these as cover, showing them to every soldier and guard as he fled through the countryside, up the mountains and over the border.

Five years on, having smuggled himself from Karachi to Montreal, he was still holding on to that tube of blueprints, as though they contained the outline of his own future. From the way he described them, it seemed that they had somehow kept him alive. Unbroken, he was determined to make a new life and was fighting to have his architecture licence recognized in Canada, even as he drove a cab to make ends meet.

Why, I asked, did he wait so long to leave Iran?

"We had made the revolution," he said, "and we thought we had to stick by it. It took us a long time to admit that the only rational option was to run."

He described how hard they had struggled to understand the situation. Was this a bourgeois regime or a petit-bourgeois regime? A reactionary transition or a revolutionary moment? Were they to accept the *lumpenproletariat* as a revolutionary force? How about the religious proletariat? Every week, some group or other would attempt a new socio-historical analysis, and before the end of the week it would completely fall apart—first the analysis, then the group.

"It got to a point," Ahmad told me, "that 'History,' 'Progress,' 'Society'—all the big concepts of the twentieth century—fell apart."

Without a forward march, or a framework for understanding the world, individual survival became his only concern.

The sound of those concepts crashing to the ground—like statues pulled down in public squares, "cast, hollow and unsupported," as Osip Mandelstam once wrote—is still ringing, and not just in Iran. No one can pretend anymore to know where History is headed, or design what Society ought to look like. No one can earnestly imagine humanity as a kind of fellowship, or propose for it a greater sense of purpose in the world. So for now, the only remaining ethos, as Ahmad pointed out, seems to be survival. There are other names for it—names ranging from "the free market" to "the selfish gene"—but that's what it comes down to. Bare survival.

When last I saw Ahmad, the ex-architect and revolutionary was a draftsman on payroll, his hair grey and thinning, back curled over a desk and an ashtray. He was touching up a redesign of a mall entrance for his corporate bosses. What the Islamic regime had not managed to break in him seemed to have been broken by a solitary and inconclusive career path.

For a moment, in the round patch of light slanting across the drafts of his blueprints, I saw the wheels of the other Ahmad's overturned moped, still spinning aimlessly—over his head, and over ours.

HONEYMOON'S OVER: WHAT'S NEXT FOR THE GAY RIGHTS MOVEMENT

PAUL GALLANT
This Magazine

LAST JANUARY, HELEN KENNEDY sat behind the *Hockey Night in Canada* desk with CBC's Ron MacLean, explaining why her organization, Egale Canada, had filed a complaint about sports commentator Mike Milbury. Milbury had worried on-air about the "pansification" of hockey. To suggest that a pansified league is inferior is to say that pansies are inferior, Kennedy argued.

"Why can't young boys be effeminate?" asked Kennedy, a lesbian with a devilish glint in her eye. "Why is it seen as lesser? You're less a person if you're not macho?"

Since taking over the national lobby group for lesbian, gay, bisexual, and trans people in April 2007, Kennedy had spoken at many rallies and public meetings. But that six-minute TV conversation took her into 1.3 million of the most testosterone-filled homes in Canada, where she evidently touched a nerve. "I received hundreds of emails after *Hockey Night in Canada*, and some of them were vile, absolutely vile," says Kennedy. "That level of discrimination and homophobia is still there."

The "pansygate" confrontation allowed Kennedy to speak to a wide audience about homophobic bullying and safe schools, one of Egale's key projects. But the kafuffle was a sticks-and-stones debate over a made-up noun. Arguing semantics would not likely woo the hearts and minds of Canadians who have a problem with LGBT people, nor was it likely to improve the quality of life for LGBT people who are harassed and discriminated against. The pansy issue, while important, just didn't have legs, and it slipped off the agenda in one news cycle. It was an illustrative episode for Egale, an organization used to making front-page news. For Egale Canada, nothing has ever equalled the remarkable three-year final battle for same-sex marriage. The group was nearly ubiquitous on the national stage from the same-sex "summer of love" in 2003 through to Parliament's final vote in December 2006. Those years put lesbian and gay issues at the centre of the national consciousness. Egale Canada and its spinoff, Canadians for Equal Marriage, raised nearly $1 million to back the court challenges that started the nuptial landslide, then led the lobbying to persuade Parliament to uphold marriage equality laws.

Same-sex marriage was, arguably, the final piece of a decades-long project for full legal equality for gay men and lesbians. In the words of Michael Leshner, a lawyer and long-time activist, "With marriage, you win the pot of gold at the end of the rainbow." His marriage to Michael Stark was one of the first legal same-sex marriages in the country. Mission accomplished. Right?

If queers were going to advocate for something more—and Canada, pink as it is, is still not quite a gay utopia—activists would have to look beyond changing discriminatory laws. But the transition from wartime to peacetime has not been easy. At the height of the marriage debate, Egale's annual operating budget peaked at $538,000; now it's about $160,000, plus donated office space in Ottawa and Toronto. This year the Coalition for Lesbian and Gay Rights in Ontario packed up shop after more than thirty-three years, during which time it had successfully advocated to include gay and lesbian people in Ontario's Human Rights Code and get the Toronto District School Board to adopt a non-discrimination policy that included LGBT people.

In January a group of six queer health activists launched a human rights complaint against Health Canada, accusing it of discriminating against gay, lesbian, and bisexual people in its spending. The complaint got limited mainstream media coverage. "I naively thought our complaint was going to be a sexy issue, but it's not sexy like marriage," says Gens Hellquist, executive director of the Canadian Rainbow Health Coalition and an activist since 1971. In 2004 the CRHC had a budget of $2.3 million to promote better health care for LGBT people. Now it has an annual budget of approximately $10,000.

Marriage was a victory that came with a price—complacency. Activists who believe that LGBT people are still oppressed are struggling to find issues to rally the troops. Kennedy has taken Egale into schools with a student survey about homophobia in the classroom and into the world beyond Canada's borders, asking that musicians who sing anti-gay lyrics be denied entry to Canada. The new directions are expanding to include more health care workers, teachers, artists, and people of colour. Kennedy seems prepared to throw lots of ideas at the wall and see what sticks, but some of her peers wonder if the issues that attract the most public attention—and the most donations— are actually the most important ones for LGBT Canadians.

Susan Ursel came out in the late 1980s, when Canadians could be fired or refused housing for being gay or lesbian, a time when police would turn a blind eye to—or worse, perpetrate—harassment and assault. At first Ursel confined her lesbian life to socializing, but then, as a lawyer, she started doing activist work. Ursel joined a legal community that had successfully removed several forms of institutional discrimination, but still had much more to accomplish. Going into the 1990s, gay men and lesbians were legally acknowledged as people, but not as couples, and with tangible rights like pensions, child custody, hospital visitations, and inheritance riding on relationship recognition, the next step was obvious. "The work around same-sex relationship recognition is what brought in the churches and other groups," says Ursel. "It was a tremendous focal point and it crossed all kinds of lines to unify people."

In 1995 Egale and several lawyers who had been handling the relationship-recognition cases convinced a gay couple to walk away from a Supreme Court challenge over the right to marry. The lawyers, believing that the courts and the public weren't ready, worried that a negative ruling would ruin their momentum. But in 1999, the Supreme Court of Canada ruled on the famed M. v. H. case concerning the acrimonious split of a lesbian couple. The court ruled that they had financial obligations to one another—effectively granting same-sex couples the same status as heterosexual common-law spouses. The M-word was, at long last, openly tossed around. Suddenly, longtime activists found themselves surrounded by gay and lesbian couples they had never before laid eyes on.

"I could tell at fundraising events that it mobilized a segment of the queer community that had more money," says Cynthia Petersen, a lawyer who worked on M. v. H. and many other groundbreaking Charter cases.

Earlier activists usually had more radical roots. They wanted equal treatment before the law, but they were also interested in what made gay and lesbian people different: a more open approach to sex that included promiscuity, open relationships, and the commercial sex culture of bars and bathhouses. Their defiant attitude toward public morals and mainstream expectations alienated gay and lesbian people who just wanted to fit in. Marriage, with its formal clothes and kitschy cakes, changed the equation.

Same-sex marriage was, in fact, a perfect storm. Established middle- and upper-class gay and lesbian couples who normally avoided anything other than traditional party politics wanted it. Sympathetic straights—people who didn't understand things like cross-dressing or anonymous sex in parks—could relate to the desire to marry. And the vehement opposition, which highlighted the sway religious beliefs still have over public policy, was a tremendous motivating force. Everything was so delightfully black and white: at some specific moment, there would be a definitive thumbs-up or thumbs-down. Queer Canadians would be equal or not. For pure drama, no other issue could touch it.

Not even a legal case that dealt with actual depictions of sex could compete with the sex appeal of marriage. Petersen had represented Little Sister's, a Vancouver gay and lesbian bookstore, against Canada Customs, successfully arguing to the Supreme Court in 2000 that the border cops were targeting gay and lesbian pornography. People offered Little Sister's good wishes, but not much cash.

"Marriage affects everyone, even if you choose not to marry,"
says Petersen. "With Little Sister's, censorship affects everyone,
too, but a lot of people would say, 'I don't consume pornography
so it's not my issue.' "

It would shock most outsiders to know how much of the equal-
marriage leadership was, in fact, quite cold to the idea of marriage itself. The activists leading the charge were the ones who
had honed their skills during the bathhouse raids, the AIDS crisis,
and anti-censorship campaigns, and many saw the institution of
marriage itself as a tool of the patriarchy and symbol of assimila-
tion. Like Christian missionaries who shrug when Jesus's name is
mentioned, this faction had no appetite for church weddings and
happy honeymoons—only for ending discrimination.

"I was supportive of the equal-marriage campaign, but I wasn't
enthusiastic," says Kaj Hasselriis, a journalist and former Winnipeg mayoral candidate who, in 2006, was the chief spokesperson
for Canadians for Equal Marriage. "I think, 'Why can't we do our
own thing, define our relationships our own way?' But I believe
in choice. And once the courts had given us the right to marry, it
would have been a disaster to have that taken away."

The community's marriage skeptics waited quietly and patiently
for the circus to end, knowing there were many other things that
needed attention. Marriage had steamrolled most other issues: in
1998, for example, Ontario delisted sexual reassignment surgery
from the list of procedures covered by the province's Health Insurance Act, forcing transsexuals to pay tens of thousands of dollars
for the procedure. Canada Customs (now operating as Canada
Border Services Agency), mostly ignoring the Little Sister's ruling, continued to target gay and lesbian materials at the border. In
2004, Hamilton police raided a gay bathhouse, charging two men
for consensual sexual activity.

There were rumblings that activist groups, Egale in particular, had become too focused on marriage and too distant from racier topics like sex laws and censorship. "I think we allowed the issues of sexuality to get buried. It was an apologetic position—'Please like us because we're just like you,'" says Hellquist. "If you were skeptical of marriage as the most important issue, you had to be careful what you said."

The Civil Marriage Act, introduced by the Liberal government of Paul Martin, was passed by the House of Commons on June 28, 2005. After defeating Martin the following year, Prime Minister Stephen Harper put the issue to another free vote on December 7, 2006. Harper's motion lost, 175 to 123.

The Conservatives wouldn't be snatching back the pot of gold. The question was not only settled in law, but in the court of public opinion. In 1997, 63 percent of Canadians opposed same-sex marriage, according to one survey. By 2006, the percentage of Canadians who supported it was as high as 60. No wonder people are always asking Kennedy, "We have same-sex marriage. What else do we need?"

The list of remaining LGBT issues in Canada can be filed under two headings: "Complicated" and "Divisive." Ask an activist to name the number one issue and the answer is bound to be safe schools—which fits under the "Complicated" heading. Schools are where gay kids still get beat up, children of same-sex parents get taunted, and straight children form their impressions about queers.

Under Helen Kennedy, Egale Canada's largest project has been its National Climate Survey on Homophobia in Canadian Schools. Phase One, released in March, found that 75 percent of self-identified lesbian, gay, bisexual, trans, queer, and questioning students feel unsafe in at least one place at school. Six out of ten LGBT

students had been verbally harassed at school, one in four physically harassed. (An earlier study suggested that 32 percent of lesbian,
gay, and bisexual youth contemplate or attempt suicide.) The report recommended that schools implement anti-homophobia and
anti-transphobia policies—things as simple as assuring students
that it's okay to bring a same-sex date to a dance—and supporting
Gay-Straight Alliance clubs. Some principals and school boards
actively block the clubs, which allow students to talk peer-to-peer
about sexual orientation and homophobia.

If marriage was about getting the Supreme Court and Parliament to do the right thing, education advocacy means getting
nearly 500 school boards across Canada to do the right thing—
and spend money doing it. Some boards are receptive to LGBT
issues, while some are emphatically not. Some have policies about
issues like homophobic bullying but don't have the money or the
will to enforce them. A national group like Egale, which is accus-
tomed to supporting court challenges and lobbying politicians,
now runs around responding to the disaster of the moment. It's
important work, but negotiations with ministry bureaucrats seldom garner headlines. Unlike marriage, school issues are also hard
to keep resolved. Responding to a human-rights complaint, British Columbia has introduced an optional high school course on
social justice that would include sexual orientation, race, ethnicity,
and gender topics. The case started in 1997 and even now, two
years after implementation, the issue is still with the BC Human
Rights Commission and the original complainants, Peter and
Murray Corren, claim that the Abbotsford school board continues
to create obstacles to the course being offered.

"I've seen great documents coming out of the education ministry recently," says j wallace, a trans man whose job description
for the Halton District School Board includes facilitating GSA

clubs. "But there's such a gap between the policy and the implementation, especially at the Catholic school boards."

The rights of transsexual and transgendered people—those whose gender identities don't match the physical characteristics they were born with—are also a top priority for Egale.

Like gay and lesbian people thirty years ago, trans people continue to suffer blatant discrimination and are often the victims of violence—they're easier to target if they have trouble "passing" as their chosen gender. Though adding gender identity to the hate provisions of the Criminal Code remains a political priority, access to good health care is considered the most pressing concern. The hormones and surgical procedures that help trans people change their gender are expensive and difficult to access, especially outside major urban centres. But, as with education, health care decision-makers are spread across the country, and just when one problem is dealt with, another emerges. After several human rights complaints spent years wandering through the labyrinth of the Ontario Human Rights Tribunal, the province relisted sexual reassignment surgery last year. Hooray. Then Alberta delisted SRS this year. Boo.

Though Ontario expects to pay for eight to ten SRS procedures annually—Alberta paid for fifteen last year—many trans people choose not to have surgery, using hormones, clothes, language, and sensibility to shape their gender identity in distinctive ways. Many live mainstream lives, choosing not to call attention to their trans identity. All of which makes their concerns a hard sell. Trans health issues involve money and training as much as they do political will. Even obvious allies like gay and lesbian people tend to have a shallow grasp of their needs and even of their numbers.

"There's a lot of preconceptions about transsexual people," says Diane Grant, one of the organizers of Toronto's Trans Pride

March. "Throughout my life I've taken as much grief from the gay community as I have from the straight community."

There are also simpler issues to grapple with, but little consensus around them. Before it decided to close up shop, the Coalition for Lesbian and Gay Rights in Ontario had campaigned against the Conservative government's raising the age of consent to sixteen from fourteen while maintaining the clause that restricted anal sex to married people over eighteen. That clause is seen to target gay men. CLGRO argued that the Conservative bill criminalized consensual sexual relationships between young people and did nothing to address the discriminatory clause.

But more conservative gay and lesbian people, especially those who had been attracted to activism by marriage, didn't want to touch the issue, which conjured stereotypes of gay sexual predators who wanted to fuck fourteen-year-olds. CLGRO has also lobbied against Canada's bawdy-house laws, which criminalize anyone found in a place used for prostitution or "acts of indecency." Depending on police attitudes, gay bathhouses or even homes where group sex takes place might be considered bawdy houses. Despite some attempts at partnering with prostitutes' rights groups, a coherent sex-law reform campaign never took off. "In the end we didn't have an issue we were able to take up and engage the community," says CLGRO co-founder Tom Warner. "We had a membership that was dwindling and aging, making it difficult to get things done."

Some have accused Egale of pushing questions of sexual freedoms to the bottom of its to-do list, and although Kennedy says these concerns remain, she does not bring them up herself in conversation. Call her prudish, but the fact is there's not enough pressure for Egale to take up this work. And though HIV-AIDS has been an integral part of gay activism since the 1980s, Kennedy says the issue is not in Egale's mandate (though some of its legal repercussions, like the Canadian Blood Services ban on gay men donating blood, are). She's also quick to point out that most HIV-AIDS organizations, with their access to government dollars, are much better funded than her organization.

The legal atmosphere has changed too. Though the courts were the main engine of the marriage train, they have become harder to use. In 2006, the Conservatives suspended the Court Challenges Program, a federal grant system that had helped fund many previous LGBT rights cases. Now Egale must rely solely on its own dwindling funds and the pro bono work of lawyers. Its current flagship case, Heintz v. Christian Horizons, is expected to go before the Supreme Court in December. The case pits a publicly funded Christian service organization against a lesbian employee who says she was fired because of her sexual orientation. This perfect charter duel—religious freedom versus gay rights—is sure to generate headlines, but there are some who would rather leave established religion alone to lick its wounds after its marriage defeat.

Egale's Stop Murder Music campaign, launched in 2007, urges the government to deny entrance to Canada to certain Caribbean singers, and this stance has also raised eyebrows. Few would defend Elephant Man lyrics like "Battyman fidead! Tek dem by surprise!" (translated as "Queers must be killed! Take them by surprise"). But demanding that the government ban hateful singers is, for some, a little too close to censorship—a practice that gay activists, in cases like Little Sister's, have historically fought against.

"If I'm saying that I should be able to produce or write pornography without committing a criminal act, then I think I'm also saying that hate mongers have the right to do what they do without committing a criminal act," says Warner. "Frankly, I think there's something to be said for letting some idiot get up and spew hate."

But Kennedy says it's a matter of life and death for LGBT people in the Caribbean, who are frequently harassed and beaten by people singing these songs. The lyrics are not just insults, they are threats, she argues—and therefore covered by the Criminal Code. And the symbolism will hopefully resonate back in the singers' home countries.

"We are very mindful of free speech," she says, "but if something violates hate-crime laws, we are going to speak up. You have to take responsibility for what you say."

Though the Stop Murder Music campaign has alienated some free-speech advocates—and many activists whose roots go back to the 1970s fit in this category—it has helped Egale grow in other directions. Often seen as a white, middle-class organization, its increasingly international perspective has attracted more people of colour, while Canada's relatively welcoming attitude to LGBT refugee claimants has brought fresh blood from the Caribbean, Latin America, and the Middle East. These are places where state-sanctioned or state-tolerated attacks on queers are ongoing realities, not things that happened thirty years ago. Marginalized by their sexuality in their native countries, the new arrivals are often marginalized again here by their skin colour or accent. New Canadians have the least to lose and the most to gain by advocating for change, and any advocacy group would be foolish to leave their energy untapped.

Leonardo Zuñiga arrived in Canada in 2004 as a refugee from Mexico, where he was persecuted for being gay. He didn't think much about the marriage debate that was going on around him when he arrived because he had a more pressing concern—not getting deported. He joined Supporting Our Youth, a program for queer young people, and soon became a volunteer. He joined the Toronto Youth Cabinet and is still active in the Youth Advisory Group and the Toronto LGBT community police consultative committee, as well as organizing No One Is Illegal, a grassroots movement to stop the mistreatment of undocumented people living in Canada. Zuñiga is typical of his generation—it's hard to know where his queer activism ends and his immigration activism starts.

Back in Mexico, Zuñiga had no interest in social change. "But when I got here and got myself settled, I wanted to do something for other youth and to pay back the support I'd been receiving," he says. "For me, queer activism is a human rights platform where I can connect other issues."

While partnering with sex workers to get the bawdy house laws repealed now seems like a stretch, "imported activists" like Zuñiga are creating intersections between communities and issues that nobody would have imagined existed as recently as a decade ago. Of course, nobody realized what a monumental project marriage would be until we were in the thick of it.

"I don't know what the next issue is," confesses Hasselriis, who has forsaken politics for a writing career. "I don't know if we'll bring it up ourselves or have it forced upon us. I look at Winnipeg Pride, which I'm involved in. We have it at the steps of the Manitoba legislature as if we're still asking for things. But we're not. Why are we still there?"

In the US, of course, gay activists are very much engaged in the marriage fight. In May, California's Supreme Court—which had granted marriage rights to gay and lesbian couples the previous year—upheld the results of last November's referendum on Proposition 8, which rescinded the legal victory. In contrast, Vermont, Maine, and Iowa have established marriage equality rights in the past year. With US politics so much more polarized and freewheeling than Canada's, marriage will unify American gay activists for years to come.

At Egale, people talk about finding a wedge issue such as safe schools, something that will push buttons. But usually that means the buttons of urban middle-class people with time and money. Marriage has been so successful at helping these people integrate into the mainstream, it's become hard for them to imagine the lives of queer teens committing suicide because of homophobic bullying, small-town landlords denying housing to same-sex couples, or transsexuals unable to find a doctor who will see them.

"What ramparts are there for us to mount at Bloor and Bay?" wonders Leshner. Youth issues? He and Stark don't have kids so it's not something he's thought much about. Supporting people from ethnic communities where it's harder to come out? "I'd love to be involved in being a symbol for Orthodox Jews and Hasidic Jews who want to be gay, but when I think of what it's like to be gay in that community, I figure the only way for them to deal with it is to leave," says Leshner, who does support Toronto's Inside Out Lesbian and Gay Film and Video Festival because it's celebratory.

"I understand there are other issues," says Leshner, "but, in all honesty, trans issues matter less to me than gay issues because when I look in the mirror, I don't see a transgendered person."

Kennedy has inherited a community filled with Leshners, people who have found their pot of gold and know the neighbourhoods they should stick to to avoid being called a pansy. The big money has come and gone, leaving behind a small group of activists who feel burnt out.

Kennedy's no fan of the institution, but does admit that marriage has made things a little easier, at least on the personal level. Although equal marriage no longer dominates the headlines, every same-sex wedding brings a new crop of aunts and nephews and grandparents into contact with queer people, forcing them to re-think their prejudices. Married couples may not give the most ac-curate or comprehensive picture of queer people or what they want, but with every wedding invitation they send, they're announcing their right to exist and to love people who would otherwise have no reason to rethink their relationship to LGBT people.

But awareness only gets you so far. It can make governments, institutions, and citizens more conscious of the needs and de-mands of LGBT people, but it doesn't get these needs met. That job requires more hard work from a community that has earned its laurels, but must fight the temptation to rest on them.

TERRITORY OF UNREQUITED DREAMS

LISA GREGOIRE
Canadian Geographic

JUDY KUNNUK MAKTAR PULLS her black tank top down over narrow hips and tosses back the thick, waist-length mane of hair she's been growing since she was three years old. Then, with the cheeky flourish of Hilary Duff or Alicia Keys—her favourite recording artists—the eleven-year-old performs an Inuktitut song and dance she learned in school. There's barely enough room to contain the fancy footwork in her modest public-housing unit in Pond Inlet, Nunavut, a community of 1,300 across Eclipse Sound from the glacier-encrusted peaks of Sirmilik National Park. After my applause, she offers an encore of giggling gymnastics, bending backward like a supple reed until her hands touch the floor near her feet, three necklaces dangling near her nose. She later presents me with a tissue rose she made for me during recess and a card with my name written over and over in Inuktitut syllabics. She is thrilled to be hosting someone from somewhere else.

Judy's mother Maina, just coming off a ten-hour retail shift at the Northern Store, grabs a soda from the fridge, sinks into a faded couch, and puts her feet up for a few minutes before tackling the dishes in the sink and popping a frozen pizza into the oven for Judy, Michael Angelo, 9, and husband Jacobie, an apprentice electrician who is, at the moment, replenishing his and Maina's supply of home-rolled cigarettes. Her gaze, a blend of pride and amusement, flits between me and Judy. Jacobie left school in grade eleven to get a job to help his family pay the bills. Since then, he's been a stock boy, a community-hall supervisor, a recreation coordinator, a bylaw officer, and a carpenter and bear monitor at the nearby Mary River iron mine.

Maina and Jacobie work hard and yet seem to have little to show for their exertions. Judy and her brother sleep on mattresses on the floor, and there are blankets on the windows. The kitchen holds tonight's dinner but not much more. There's no Nintendo Wii, no rug on the linoleum tile, little adornment save for Christian icons, family photos, and some children's artwork, but the Maktars are generous, and they give thanks before eating.

I ask Judy what she wants to be when she grows up, to which she replies, "A telephone operator." Her father winces.

"Why do you want to do that?" he asks. "It's too easy. I would rather you be a lawyer." His words and this spartan home—like so many spartan northern homes—remind me that even though a decade has passed since Nunavut was born on

April 1, 1999, two threads still compete to unravel and mend this place: scarcity and aspiration.

There are not enough senior accountants to audit government spending here, not enough teachers or doctors or Inuktitut-speaking police officers—there never were. Houses are still scarce, and so are fresh vegetables, furniture, university graduates, hardware supplies, fishing quotas, computers, and affordable airline tickets. This family and this territory survive one paycheque to the next.

Despite these acute needs, the Nunavut government dreams of making Inuktitut the working language of government by 2020 and has just passed a pair of language laws that legislates its use in the public service, municipal offices, courtrooms, clinics, schools, and private businesses. It's a cultural victory, to be sure, but prohibitively expensive given compliance deadlines, Nunavut's limited control over government revenues and the insatiable infrastructure demands of a new territory.

But Nunavut has always been stubborn that way. Just as the tundra's ubiquitous lichen clings to rocks, erodes the surface, and grows by micrometres each year, so does Nunavut change: slowly, bewilderingly. Momentum seems impossible in a place where adversity smothers any sign of progress. On the surface, anyway. Look closer, and you'll find individuals for whom Nunavut has given hope and opportunity, people who inch forward not in spite of scarcity but because they've lived with it so long that it's normal. That's why little girls in Pond Inlet can sing and dance and become lawyers if they so choose.

ASK RESIDENTS WHAT'S CHANGED in the ten years that have passed since Nunavut was created by carving almost two million square kilometres from the Northwest Territories, and you'll likely get a blank stare. Some say nothing has changed, aside from

explosive growth in the capital city of Iqaluit, which has doubled
to more than 6,200 residents since 1995. Nunavut Arctic College
was on the northern edge of town when I was a newspaper reporter here a dozen years ago. Now there's a whole neighbourhood
behind it with Inuktitut street names that southerners can't pro-
nounce. Multicoloured mansions overlook the bay, multicultured
customers buy fresh parsley at the grocer's, and homeless men
urinate in front of the new Salvation Army shelter every morning
because there's only one bathroom inside.

Inuit have been trying to shape their role within Canada since
long before Nunavut was born. Traditional society in the eastern
Arctic has been unravelling for 100 years, most dramatically since
the 1950s, when Inuit shifted from a self-sustaining nomadic lifestyle to a sedentary, wage-based economy largely controlled by,
and beholden to, Ottawa. Inuit have sought ever since to recover
their autonomy and become self-sufficient again. They've done so
with varying degrees of success, led sometimes by people ill-pre-
pared for public office, who were repeatedly returned to power in
a cycle of denial that says as much about the electorate as it does
about the elected.

Nunavut was supposed to be different: a model mixture of in-
digenous and public government with transparency and account-
ability. But a decade after Nunavut adopted its inuksuk flag and
stirring motto—Nunavut Sanginivut ("our land, our strength")—
scandal, conflicts of interest, government accounting disasters, and
social problems persist. Some Nunavummiut have lost patience
awaiting the cultural renaissance and say the Northwest Territories was preferable to the Nunavut carousel that turns furiously but
goes nowhere. Such doubts would have been heresy thirty years
ago when, fuelled by Inuit nationalism, enthusiastic and fiercely
proud twenty-something Inuit political activists began the intense

discussions and negotiations with Ottawa from which Nunavut eventually emerged.

Jack Anawak was a young man during that heady awakening. A one-time Liberal MP and a father of fourteen—twelve of them adopted—he is committed to self-determination for Inuit, and is a bit of a heretic. Nunavut was created before its time, he says: Inuit were uneducated and unprepared in 1999 to run a territorial government. However, he adds, sounding very Buddhist, what's done is done, and Inuit should focus not on what Nunavut is, but on what it could be.

"We need visionaries and dreamers," says Anawak. "We need a Department of Imagination in government. Why should we just copy the British parliamentary system? This is Nunavut. We didn't survive for thousands of years just to copy someone else." He's just completed a contract with the Nunavut Employees Union, and aspires, once again, to political office. "A boat in a harbour is safe. That's what the Nunavut government is now. But that's not what a boat is for. It has to go out and explore. We need bold, decisive action on issues, and there isn't the leadership to say we are going forward. Nunavut is comprised mostly of young people. They're more idealistic. When that population gets to be in charge, Inuit nationalism will come back." We're sitting in the restaurant of Iqaluit's Navigator Inn buzzed on caffeine. I ask Anawak the time. Judging by the angle of the sun, he says, it's just about 3 p.m. As I marvel at his precision, he points to a clock over my left shoulder and laughs softly into his mug. Touché.

We tend to think Inuit such as Anawak have special skills and superhuman endurance. How else could they have survived long, dark winters in the Arctic with only primitive tools and no wood to burn? And how else can they keep this start-up territory afloat? But their power lies in their shared history. Inuit know their fickle land with a kind of intimacy that has all but vanished from southern society. In few other places in Canada do residents feel such a deep sense of ownership, share such a unique past, speak predominantly one aboriginal language, and successfully maintain close family ties within a population smaller than Moose Jaw scattered across a land mass the size of Mexico.

But transforming an aboriginal spirit into a modern, effective bureaucracy with jobs for Inuit and service in Inuktitut is tedious and inherently fraught with discouraging trial and error. Add a shortage of health providers, a mounting energy crisis, and a global economic meltdown, and you might fear for Nunavut's future. Without nurses, millions of litres of oil, and robust commercial investment, Nunavut could not function. It does not even fully control its annual budget: more than 90 percent of its billion-dollar operating revenues come straight from Ottawa. The Crown still collects most of Nunavut's resource revenues, and until the right to manage resources is devolved to the territory—likely during the next few decades—Ottawa retains the accruing royalties and taxes.

While leaders look to the future for economic and political independence, residents of Nunavut's twenty-six communities—some as small as 150 people—hunt and go to work and play hockey and wonder what climate change will do to their land. Have their lives improved in ten years? Circumstances vary across three time zones and three regions: Baffin in the east, with half the territory's population; the central Kivalliq region; and the western Kitikmeot. The cost and logistics of binding such a wide, remote geography naturally fuel an east-west rivalry. Kitikmeot residents feel isolated from, and ignored by, Iqaluit, much like Albertans feel snubbed by Ottawa. But with its western boundary abutting NWT diamond country, companies are scouring the Kitikmeot for more of the same and other minerals too, positioning the region favourably in Nunavut's economic future. Despite that, says Charlie Lyall, president and CEO of the Inuit-owned Kitikmeot Corporation, western Nunavut can't even get money for training programs, let alone a new trades school like the one set to open in Kivalliq this year.

RIVALRIES ASIDE, NUNAVUT AND its corresponding land claims have brought political certainty to the region, which pleases Bay Street and has thus attracted an army of prospectors in the past decade. The exploration and mining sector spent $230 million in Nunavut in 2007, and several mines are set to begin shipping iron, gold, and perhaps even uranium within a few years. These projects vibrate with long-anticipated promises of security and jobs, but some Inuit balk at the potential impact on caribou, sea mammals, and fish. "I've been trying to send the message that in the area of Mary River, there are migrating narwhals," says Abraham Kublu, Pond Inlet's twenty-eight-year-old mayor, singling out one of several species that will be affected by Baffinland Iron Mines' massive Mary River Project, south of his community. "I spent two weeks with two narwhal researchers from McGill University. There were thousands of narwhals."

And, as with any fledgling jurisdiction, there are signs of both progress and disarray. Last year saw the groundbreaking in Clyde River for Piqqusilirivvik, Nunavut's new cultural school, which will teach language and survival skills to Inuit and non-Inuit. Retail sales in Nunavut are up, and so are building permits. But Iqaluit's two-year-old $64 million hospital is still half empty, because government can't staff the place, and the public service is operating under capacity, with 20 percent of the jobs still vacant. In some departments, job vacancies exceed one-third. Of jobs, at least, there is no scarcity.

With half its 30,000 residents under age twenty-five (and a birth rate twice the national rate), Nunavut has the country's youngest population, which is both an asset and a liability: youth have dreams, says Jack Anawak, but they don't necessarily know how to achieve them. The first order of business, everyone agrees, is getting more kids through school, and on that front, there is modest progress. Slightly more teenagers are graduating from high school now, nearly 30 percent, compared with 25 percent before the creation of the territory. More young people are attending southern colleges and universities, and fewer are smoking. Despair still drives far too many Nunavut youth to suicide, but for those bold enough to snatch a job among manifold opportunities—teacher, outfitter, receptionist, entrepreneur—their inheritance is a territory ripe for a creative makeover; indeed, starving for it. Aside from its youth, Nunavut's greatest asset might be the absence of obstinate status quo.

"I think the socio-economic conditions of our people are getting better," says John Amagoalik, an Inuit sage raised in Resolute and now director of lands and resources for the Qikiqtani Inuit Association in Iqaluit. "The younger generation seems to be in a much better position than we were. I notice they are more healthy and staying in school longer." Amagoalik, known as the "Father of Nunavut" for his work as a negotiator in the 1970s, is now sixty-one, paler and thinner than he was ten years ago, with a grey ponytail hanging between his shoulder blades.

"Back then, it was very difficult to envision what we were going to experience in thirty or forty years, but we knew things had to change," he says. "We had lost control of our land, and we discovered oil companies and mining companies could do what they wanted, with the blessing of the federal government. It was a colonial situation." Circumstances soon changed. Within one generation, Inuit mapped their homeland and negotiated Canada's largest ever land claim and a new territory, both of which re-established Inuit traditional rights and decision-making powers. Formally educated at a residential school, Amagoalik used his newfound language and skills to help negotiate his people's future. Responsibility and prestige must have been equally intoxicating, and youth a definite asset. "We were pretty young but so full of energy back then," he says. "Most of the time, we were running just on adrenaline." But even revered statesmen and winners of National Aboriginal Achievement Awards like Amagoalik are not immune to burnout. In 2001, he served six months' probation after pleading guilty to assault. Police said alcohol was a factor.

AMONG THE ARTWORK AND photographs crowding the walls of Leona Aglukkaq's Legislative Assembly office, a snapshot of her with Jean Chrétien on April 1, 1999 stands out. She is smiling and radiant in a resplendent coat made from *siksik* (ground squirrel), caribou, wolf, and wolverine. Her grin belies a very stressful year.

A centennial baby born in Inuvik, NWT, Aglukkaq grew up in Taloyoak, Gjoa Haven, and Thom Bay, an outpost camp on the central Arctic's northern coast. In 1985, she moved to Yellowknife to attend high school, with tentative plans for a career in health care or teaching. But after working as a page for the NWT Legislative Assembly and watching firebrand MLAs such as Nellie Cournoyea and Lynda Sorensen, she discarded conventional "female" professions and entered the public service. Aglukkaq then ran for office in 2004, beating out six men to become MLA for the riding of Nattilik, one of only two women elected to the nineteen-member legislature. She took on the daunting Finance portfolio first, then Health and Social Services. In September 2008, she resigned her seat to run federally for the Conservatives. She is now MP for Nunavut and the federal Minister of Health.

But let's rewind to 1998, when she was a thirty-year-old acting deputy minister of human resources in the Office of the Interim Commissioner, Nunavut's bureaucracy-in-waiting. After addressing practical concerns—such as finding office space (the new legislature didn't open until October 1999), skilled staff (hundreds of them, preferably Inuit), desks, trash cans, and computers, and then installing networks and servers—Aglukkaq was expected to prepare briefing documents and budget priorities for incoming MLAs. As Nunavummiut ate cake on April 1, 1999, government staffers were still scouring NorthMart for office supplies. "I took every job skill I'd learned and put them into one task. It was a test of what I know and what I don't know. It was very stressful," says Aglukkaq. "At the end of the day, I thought, 'Something will go terribly wrong. There's something we missed.' But no. We'd done enough."

Today, despite the territory's perpetual job-creation machine, less than 70 percent of the labour force is working, with a higher representation of Inuit among the unemployed. Other territorial indicators are equally vexing. Violent crime is up 50 percent since 1993, and life expectancy is ten years below the national average. Since 1999, 267 people here have committed suicide, mostly boys aged fourteen to twenty-four—the equivalent of wiping out my entire university graduating class. A century ago, those young men would have been formidable hunters who found food when everyone was starving. Now, they are killing themselves. But when it comes to other health issues, such as teen pregnancy, fetal alcohol syndrome, lung cancer, and diabetes, notes Aglukkaq, Inuit can't always blame "the system" or a lack of funding for their own bad choices. "Building dependency creates a sick society, she says. "Where did this dependency come from? Why not brush your teeth? Stop smoking? Eat better? It's complacency, and complacency has grown into dependency."

Nunavut's flaws have always been on display, like bleached bones on the tundra, periodically nudged by the wind but never buried. With vast expanses of treeless land and long stretches of unrelenting sunlight, there's nowhere to hide: not in a small statistical sample where bad news gets amplified; not from police when you're high and homeless; not from conflict-of-interest guidelines when you're a politician approving million-dollar construction projects; not from your ex-husband in tiny towns of overcrowded households where nearly everyone is related by birth or marriage.

"You feel as if you're in a fishbowl, with everyone watching. There's a lot of pressure," says Qajaq Robinson, a thirty-one-year-old Crown prosecutor born in Iqaluit and raised in Igloolik by her teacher father and librarian mother. Fluent in Inuktitut, Robinson earned her law degree in 2005 with ten other Nunavut residents through the Iqaluit-based, University of Victoria-affiliated Akitsiraq Law Program. She also coaches high school basketball and says Inuit pride is on the rise. But pride demands something of the proud: action. "We can't remain in a bubble. We have to become worldly—do what we do here and also on Wall Street if we have to," she says. "The survival of Nunavut depends on becoming more grounded *and* more worldly."

In Resolute, a tiny smudge on the gravel coast of Cornwallis Island and Canada's second most northern community (pop. 230), Zipporah Kalluk Aronsen sits on the floor of her kitchen. Next to her is a piece of cardboard, upon which rests a caribou leg, hoof still on, strands of coarse fur clinging to the flesh. "Have you ever spent time with Inuit?" she asks smiling. "This is real Inuit here." She slices open the bone with an ulu and sucks out the marrow, which she says prevents cancer. The walls swarm with photos—among them, old black-and-whites from the 1950s of Kalluk Aronsen as a child in caribou skins, when people called her Ootoq ("seal sleeping on the ice").

"We were so proud when we were told that we would have our own Inuit land, with Inuit rights, and our way of living would come back," says Kalluk Aronsen, a court worker who helps accused people navigate the legal system. "That's what we were promised. Lots of people probably could not go back on the land, but at least they could preserve it and remember it." Remember how to track polar bears and sew skin boots, for instance. Kalluk Aronsen articulates what many of her generation—and others—fear most in this struggle to modernize: losing that which makes Inuit Inuit. She represents the grounded part Robinson talked about. Her daughter Celina Kalluk, who runs a graphic-design firm in Iqaluit and helped incorporate traditional images into an urban graffiti project there, represents the worldly part.

And if the term refers to your genes, then Kalluk Aronsen's fourteen-year-old granddaughter Cassandra is worldly too: the offspring of an Inuit mom and a Jamaican dad who works as a mechanic for the hamlet. Cassandra gives me a tour of Resolute in running shoes and a fleece jacket lazily half zipped against -17°C weather. A trio of pre-teens—Amy Salluviniq, Melissa Idlout, and Belinda Oqallak—joins us for a lark. Belinda is chewing something that looks like white plastic, and I ask her what it is. *Qaqulaaq*, she says, cartilage from a polar bear toe. They tell me they've been learning to throat-sing from an elder and take turns proving it. Amy and Melissa grasp each other's elbows and sway, exchanging ancient, inhuman vibrations until one laughs and loses the game. When they finish, they ask me about West Edmonton Mall and listen, agog, to every detail.

Trendy clothes and indoor swimming pools might be scarce in Resolute—and Pond Inlet too—but cultural traditions and family bonds are not. And perhaps that's what propels Nunavut forward in the face of diminishing odds, something Robinson calls "collective duty." Nunavut has a long history of cyclical scarcity. For forty generations, as the tundra warmed and cooled and the spirits chased away the animals, Inuit have understood that survival depends on decisive action. When food was scarce, groups leaned into the wind to search for caribou, and those too old or weak stayed behind, knowing their souls might soon be reincarnated in promising new flesh: a baby named for a grandmother, the past thrust into the future and the line between them forever blurry. Today, even among naysayers and heretics, there is commitment to move forward together, however slowly and painfully. It begins when someone starts walking.

"People need positive influences. They need role models, words of healing, love, comfort, support," says Cheryl Akoak, 22. "Once you're given the proper support, you take baby steps, and they lead to bigger steps, and you stop and look back and say, 'I can't believe I've gone this far.' "

Ten years ago, Akoak was an eleven-year-old cadet parading about in uniform and brimming with pride at events in Cambridge Bay celebrating the creation of the new territory. In the decade that followed, she succumbed to addictions and depression, like so many of her friends, but managed to get healthy and sober with the help of her family. Now, Akoak and I sit beneath a poster that declares "There is hope for the future," in classroom 22 of Nunavut Arctic College's Iqaluit campus, where baby steps lead to bigger ones. She is hoping to complete a two-year mental-health diploma, though she has recently taken a break from school to take care of some personal problems. Despite her desire to help others, she has to stop and mend herself. If her struggle and success are any indication, there is hope yet for Nunavut.

But I am skeptical. We've talked for hours when I finally ask how she got the purple mark beneath her right eye, because it looks as if someone has punched her. Not so. It's a scar from an accident seven years ago, when she was struck by an ATV and her eyeglasses cut deep into her cheek. It's a scar she can't hide from an event she can't change, and she tires of explaining it. I tell her it makes her look tough, but like most young women, she'd rather be pretty.

We make assumptions based on what we see, and Nunavut is no exception. The cold, the darkness, the scars are all distractions from Nunavut's powerful vitality. One thing's certain: scars tell you something about the past but nothing of the future.

THIS IS YOUR BRAIN ON LOVE

DANIELLE GROEN
Chatelaine

ANTHROPOLOGIST HELEN FISHER IS being very patient. I have cracked some weak jokes; she laughed politely. I talked too long about myself; she indulged my rambling. And now she's trying to convince me—with intermittent success—that my relationship isn't doomed.

Fisher knows something about love. She's written several books on the science of attachment—that is, the biochemical reactions behind everything from a first crush to a lasting marriage. She has stuck the hopelessly smitten into MRI machines and peered at their brains. She has even popped up on Oprah. And four years ago, she was tapped by executives at US-based Match.com, one of the world's largest dating sites, to study the neurological mechanisms that direct our romantic choices.

There are well over 100 chemicals firing in our brains at any given moment. Some keep our hearts beating, some keep our eyes blinking, and, according to Fisher, four of them—serotonin, dopamine, estrogen, and testosterone—help govern a wide range of behavioural traits. These chemicals interact in different ratios in different people, creating what Fisher considers four primary personality types. Each type has a natural match as well as a few decidedly unnatural ones. You can see where this is going.

Armed with her knowledge, Fisher developed a lengthy questionnaire centred on neurochemistry, tested with 40,000 Americans and perfected on more than 6 million men and women across thirty-five countries. The questionnaire now pairs up potential suitors on Match's sister site, Chemistry.com, for which Fisher is chief scientific adviser; it can also be found in her new book, out this month, called *Why Him? Why Her?*, a guided tour through these personality types. I took the test. It was a lovely, sunny morning. My boyfriend had just made pancakes and, better still, an enormous pile of bacon.

I cracked the book open. Am I patient, cautious, domestic? Er, not exactly. (Note: I did not make the pancakes.) Then I can't call myself a Builder, Fisher's term for a personality powered by the chemical serotonin. Would my friends say that I was impulsive, adaptable, or obscenely late? Maybe just that last one. It wasn't looking good for me as a dopamine-fuelled Explorer. And no, I'm not overly trusting, and I'm pretty sure no one's ever compared me to Gandhi. So scratch the estrogen-driven Negotiator off my list. But analytical, skeptical, extremely competitive? Someone who can be demanding? Was my childhood nickname not Bossy Boots?

I am a Director. My brain is flooded with testosterone. This explains the high cheekbones, the man-sized hands and why I kill at Tetris. (Directors are highly skilled at spatial games.) It also explains why I immediately thrust Fisher's questionnaire at my boyfriend: I had managed to turn a personality quiz into a competition. Because he is also competitive, he grabbed a pencil. This should have tipped us off; sure enough, he's a Director, too. We flipped through the book, learning that Builders pair well with Builders (they're both devoted to family), Explorers gravitate to Explorers (they seek out adventure), and Directors and Negotiators complement each other's temperaments.

But our match sounded toxic: "Two Directors sometimes question each other's facts or logic when they talk, or hurl criticisms that make each other angry . . . Neither wishes to be intimidated. Both want to win." So a few weeks later, I was on the phone with Fisher, looking for a little reassurance. "You're not doomed," she said. "There are lots of things that can keep two people together, even though it's not a natural match. You can work with the problems. You might decide, Well, I don't think I am going to pick on his logic this time. I'll just let that one go." That sounded unlikely. The conversation went downhill. "I don't want someone always competing with me," admitted Fisher. "But it might work for you." I imagined the Chemistry.com website, where millions of estrogen-laden, Gandhi-like Negotiators waited, keen to let me win an argument. I'd have my pick of dating sites, too, each touting its own algorithm for love. It's big business these days: Match.com attracts more than 15 million users, and eHarmony has actually patented its matchmaking formula, which pulls in US$200 million a year from millions of visitors. Here at home, Vancouver's Plentyoffish.com culls a yearly revenue of $10 million from 600,000 users. And it's not just about the money. The study of romance—particularly the study of our brains in various stages of romance—has become a serious academic pursuit. It seems that every year, more lovesick brains are scanned, more sweaty garments are sniffed for pheromone responses, more affairs are cross-checked against menstrual charts. Science stands on the brink of telling us everything there is to know about love. Will we like what we hear?

For all our preoccupation with love, its serious scientific study has often lagged behind sex research. In the 1910s, John Watson first brought arousal out of the bedroom and into the lab; however, the dearth of willing participants meant he had to improvise. "Watson used himself as a subject," says Mary Roach, author of *Bonk: The Curious Coupling of Science and Sex.* "He also used the woman he was having an affair with, which caused all manner of complications in his later divorce proceedings."

Love research, on the other hand, has far less salacious origins. Although it's now a booming field—with experts across Canadian universities (there's even a relationship research lab at the University of Waterloo) and scientific studies conducted everywhere from Japan to Brazil—it began, innocently enough, with a monogamous rodent. The prairie vole, a sort of field mouse from the Midwestern US, is, along with humans, among the scant three percent of mammals that form exclusive relationships. In 1995, Sue Carter, now a professor of psychiatry at the University of Illinois, found that when prairie voles mate, the hormones oxytocin and vasopressin are released. Additional investigation showed that the brain receptors for these hormones existed alongside those for dopamine—a pleasure chemical associated with ecstasy, focused attention, and reward. It appears that the voles remain monogamous because monogamy feels good to them.

With the advent in the 1990s of functional magnetic reson-
ance imaging (fMRI)—a technology that measures tiny metabolic
changes in the brain—scientists could begin studying the chemistry of human romance. In 2000, British researchers harnessed
this technology to scan the brains of subjects who were deeply
in love. They put these subjects into the machine and showed
them pictures of their partners, as well as photos of friends. The
researchers discovered that a much smaller part of the brain becomes active in love than in friendship. With a surprisingly poetic
flourish for a neurological report, they noted, "[It is] fascinating
to reflect that the face that launched a thousand ships should have
done so through such a limited expanse of cortex." Something
else stood out. The regions of activity in the lovers' brains didn't
much resemble those of people feeling other strong emotions,
such as anger or fear; instead, they looked like the euphoric brains
of people high on cocaine. It would have been sweet vindication
for Robert Palmer—cue the swelling synthesizers and the babes
in black minidresses, because we might as well face it: We're addicted to love.

At the same time, Helen Fisher and her fellow scientists in the
US were comparing their own fMRI scans of forty love-addled
brains. The results were identical: They found heightened activity
in the caudate nucleus, a shrimp-shaped region deep in our brains
that evolved more than 65 million years ago. This region is part
of the brain's reward system and helps us to detect, favour, and
anticipate a particular prize. The more passionate Fisher's subjects
reported being, the more active their caudates.

Fisher also saw activity in the ventral tegmental area, a section
of the reward network that she calls a "motherlode for dopamine-
making cells." Euphoria, infatuation, even arousal—chalk all
these feelings up to dopamine. And dopamine-saturated areas of

the brain are home to our oxytocin receptors, which means that, just like our faithful prairie-vole friends, we think monogamy feels pretty good, too.

In that first flush of love, when we can barely eat, and sleep even less, the brain turns into a see-saw of chemical reactions. Dopamine goes up. Levels of serotonin—the compound thought to help control obsessive-compulsive disorder—go down. Little wonder you can't get him out of your head. Testosterone levels increase; you find yourself lustily eyeing the bedroom. Once there, touching and orgasm release a flood of vasopressin and oxytocin, the chemicals associated with attachment and trust. (Kissing also elevates levels of oxytocin in men, but not in women. It seems we need more than a little smooching to feel connected.)

Lust, love, and attachment: all are accounted for in our frenzied brains. According to Fisher, that's because these are three neurological drives as potent as hunger and thirst, each serving to control a different aspect of reproduction. Lust emerged to encourage us to get frisky with almost any suitable sexual partner. Because that can be exhausting, romantic love developed so we would focus our efforts on one partner. And since a baby's chances of survival would improve with two parents, attachment evolved to keep our ancestors together.

These reproductive drives might also account for the differences Fisher perceived in male and female brain scans. Unsurprisingly, men showed more activity in regions associated with visual processing, especially of the face. This may be because shiny hair, smooth skin, white teeth, and a strong body all indicate a healthy woman with good child-bearing possibilities. (It may also explain why more Canadian men than women say they believe in love at first sight.) On the other hand, it was only women who demonstrated activity in regions of the brain associated with the retrieval of memories. It's no easy task to raise a kid, so it's important to remember, in Fisher's words, "whether [your mate] can hit the buffalo on the head and share the meat with you."

It would seem, then, that the three reproductive drives progress quite tidily from each other: Lust begets love begets attachment. Not so fast, says Fisher. "I don't call them phases; they're brain systems," she explains. "You can fall madly in love with someone you've never slept with, you can go to bed with someone you could never love, and you can feel deeply attached to a college friend and, years later, it turns into a romance. So you can start with any one of these brain systems and have it develop into others." But it appears as though the brain can be tricked. Danger triggers adrenalin, a stimulant closely related to dopamine. In one experiment, researchers wrangled dozens of men into crossing Vancouver's Capilano Suspension Bridge, which teeters seventy metres above a rushing river. At the centre stood an attractive woman, who handed them a basic questionnaire and then passed out her home phone number, telling the men to call with any questions. The experiment was repeated with new subjects on a low, secure bridge. More than four times as many volunteers from the suspension bridge called the woman. Those breathless boys thought they were experiencing the thrill of new love, but it was really just the rush of standing on a plank of wood more than twenty storeys high. And couldn't a casual one-night stand—with its groping-induced release of oxytocin—prompt unexpected feelings of attachment? Fisher isn't convinced.

"We're not simply puppets on the string of DNA; biology and culture are constantly interacting with each other. A person who's prone to alcoholism can give up drinking." She points out that, in the heady moments of sex or love, there are many systems working together. "The cortex is assembling data and making decisions; the limbic system is feeling various emotions; and then there are the basic passionate drives." Turns out our brains are better at distinguishing between lust and love than we might think.

"Don't forget, somebody has to fit with what you're looking for in a mate," Fisher says. "You can drive up dopamine in the brain just by taking cocaine. But if you're kissing a frog, you're kissing a frog."

So we aren't cavemen worried about surviving the cold winter or passing along our DNA before that thirty-year life expectancy kicks in. But love still can, in some cases, be a matter of survival, with implications for our financial well-being and the longevity of our relationships.

Studies have shown that during ovulation, a woman appears more attractive to men and tends to be guarded more vigilantly by her partner. From a cold Darwinian perspective, that sounds about right: She is signalling her fertility, and, if a man doesn't want to raise another guy's baby, he'd better keep his woman close.

Researchers from New Mexico took this show on the road, looking for the "first real-world economic evidence of male sensitivity to cyclic changes in female attractiveness." On the page, that sounds dryly academic; in reality, they headed for a gentleman's club. The team asked lap dancers to monitor their menstrual periods, their work shifts, and their tips for sixty days. The results are astonishing. Ovulating dancers pulled in US$70 an hour; those in the middle of their cycle made $50; and menstruating dancers took home a lowly $35 an hour. Now here's the caveat: Those are the statistics for normally cycling women. Dancers who took the birth-control pill saw no mid-cycle increase in their tips. But Pill users made an average of only $193 per five-hour shift, while the other women pocketed $276—which means that patrons found them less attractive to the tune of sixteen bucks an hour.

It gets worse. Women are particularly responsive to olfactory cues, and researchers wondered if that might serve a reproductive purpose. Our chances of giving birth to a strong, healthy baby increase if we partner up with someone who has a different immune system from ours. So a team of Swiss scientists handed women a stack of sweaty T-shirts and asked them to take a whiff. Normally cycling women consistently preferred the smell of men with immune systems that were distinct from theirs. Women on the Pill picked the wrong shirt.

As if genetically compromised babies weren't bad enough, couples with similar immune systems have a host of relationship problems to look forward to. As the proportion of similarity increased, women's sexual satisfaction decreased, their number of affairs increased, and their attraction to men other than their partners increased—particularly during ovulation.

The Pill gave women sex without fear, but it may have come at a cost. Even scientists are now advocating that consequences of the Pill "need to be known by users." We already have warning labels on cigarettes—those dramatic pictures of bleeding lungs—so why not on your pack of Yasmin? I suggest a lap dancer looking forlornly at her paltry pile of tips. But adultery omens and lap-dance economics aside, why do we study love? Fisher's reasons are fairly pragmatic. "It's totally fascinating, and it's very central," she says. "But why do I study it? Because it's there." *Bonk* author Mary Roach pushes this argument further: "People are endlessly confused, flummoxed, depressed; they feel that love pulls the rug out from under them. There's a tendency to want to control it and understand it, so you turn to science for the answers."

Yet many of the scientific observations made about love sound mighty familiar. It drives us to sheer heights of ecstasy? The Romantic poets had that covered back in the nineteenth century. It's an addiction as powerful as any drug? Those cowboys in *Brokeback Mountain* couldn't quit the habit. When we're separated from our beloved, dopamine levels go through the roof, causing anxiety, fear, even violence? Three words: *Romeo and Juliet*. Before a man with a microscope or a woman with an MRI machine stepped onto the scene, the task of explaining love fell to the poets and the playwrights—and they did a decent job of it. Scientists are now able to corroborate what artists have already intuited. To do so, they've taken the metaphor and turned it literal; chemistry is no longer just an enigmatic spark between two people but a neurological network that lights up our brains like a Christmas tree.

So why isn't the metaphor good enough? Literature offers a window onto the messy lives of others; it prompts that shock of recognition; it helps us feel, emotionally and intellectually, a little less alone. Still, because we want something more concrete, perhaps that's why we find the idea of a scientific formula for partnership so seductive. It's the closest thing we have to a guarantee.

But there is a wonderful mystery to why two people come together that I don't think the poets or the scientists will ever truly resolve. Maybe that's just my testosterone-fuelled, Director-like skepticism talking. Maybe my boyfriend does lack sufficient estrogen levels for our relationship to last, and maybe that will be of some consolation if it ever crumbles. But he provides pancakes and we lose entire days to conversation and, sure, we fight fiercely but we make up well. That's plenty Love Potion No. 9 for me.

LAST POEMS

ELIZABETH HAY
New Quarterly

WHENEVER I READ THE phrase "as ill luck would have it," I think of the summer of 1988 when the weather turned against us and so did Frank. Our daughter was two years old and rose at dawn. Mark got up with her and took her outside every morning before six. They descended from our third-floor rooms under the flat, tarred roof, passed Frank and Cathy's apartment on the second floor and Laura and Louie's on the first, then headed out the heavy oak door and down the steps to Devoe Street. They turned right and walked to Olive Street, turned left and passed the pizzeria, walked another block and turned left on Orient Avenue and came to the house with all the cats. An old man lived there and every morning he came out early to sweep his dirt yard while at least a dozen cats wandered through the bushes and between his legs. Our daughter stood with her hands in the wire meshing of the fence and watched them intently until Mark grew restless and they moved on. The rest of the route included McCarren Park, beautiful in its layout and its mature trees, but badly run down, and a certain greasy spoon on Metropolitan Avenue where they had breakfast.

While they were gone I would write. Frank had said to me soon after we moved in, "I hear that typewriter of yours all the time. I want to see what you write." He paused, then gave me a rare smile. "Maybe I'd like it." Slender, macho, tattooed Frank Graziano with the Brooklyn swagger, the browbeaten wife, the three kids who had numbered four until Frank Junior was killed in a car crash at the age of seventeen.

We had moved into his house in October and that first autumn was so long and warm I thought all New York autumns were the same, one sunny day extending into the next with a clarity you find at sea. Winter never came. Autumn lasted six months and turned into summer. We lowered the Venetian blinds and lived in the shady, windy world underneath the ceiling fan. Summer passed into fall. That November I realized my mistake when cold and rain arrived in unison and never left. On the first day of May I would still be wearing a winter coat and the heat wave to come was inconceivable.

Laura, the elderly, self-possessed woman who lived on the first floor, took a protective interest in us. At Christmas we had travelled to Canada to see my family and upon our return she greeted us warmly and volubly. There was trouble with the burler, she said. The burler? Yes, the burler. You know. That you put the url in.

In March I told her that I was pregnant again and she warned me that if I saw a rat I should hold my hands above my head until it disappeared or the baby would be born with a grey birthmark exactly where I had touched myself. Satisfy every craving, she said. Don't sit with your face in your hand longing for strawberries or red wine, or the baby will be born with a red smear on his cheek.

That was the month Frank replaced the old front door of solid oak with a suburban-style aluminum door on a steel spring that snapped to like a leg-hold trap. He was as proud as could be of his fancy new door. Soon there were scuffs on it from heroic attempts on my part and on a friend's part to bring strollers inside without loss of life.

Within a few weeks people were saying grimly, "There's not going to be a spring." Certainly our neighbourhood resembled outer Mongolia: blowing dust, gritty cold, havoc in the streets under repair.

On the first of May, as I say, I was still in my winter coat.

That weekend we went for a walking tour through the neighbourhood adjoining ours, a section of Williamsburg between Union and Bushwick Avenues. Two park rangers led the tour and both of them had red hair. In that part of Brooklyn, red hair was most unusual. Perhaps I should have raised my hands above my head until they disappeared. The one with short red hair talked most, because the one with long red hair had to keep pulling strands of it out of her mouth. They told us, the eight of us on the tour, that the creamy white bark of the American plane tree made it stand out and so the London plane tree with its darker bark, also peeling, was preferred by city planners. Someone joked (I don't know why I say someone, it was Mark) that the preferred city tree was the one nobody notices, but they paid him no mind.

The woman beside me had peeling lips, which her lipstick only accentuated. She became for me the woman with the plane tree lips. Because of all the wind, the car alarms, the car radios, and

the trains, it was nearly impossible to hear the rangers. They took
us to an empty lot to show us what was meant by "a tree grows in
Brooklyn." *Atlantis Altissima*, they said, and I jotted down what
I misheard. In fact, *Ailanthus*, as I realized years later when I was
reading Grace Paley and saw that you could write a story that
included poems. The tree of heaven. Scrawny and sumac-like
with soft grey antlers still leafless in the cold April air. After showing us the tree, the rangers took us to Henry Miller's house at
662 Driggs.

Later, my friend Monica would tell me that one of Miller's
lovers had lived on our street, Devoe Street, pronounced De-voo.
Monica was a big fan of Miller's. Her son Liam was my daughter's
age and sometimes they came to visit and we drank tea as our
children played together. Hers was one of the offbeat love lives I
followed as Clara's magnolia next door came into bloom and she
unwrapped her fig tree, as the harmonica player re-emerged and
leaned out his window alternately spewing music and curses, as the
theme song from *It's My Turn* swelled to full volume from another
open window—Diana Ross at her most yearningly romantic, over
and over and over again—and as the playground nearest us filled
up with boys saying things like, "You've got no balls." "I do so, my
balls are big enough to stuff in your mouth." "You do not, a mail
slot's too big for your balls."

On May 5 summer began with a long soft rain. For supper my
daughter ate black olives, a tomato, and several capers. She sucked
on half a lemon. I was writing poems to her, that's what I had been
typing on my typewriter.

> *Conceived beside a waterfall*
> *12 miles from a ruins—Palenque:*
> *your name, Xochitl. Your father's idea*

not mine.

Over my dead body, I said
And you became Sochi.

The rain let up in the evening and the three of us went for a
walk in the soft misty air. At the house with the cats, only three
were outside. We passed two magnolias and came to the camellia
bush at the end of the street and Mark broke into a Mexican song
about Camelia who shot her lover Emilio when he tried to ditch
her in Hollywood. He sang it to the end of the block.

When we got back Laura was sitting on the stoop with Clara
from next door. They said, "It's raining because the circus is in
town. It always rains when the circus is in town. Sometimes during the day. Sometimes at night. It always rains."

Clara was a weary woman in her sixties. She often gave Laura
a hand with Louie, the abusive husband of forty-three years who
had fallen down the cellar stairs three years ago and had been bed-
ridden ever since. At the time of the fall, Laura and Louie had
owned the house. Soon all the medical bills forced Laura to sell,
and she sold to Frank, until then her tenant on the second floor.
"It's the sorriest thing I ever did," she was given to saying. "I says
to him, I says, it's the sorriest thing I ever did."

We climbed the stairs to our rooms and minutes later came the
ominous knock on the door.

Mark answered the summons and I heard Frank's youngest son
Vinnie say, "My father wants to see you."

Mark went down. Soon I heard raised voices through the floor.
I lowered the radio and cleaned off the table, did the dishes, paused
every so often to listen. Half an hour later, he came back upstairs.

"The stroller in the hallway," he said. "The fire inspector was
here this morning and saw it. Frank started in as soon as I walked

through the door. 'You're trying to make a fool of me, I told you, I told your wife.' The usual shit. He says we can't have any friends over who bring in strollers. They mark up the doors and dirty the hallway. We can't let Sochi run in the apartment. We can't let her in the backyard. Once our washing machine breaks, we can't have another. And he's going to raise the rent 'substantially.' "

He started to laugh as he imitated Frank's yelling voice: MY WIFE BREAKS HER BACK CLEANING THAT CARPET. I CAN RAISE YOUR RENT ANY TIME. IN THE MIDDLE OF THE MONTH, RIGHT NOW, NEXT WEEK. YOU DON'T HAVE A LEASE."

"He wants us out," I said.

"Sure."

I was five months pregnant. What were we to do?

That night I did not sleep. Before dawn I walked barefoot across the floor to the window, raised the blind, raised the window, and crooked my head between the child-guard and the window frame. Tiny backyards ranged below, as did Frank and Cathy's clothesline, one T-shirt hanging: *Sports Pal.* I looked out at the rooftops of the small Italian neighbourhood, getting smaller and more paranoid as blacks and hispanics closed in. "They sent me a phone book in Puerto Rican," Frank had raged one day. "I can't believe it. Threw the fuckin' thing in the garbage."

I pulled my head in and surveyed the kitchen. The offending sandals were in one corner. I picked them up (my daughter's, oversized, they clunked) and hid them. I made coffee (the tap, I thought, is that the noise he hears early in the morning? Or is it the typewriter?)

Aztec Venus
they drank chocolate in your honour,

now

you pry open my mouth (clenched
shut despite my laughter)
to get at the chocolate cake inside

In the pre-dawn light I felt tattooed. Frank was all over
my skin.

EARLY JUNE WAS COOL and rainy.

Monica was wearing large glasses with reddish frames. "Oh,"
she said, pushing them up on her nose. "My magic glasses. I never
told you?"

We were in the field near her apartment building, a ball diamond at one end and a row of cherry trees pushing through a
broken-down fence at the other.

"I don't need glasses," she said. "I've never worn glasses. In fact,
my problem is that I see too well. I have sort of X-ray vision."

A nut grows in Brooklyn. She told me about the optometrist
who had charged her eighty dollars for glasses especially designed
by him to alter her way of seeing the world. She was more desperate than I had realized, but we were all pretty desperate, those of
us who found ourselves living in this part of Brooklyn because we
were too poor to live anywhere else. We walked along smelling the
last of the blossoms while my daughter and her son chased after
two dogs named Petey and Sparky. The children ran and ran. They
wore wool sweaters and looked like Scottish children on a heath.

Monica talked about Jack. He wasn't nearly as good-looking as
her husband, she said, but he had charmed her with his talk and
his possessions, a store full of beautiful things, an apartment full
of "faces" as she put it. "A thousand different images. It's a feast
for the eyes. I keep going back," she said, "even though I'm not

attracted to him. He sees my potential, he sees how frustrated I am because I'm not doing anything. He believes in me."

Every day she bought a large Hershey chocolate bar and since she was so slim, and worked at staying slim, she ate little else. Her two-year-old son didn't eat much either, besides formula and the toasted raisin bread from Rosalee's Bakery.

From Laura I learned that our neighbourhood had been German-Irish formerly. The first Italian family arrived in 1927. She and Louie moved onto the street twenty years later. Frank and Cathy were born on the street, both of them. Clara next door arrived in 1955 directly from Italy into an arranged marriage. Her cheeks were like apples, Laura told me, but in less than two years she had two children and her husband hit her and so did her mother-in-law. Clara still cooked and cleaned for him and for her mother-in-law, who was 103 years old. She also worked in a garment factory in lower Manhattan.

I learned these things in Laura's kitchen. She was always calling to me as I went up or down the stairs, insisting that I come in and eat. "You're eating for two," she would say, serving me a big plate of pasta with gravy, as tomato sauce was called in that part of the world. In order to avoid yet another forced feeding, I took to tiptoeing up and down the stairs, my finger on my lips to caution my daughter against making a sound. Frequently, she giggled at our game.

Between stealing up the stairs and padding softly around our rooms, I felt like a sneak (a worm) in a police station. Night and day I was intimidated by Frank and ashamed of my fear. Mark didn't share my feelings and could not understand them, and our marriage became very difficult. He said, "I'm not going to let him ruin my life. He's just not that important." He was happy to stay put and ignore Frank. But I couldn't imagine staying put. And so we looked at apartments for rent. We discovered they were all smaller and more expensive than ours. And then we learned of a railroad apartment for sale in a friend's co-op in Manhattan and examined our savings and turned to our families for help and applied for a mortgage.

Then on June 12 the heat wave began, the longest I have ever known. Our rooms, directly under the flat roof, were the top rack in a bake-oven.

> *summer snowfall in New York:*
> *children out of windows. Four*
> *in the last twenty-four hours the paper says.*

Water bubbled into Frank and Cathy's pool in the backyard: the tantalizing sound of water moving, the pool free-standing and no bigger than a trampoline, but nevertheless attractive and out of bounds. Next door, Clara watered her garden, inspected her small fig tree, retreated to the second floor. At night we all gathered on the sidewalk: Cathy, Laura, Clara, me, my daughter, all in our lawn chairs, the sidewalk flush with the houses, our faces flushed with the heat, and took the breeze. The streetlights came on and we continued to sit, passengers on a gloomy sort of freighter, with the occasional smell of the ocean to remind us where we were.

"Louie was the only one that came out good," Laura told me. "Him and his sister. The rest were on boards."

"Boards?" I said.

"They couldn't move. The same sort of paralysis Louie has now."

"How long did they live?" I wanted to know.

"Oh, a long time. His sister lived till thirty."

Every night Laura put Louie to bed at six o'clock, applied some rouge to her cheeks and sat outside until ten. She was seventy-two and stout, with soft white diabetic skin. She held herself erect and carried her glasses like a confident schoolmistress. When I told her about our fight with Frank, she motioned me away from the open window in her kitchen. "Talk soft," she said.

"You know," she said, "we have a name for people like him. I knew him since he was a baby. He lived across the street and he never had nothing. *Nothing.* And now he's got this house he's a big shot. *Nigger rich.* That's what we call them. *Nigger rich.*"

Around this time, in struggling to tie back the new aluminum front door and position Louie's wheelchair in the open air, Laura caused the door to come off its spring. For a blissful week it hung loose, simple to open and easy to close. Frank accused her of breaking the door and told her she wasn't allowed to tie it back anymore. "What about Louie?" she said. After that, I saw Louie's face, pale, barely visible, through the screen of his bedroom window. He scrabbled at the screen with his fingernails whenever I walked by.

Around this time, too, as the heat wave continued day after day, Frank told Clara she could not sit on the stoop anymore, something she had been doing with Laura for thirty years. What her offence was I never learned. He also told the city that they could not plant a tree outside his house.

His wife Cathy agreed about the tree. "Raking all those leaves," she said. "Forget about it. I need a tree like I need a hole in the head."

At the end of June, Frank summoned my husband again and said, "I'm not going to kick you out, but these friends of mine offered $850 for the place. So if you're going to stay, that's how much you'll have to pay." We were paying a monthly rent of $630.

"Things quieted down for a while," he said, "but it's noisy again. Whenever other kids come over it's noisy. And your wife still has friends who bring strollers in and bang up the door."

Any stroller left outside would have been stolen, that went without saying.

GOD PUNISHES GREED. I imagined cutting the words out of a magazine, gluing them to a piece of paper, typing Frank's name and address on the envelope. A series of such letters, spaced two weeks apart. I imagined hanging one of them around the neck of Saint Barbara, the two-foot religious statue right outside his apartment door. I thought of printing: YOU LOST ONE SON, FRANK. YOU CAN LOSE ANOTHER. WATCH OUT. I thought of spray-painting TURD on his precious front door. Of saying to him, If anything happens to this baby, Frank, if all the grief you're putting me through harms this baby in any way, I will sue you for every penny you've got.

Laura sputtered when I told her the latest. "Eight hundred and fifty! He's full of shit!" Her lips were moist and pink, the dozen grey moles quivered on her pale neck.

She was on her way to the beauty parlour. Once a week she got her hair done and in the afternoon it sat six inches above her head, freshly blonde, lacquered and waved. Halfway through the week it started to itch and by Friday it lay flat. I walked with her to the corner, pushing the stroller, and told her we would try to find another place before the baby was born in September. She was wearing makeup, the rouge ragged on her cheeks and very red. The light at that early hour in the morning was reddish-blonde. It covered us like powder left over from the setting sun of the night before.

When I came back Frank was leaning out his second-floor window. He averted his eyes, I averted mine. Upstairs, I pulled down the Venetian blinds. I hushed Sochi. I hesitated about having friends over. But I did not stop typing.

> *through the Venetian blinds—banners*
> *of doubt on my desk*
> *mourning doves on the fire escape*
> *owl-sounds under water*
>
> *city loons*
>
> *a lake you've opened in me*

The air outside was the same temperature as the coffee I drank. I could put my finger out the window, or I could put my finger in my coffee.

> *I thought of writing you some pissed-*
> *off poems*
> *but with you*
> *my anger doesn't last.*
> *With everyone else*
> *it never ends.*
>
> *You have discovered how to kiss*
> *my knee, my neck, my hand*
> *repeating till you get the perfect "pop."*
> *So musical! your father says.*

Monica dropped in, lifting Liam in his stroller up the two flights of stairs. I worried about Frank seeing her and despised myself. She told me that she and Jack had made love and the mo-

ment they finished he reached for the remote and flicked on a
porno movie.

"He's crazy," she said. "Excessive. I can't get a word in edgewise
he talks so much."

Yet a week later she told me she was moving.

"Really?"

"In with Jack," she said.

ONE NIGHT MY DAUGHTER and I were standing by the window
looking out at Devoe Street when a car pulled up to the curb
and the passenger door opened. To my surprise, Frank got out. I
stepped back quickly, as though slapped.

"You can't let him do that to you," Mark said. "You can't let
him dominate you. You can't care about what Frank thinks."

But I did care. Frank was in my head and too much light was
in my eyes.

It seemed to me that our neighbourhood was a series of skins
and the skins were heavy coats, one inside the other. I was a heavy
coat for the baby in my womb. The kitchen was a heavy coat for
me. The Venetian blinds were a heavy coat for the kitchen. The air
outside was the heaviest coat of all.

In the morning it was already ninety degrees when I took my
daughter over to Maria's, the subsidized babysitter we had been
lucky enough to find. It was nine o'clock. An old woman walked
by wearing a hat, scarf, boots, coat, mittens. Her mittens were
brown and yellow. She carried two bags of groceries. She was the
Fever walking by. At ten o'clock Maria called me to say my daughter had it.

I brought my daughter home and we lay side by side on the
bed. I put a cold wet cloth on her forehead. She played with a
small white purse. The blinds were drawn and it was quiet, except

for the zip of the purse and the sound of her fingers.

I saw the old woman in her winter coat several more times. Her name was Anna, I learned. Her son Peter almost always accompanied her, but when she was alone she would speak to me. The son was fat and bearded and used a walking stick. He could have been thirty or he could have been forty and he had an educated air out of keeping with the neighbourhood. Anna called him "that son of mine." He was her only child, I learned. She had sent him to private school, then college, and now they lived in the projects, like Maria.

From Anna I learned something about aspirations and something else about reality. She spoke of a former apartment not as an apartment but as "the most beautiful rooms" and her expressive, old eyes shone with the memory of former glory. I found it helpful, reassuring somehow, to think not of housing but of "rooms." The word took on a particular lustre, and I felt my Canadian expectations fall into line with the rest of the world's.

Then one day I entered Maria's building to pick up my daughter and heard screams that were piercing and out of control. Male or female, I couldn't tell. I climbed the stairs towards the screams and made out another voice saying quietly, just inside the door, "Get away from me. Get away from me, Peter." The door opened and Anna backed out. I paused, but she didn't look around. She went back inside and shut the door. Her son continued to scream.

"Do you know them?" I asked Maria when I got to the fourth floor. "The old lady and her fat son?"

Oh yes, she knew them. "Since I came here seven years ago it's like that. Saturday night, midnight, it's terrible. We call the police, but he won't open the door. You see her in summer wearing a coat. He's a very bad son. They go to the store and all they buy is Pepsi. He carries a little bag and she carries two big bags."

Usually Maria was buoyant, but not today. She started to cry. She was pregnant, she said, and the news had depressed Willy, her loan shark lover and a married man. Maria had a round, pretty face and the kind of shapely body that is very firm. Perhaps the skin is thicker, tougher. Her hair was curly, almost shoulder-length, and coppery brown. "He doesn't pay attention to me like before, and I told him not to come back here no more. He just talks about his family." His family had everything—a big house, a swimming pool, two cars. His wife had everything and Maria had nothing.

When I went downstairs, Peter's crazy voice was still screaming. I paused outside the door. Anna's quiet voice was saying, "My face and neck. I'm going outside to show everybody." But she didn't come outside.

We got away on weekends. Packed the old Chevette with our camping equipment and drove to state parks on the Hudson River, set up our tent, cooked over an open fire, swam in any lakes we could find.

last summer slid off
the faces of three black women
like rhododendron petals on the ground

In Clarence Fahnstock Park the humid night circled into me, a vast liquid, and I peed it out. "This is ludicrous," I said to Mark, filling the chamber pot yet again. "The whole summer is ludicrous."

At dawn, however, I slept for an hour and dreamt a beautiful dream. Michael Ondaatje had made especially for me a series of dishes of food, all of them small, soft, delicious, each in its own bowl set upon crushed ice.

my father teethed on amber
left marks on five million years
of coming-to-be

And here you are.
In fake amber down to your knee.

Already you know
there's no love without luck
and place just so
these beads around your neck.

We brought back a container of country strawberries for
Laura, and the next afternoon I took them down to her, the
dark hallway cooling with the descent, the container cold from
the refrigerator. I gave them to her, then continued on to the
air-conditioned library several blocks away on the other side of
Graham Avenue. In the library a woman wearing flowered blue
gloves shelved books. She wiped her mouth with a tissue and
dragged her feet as she walked. The library was almost empty,
the ceiling low, the lights fluorescent. There was the steady whir
of air-conditioning and the patter of typing in the back. The
soundlessness of books being put away by gloved hands. The occasional ring of the telephone.

My sunglasses were on the table. A partially written letter to
an old friend. A book about the Arctic lay open in front of me. I
was rereading the account of an anthropologist who stayed with an
Inuit family near Gjoa Haven and was ostracized because of her
temper, a loss of self-control for which the Inuit had no respect. My
own anger scalded and splashed me. I thought of telling Frank we
were getting a lawyer and taking our case to the human rights com-

mission. I thought of killing him, then trashing the apartment.

Walking home I crisscrossed the street, drawn by pitiful spots of shade until there was no shade at all. I entered the dark hall of Frank's house and climbed to the third floor where an old skylight gave onto a yellow dusty sky. The rooms were perfectly still. Less so when I turned on the ceiling fan. The kitchen, its blinds lowered against the heat, was grey, and the windowless bedroom was dark. I saw myself in those rooms in the heat wave that would not end, avoiding wool the way I avoided Frank, my body slow and wide, my mind frantic and repetitive with plots of revenge.

> *Clara sweeps magnolia petals*
> *off the walk*
> *for high-blood pressure, your father reminds me—*
> *the buds. Made into a tea.*

> *Your life*
> *will be long, he reassures me.*

> *You litter the floor, the magnolia*
> *the ground.*

> *In New Orleans I saw magnolia blossoms*
> *the size of your head.*
> *Carved one off and carried it home,*
> *precursor of you.*

When Monica came over she was wearing her red-framed glasses again, back to altering her vision, having so miscalculated with Jack. To her great surprise he had chickened out. Now she would have to continue to share an apartment with her husband, since neither had enough money to move, even though the marriage was over. She said, "Distraction has been replaced by reality and it's very hard. The reality of what I've done."

During the visit my daughter pushed her son into the wall and he didn't react. Monica said, "He really doesn't mind. He must be just like his father."

We talked a lot about the weaknesses of men, a favourite subject back then. We thought something was wrong with these mild husbands who didn't fight back, some element of reasonable anger was missing.

At the end of July the bank turned us down for a mortgage. Not enough credit history, they said. Then we really had to scramble. We would have to finance the purchase ourselves by using every cent of our savings and by borrowing from our families. Even Mark showed the strain and I became aware of his kind of anger. It would have earned him respect among the Inuit because it was never self-indulgent, never childish.

In August Maria said, "I think the summer don't want to go."

She held out her wrists to me. "I hold them under cold water and I feel all the heat coming out. It feels wonderful."

She began to put clothes into the washing machine, a brassiere, a long T-shirt. It was the same old story. Willy was off to Florida to buy a house and "for Maria, nothing. I tell him I hope nobody else ever loves me the way he loves me. All he gives me is love, pure love, nothing else. What good is that? I have expenses. My car is always breaking down. He has two new cars. He could buy me another car, at least. His wife has everything. *EVERYTHING.* And I have nothing. It's been four years like this. I'm sick and tired. All my friends tell me to change the locks on the door, but I can't do that."

That morning my daughter cried when I left her there. She had never done that before. Maria pointed at Christopher, her other charge, and said, "She's just like you."

I walked home slowly and with a handkerchief, mopping my face and neck, shade-seeking and slow.

> *a hollow mournful ooah, cooo, cooo, coo*
> *on Clara's roof*
> *4 sounds, short*
> *symphony*
>
> *on the radio Alice Munro says*
> *there's a moment*
> *when a child realizes*
> *her parents can't protect her.*

On August 14 the newspaper said we had had forty-two days and forty-two nights of unbroken heat, of temperatures above ninety during the day and above eighty during the night. Ice cream sales had fallen off, but shish kebab and hot dog sellers were doing a roaring business. Salt. Everyone wanted the salt. On August 15 it was 100 degrees and the next few days were almost as bad.

Then on August 19 everything changed and nothing was the same again. In the evening strong cool breezes swept through the apartment and blew the smell of my nightgown into my face. I went to the kitchen window and opened it as wide as it would go and I stuck my head out into cool tumbling darkness and the sound of crickets, immutable, a late-summer sound I've heard all my life, and I was overcome with joy at the northern turn the world had taken. Clothes billowed on every clothesline just as the apartment billowed with wind and my nightgown billowed around me.

When I am dying, I want to remember the rapture of it.

I lay down and picked up my book. The scent of those pages came into my face. Then a new surge of breezes blew through the room, stirring my nightgown once again. The book was *Emoke* by Josef Skvorecky. It began, "A story happens and fades and no one tells it." The words dovetailed with the cool air and I felt stories stirring all around me and in my soul, so close I could touch them with my hand.

Mark lay down beside me. We turned out the light and he murmured to me as I questioned him about a book he was reading. Panama. A northern wind blew over us and we talked about Panama. I remembered what Clara had told me earlier in the day. She was sitting in Laura's kitchen, her eyes full of tiredness and pain, as they often were. "You haven't been sleeping," I said. She said, "I can't." And she told me about something she had seen when she was very small: an old lady sitting in a doorway in July with woolen socks pulled up over her knees. Clara could not believe that anyone in the heat of an Italian summer could be cold. "Are you cold?" she had asked, and the old lady answered, "In my bones I'm cold."

"Now I understand," Clara said. "Now I know what she felt." She pressed her lower back with her hands. "Maybe it's the fan at work," she said. "It hits me right in the back. I'm in pain all the time. In my bones."

Across the river was Manhattan. On the other side of Manhattan was the countryside to which we still escaped, packing our car to the brim, leaving the treeless, tortured lives on Devoe Street and taking ourselves to the woods. If I had been less afraid of Frank, then I might have sat down with him and said, Tell me what noises you hear and when, tell me what disturbs you and we'll do our best to fix it. I would have brought little gifts to him and Cathy in keeping with our feudal relationship. But then he wouldn't have had the great sadistic pleasure of treating us the way landlords had treated him.

We had picked up *The Village Voice* to see the ad he placed. "Five rooms, two blocks from subway, working couple, or couple with child okay. $750 negotiable. No fee." And his phone number. And Mark said, "$750 negotiable. That means $700. We would have paid that." But Frank wanted to be rid of us and it shamed me to be unwanted, even by him.

> *Supper at El Viejo Yayo. Sochi and her yellow horse.*
> *The cashier had a bad back and couldn't*
> *lift her up, but gave her quarters*
> *to make the yellow horse go.*
>
> *Her brave face crumpled when a man*
> *got between us. I gestured*
> *come around him,*
> *and she came into my arms. Oh, these sorrows.*

I FINISHED *EMOKE* BY Skorvecky. Within the stories we write are other unwritten stories, the more important ones, and within the stories we live are all the stories we don't realize we are living. In each of us stories happen and fade and no one tells them. Early in September my daughter and I walked over to the projects to say goodbye to Maria. Afterwards, Sochi played in the dusty, semi-shaded park that the projects shared. A small white-haired woman sat down beside me on the bench and pointed out an even smaller man. "He feels bad," she said, "he and his wife did everything together." She's in the hospital? "Yes, she broke her hip, and in the heat the bones often don't knit back together."

You hate milk
until I remember Morir Sonando.

Cold milk and orange juice:
Die Dreaming

I add the yolk of an egg
with the "yemas" of my fingers,
soft yolks, the tips,
running my egg/hand
over your body as the brujos do—
to protect you

At home that night I watched the shadow of the child-guard
play on the living room wall, three bars across a soft square of
light made by the streetlamp outside. We could see the Empire
State Building from the window. That meant, Mark said, that if
we were on top of the Empire State Building, we would be able to
see this house.

He drew the rocking chair under the fan and that made for
even more movement: the breeze, the fan, the rocking chair. Towards the end of September I went into labour and while I was
in the hospital he moved our things with the help of many kind
friends into our new place in Manhattan, the small, dark, railroad
apartment that I have written about elsewhere.

Our son was born with red hair and two red birthmarks on his
forehead. "The birthmarks will disappear," the doctor said, "except
when he's angry."

I came out of the hospital two days later into a beautiful fall.
Manhattan was beautiful, the graceful old buildings, the flower-
boxes, the trees. We were within three blocks of the Hudson River
and Riverside Park stretched for miles, grassy, shaded, sloping.

The doctor was right, my son's birthmarks faded away. He remained, however, a redheaded boy full of thwarted passion. On his second birthday, among other gifts, he received a goofy-looking, blue stuffed dog. He pulled the name "Frank" out of the air and gave it to the dog. For quite a while he was so fond of Frank that he slept with him every night.

My last poems were written in Brooklyn. In the sad and unforeseen way of things, my son displaced my love for my daughter without generating an equivalent love for himself. There were difficult years when I didn't love either of them as much as a parent would hope to. That changed too. The love came back. This is something I can attest to: love comes back.

But not the poetry. It got supplanted on that windy night in Brooklyn when I was filled with the thousands of stories I have been looking for ever since.

PREPARATIONS FOR THE END OF THE WORLD AS WE KNOW IT

JASON MCBRIDE
Toronto Life

ON THE FIRST DAY of what my girlfriend, Liz, and I are calling apocalypse week, I get up at 6:30 a.m.—the cats are begging to be fed—and try to make a cup of coffee. I'm pretty well prepared, I think, having bought several ten-litre jugs of spring water, a jar of instant Maxwell House Dark Roast, and a sleek, Swedish-designed multi-fuel camp stove that can, its packaging says, boil a pot of water in less than three minutes. My stove, however, can't boil anything in any minutes. It's a perfect late-May morning, just a touch gusty, and I set up the crab-like contrivance on a glass table on our deck. After carefully filling it with kerosene and priming as instructed, I go through an entire box of waterproof matches in my attempt to start it. No dice. Twenty minutes and another box of matches later, caffeine withdrawal already clouding my brain, the stove still isn't working. I crawl back into bed. "I'm not surviving very well," I say weakly. Liz and I have just celebrated a year of living together, during which she's become intimate with my domestic incompetence. She offers to give the camp stove a shot, and when even she—the MacGyver to my Michael Scott—can't get the thing going, I know I'm really screwed. I threaten to make a fire in the backyard, though God knows how that'll happen now that I've run out of matches. "You know," Liz says, "you don't actually need hot water to make instant coffee."

Turns out that there are a lot of things I don't know, as the next several days will prove. Apocalypse week, briefly put, is a kind of experiment to see how I might make out at the end of the world. I'm increasingly jittery about the future these days, with its grim quadruple threat of climate change, vanishing fossil fuels, pandemics, and terrorism. The end, if not nigh, certainly feels nigh-er. I've always been a bit of a Chicken Little when it comes to environmental stuff—every mild February day fills me with global-warming dread, and my heart sinks whenever I see an SUV fitted with a child's car seat. (Don't those parents care about the world they'll leave behind for their kids?) The speed and severity of the global financial meltdown—plus the more worrisome fact that no one saw it coming—seems to me just a harbinger of a more horrific, abrupt, and irrevocable eco-collapse, when birds will fall from blackened skies, drought will decimate the prairies, and spoiled, soft North Americans like myself will have to fend off climate-change refugees with the useless keys to our Zipcars.

Which makes reading something like Jeff Rubin's *Why Your World Is About to Get a Whole Lot Smaller* both self-flagellation and a prophecy-confirming thrill. Rubin, a Toronto economist and the former head of CIBC World Markets, is most famous for having accurately predicted the pre-recession spike in oil prices. In his new bestseller, which he left CIBC to flog, his main bugaboo is peak oil, the theory (if you can even call it a theory now, rather than a fact) that we've essentially run out of cheap oil and that any existing global reserves will soon be so expensive to extract, no one will bother trying. And since globalization depends entirely on cheap oil, Rubin's argument goes, once it's all gone—ipso facto, no more globalization. The world will contract: travel will become prohibitively expensive, and trade will shrink. Your morning macchiato will be well out of price range, and salmon will disappear from the menus of whatever restaurants remain. Poorer countries, however, won't just see luxuries disappear; their economies will be crippled, their desperate citizens trapped in resource-depleted deserts. But one man's dystopia is another's utopia. Rubin's silver lining, for Canadians, anyway, is the return of manufacturing jobs, a boom in local agriculture and, if we're lucky, a reduction in greenhouse gases.

Even so, the transition to a post-oil economy is going to be frustrating and bewildering and probably painful. And, while temperamentally I'm an optimist, the more I think about it, the less ready I am for a future that could look more like *The Flintstones* than *The Jetsons*. Your average urban bohemian, I know how to neither hunt nor forage. I don't know how to fix my bike, perform CPR, tie a proper knot, or clean a fish. Fire a gun? I've never even seen a real gun. I was a lousy Cub Scout (in 1977 I earned precisely zero badges), and I dropped out of shop class after building a footstool too small for the cast of *Little People, Big World*. Not only did I refuse to trap the mice that ran around my kitchen for years, I named them. The only real skill I have—arranging words on a page—is of dubious practical value, and it certainly isn't going to prove useful when, to use an acronym beloved by the practical-minded doomsdayers who call themselves survivalists, SHTF—the Shit Hits the Fan.

Which is why I began taking baby steps toward some form of self-sufficiency. Remedy my uselessness, I thought hopefully, and I'd reduce that sense of powerlessness. Man up. Be prepared, not scared. I purchased a library of survival manuals, crammed our small mud room with hundreds of dollars' worth of canned food, several jugs of spring water and, for moments of low blood sugar and even lower spirits, some outrageously expensive dark chocolate. Bought the aforementioned stove and a 150-litre President's Choice rain barrel, and started taking classes and workshops in wild edible plant identification, fire making, self-defence, and gardening. An old backpack became a "bug-out bag," my survival kit, complete with water purification tablets, protein bars, a handful of multi-tools and knives, a decent first aid kit, and a freezer bag containing my passport and emergency cash. Finally, I hooked up with a group of survivalists who weren't the reactionary, militant, paranoid, bunker-dwelling stereotype I expected but rather a cuddly bunch of outdoors enthusiasts and DIYers brought together by a hate-on for our consumerist, tech-addicted, nature-destroying, suicidal culture. There was nary a Ted Kaczynski in the group—at least among the members I met—though, not surprisingly, most possessed a somewhat jaundiced outlook on the future. They're counting on catastrophe, and a few will even admit it's something they're looking forward to. While jarring at first, it was a worldview that I eventually took solace in, a bulwark against hopelessness. Come, Armageddon, come.

"LIVING IN A HOUSE without utilities," the legendary American wilderness guru Tom Brown Jr. writes, "is not too different from living in a cave." In his *Field Guide to City and Suburban Survival*, he recommends, as preparation for a disaster or emergency, that readers "set up survival scenarios and act them out. Try living for several days without electricity. Try evacuating the home in three hours. Try subsisting on survival rations." Check. Check. Check. But during my off-the-grid week, I'm also doing Brown one better, pretending that the entire GTA is in the same powerless boat, so no 7-Elevens or Starbucks, no streetcars or gas stations, no movies, no pints on a patio, no baseball games, no ATMs, no brunch.

Liz isn't 100 percent into this—she still has to go to work, after all, and usually likes a hot shower and meal before doing so—though at night she graciously leaves the TV and lights off and joins me for games of candlelit Boggle. As caves go, our west-end apartment is pretty cozy; caves don't often come with skylights, queen-size beds or 200-square-foot decks. Still, as anyone who's lived through one of our recent blackouts knows, forced off-the-grid urban living is inconvenient, tedious and, on occasion, downright miserable.

The City of Toronto maintains an Office of Emergency Management whose *raison d'être* is to help residents prepare for and deal with disasters of all kinds. Its staff of eleven works closely with many other city agencies, like Toronto Water and Public Health, as well as first responders, like police, fire, and EMS. Emergency Management's Program Committee, chaired by the mayor, meets quarterly or, in response mode, as frequently as necessary. While the OEM is responsible for preventing and mitigating disasters, its chief role seems to be informing residents, as placidly as possible, about the precise threats the city faces and instructing us on how to prepare for these threats. (The OEM's website even has a "Fun

Stuff" section, though their idea of fun is a puzzle containing such hidden words as "terrorism" and "pandemic.") When I ask Warren Leonard, the OEM manager, how nervous Nellies like myself might feel more secure, he suggests that I undertake a personal preparedness plan. "It's going to give you that immediate comfort," he says, as if providing voice-over for a tampon commercial, "because you've done something yourself."

It is comforting, at first, to simply stockpile food and bags of powdered milk, to read how-to guides on making flour with a manual grain mill. It's comforting in the way that going to church or dutifully contributing to your RRSP can be. Except I've never gone to church, and I haven't opened a bank statement in months. And my reassurance is soon undermined by the fact that no one really knows exactly what to prepare for. It's one thing to dream of a post-petroleum economy, but catastrophe could also come in the guise of a North Korean nuke, a swine flu pandemic, a wayward asteroid, or the collapse of the oceans. All the powdered milk in the world won't help you avoid an asteroid.

The OEM recommends that all citizens stock at least seventy-two hours' worth of food and water in case of an emergency, and we've got, by my quick estimation, at least a week's worth of food and even more water. (I also laid in a couple bottles of rioja, but those went fast.) I bought mostly canned stuff, No Name beans and tomatoes and lentil soup, non-perishables that don't necessarily require cooking though would probably taste a lot better if I could heat them up. I'm a vegetarian who occasionally eats fish, and Liz is a meat eater allergic to dairy and wheat, so our little supply room is larded with tins of cheap tuna (I expect mercury poisoning will kill us before anything else). I hoped that the small garden I started on the deck—my first ever—would provide something edible, but it's way too early in the season, and the best

I'll get out of it is some fresh basil. On the first morning, instead of a customary omelette or oatmeal, breakfast consists of a PowerBar and some peanut butter and crackers. And that cold coffee.

Though I'm kind of looking forward to the simplicity of this diet, I'm less excited about where the food will go after I eat it. Technically, if the grid really were down, the city's sewage system wouldn't be operational and human waste would quickly fill our backyards and alleyways. My apocalypse week version of this is to not flush the toilet. Or rather, I lug a bucket of water from the rain barrel and use that to flush, letting gravity do the work. A pain in the ass, but it does the trick. (At least for a few days.) I'm thinking I can also use the rainwater to bathe in, if I really have to, but it's piss-coloured, chilly, and funky-smelling. Instead, Brad Pitt style, I resort to baby wipes, which turn out to be pretty effective. Even by day five, I don't stink too bad.

I'm writing this not on the MacBook I normally use but with a ballpoint pen, on sheets of loose-leaf paper bought a decade ago. The iPod that usually blares while I write is cold and silent. My penmanship, like pretty much everybody's now, has become atrocious. (Retyping this later on my computer, I'm just guessing that that word is "atrocious"; could be "abysmal" or "attractive.") Ignoring my cell, TV, Gmail, Facebook, and recently acquired Twitter account is delicious torture: I feel like a cokehead sitting on a kilo that he can't snort. My only contact with the outside world is a hand-cranked combination flashlight and radio, tuned perpetually to CBC Radio 2. (I suspect that even doomsday won't shut up Stuart McLean.) Once I get over the perverse fact that I'm eschewing an electronic fix that lies just inches away, it's a relief, a vacation from the 24/7 distraction I'm unabashedly hooked on. And I'm pleasantly surprised by how, after a day or two, powers of concentration I thought the Internet had stunted forever return.

I can read a novel again—for hours. Sleeping is also a snap—and I do it often, undisturbed by the nagging bleat of text messages. Most nights, I'm in bed by the time the sun sets.

It occurs to me, however, that my all-too-common technological dependence also comes freighted with a substantial degree of faith in that selfsame technology. Most survivalists I've read and met are thoroughly convinced that it's too late for any tech fixes to our environmental crisis or that such solutions—nanotechnology, renewable energy, geo-engineering and so on—will bring their own set of possibly more abhorrent problems. But who could have conceived just a decade ago how dramatically the Internet would rearrange our lives? What future, unforeseen scientific innovation might rescue us from ourselves? A concurrent revelation: pretty much all of my daily communication with friends and family who don't live within a block of me happens via some electronic medium, and without that, I don't talk to anybody but Liz and the cats. The hoary notion that such virtual interaction is alienating and atomizing goes completely out the window; that stuff genuinely makes me feel part of the world, and without it, things get lonely fast. When a few friends drop by mid-week, I react like a castaway who's just seen a rescue boat on the horizon.

A POST-PETROLEUM WORLD MIGHT just mean living more like many people do right now. This new survivalism dovetails conveniently with our contemporary, recessionary moment, where the small, the simple, the fresh-and-local, the sustainable and artisanal are all increasingly prized. We bike to the farmers' market and hot yoga class, spend our Sundays knitting baby clothes and canning fruit and making beer, contemplate adding a chicken coop to our new edible garden or green roof, take furniture-making classes. Hyper-localism, for a growing number of progressive-minded folk, is a panacea for the economic, ecological, even spiritual traumas that afflict our modern age. Witness the enduring popularity of locavore-loving foodies like Michael Pollan and Mark Bittman, the sudden success of books like Rubin's and Matthew Crawford's strenuously earnest *Shop Class As Soulcraft: An Inquiry Into the Value of Work.*

Survivalists aren't necessarily removing themselves from society; on the contrary, they're embracing and trying to prepare it for an uncertain future. Or, in some cases, hurry that future along. About a month before apocalypse week, while researching urban farming, I stumbled across a website called the Post-Oil Survival Guide for City Dwelling. It's a compendium of instructional tips and strategies on everything from building greenhouses to delivering babies, run by Claudia Dávila, a thirty-six-year-old new mother and freelance illustrator. With her black bob, cardigan, and cat's-eye glasses, she looks like a hip JK teacher. She was formerly the art director of *Owl* magazine and has written and illustrated two comics, *Spoiled* and *Luz, Girl of the Knowing,* which chronicle a tween's peak oil consciousness raising. Despite the subtitle (a reference to *Mad Max*), Luz lives in a picture-book Toronto where people grow sunflowers for cooking oil and make cakes flavoured with lavender plucked from their community gardens. (Radioactive zombies and gun-toting mercenaries are nowhere to be found.)

Dávila first learned of peak oil from a friend, a hardcore survivalist who now lives on a farm near Peterborough where he raises goats and, yes, grows sunflowers. Dávila prefers the label "naturalist" to survivalist. "It suddenly dawned on me," she says, "that we have a completely unsustainable way of life, though we've been living this way for just a brief time in history. This isn't how it's always been nor how it always will be." Dávila would love to retreat to the acreage she owns in Beaver Valley, but she feels a duty to help Torontonians puzzle out sustainable survival. The majority of the world's population, she argues, lives in urban centres, and transformation has to start there. She and her husband, the artist Michael Cho, and their daughter live in a tiny Little Italy walk-up, but Dávila fantasizes about soon erecting what she calls an "eco-village," a kind of Eden made up of self-sustaining downtown homes that she'd share with her brother's family and which would be outfitted with solar and grey water systems, and an enormous permaculture garden.

It turns out that she isn't yet practising much of what she preaches on her website. Her apartment is too small to store supplies, and her deck is too shady to grow vegetables. When her husband suggests that the family car trips they take are contributing to the planet's problems, her response is basically, "Good—let's use up the oil faster." Maybe she's just sleep-deprived—her baby's only ten months old—but she seems unfazed by both a coming catastrophe and how unprepared she is for it. When I ask her what would happen if disaster were to strike tomorrow, she says, with a warm, only slightly embarrassed, smile, "We'd be screwed." But Dávila thinks the transition will happen gradually, over the next fifteen years or so. "Humankind is cocooning," she says, citing one of her big influences, the anti-globalization guru David Korten. "But caterpillars don't just sprout wings and fly out. They dissolve into a molecular goo and then become a brand new being. With this crisis, we can still turn into something new and beautiful."

ON THE THIRD NIGHT of apocalypse week, my genius culinary idea is to combine a can of tomatoes, a can of chickpeas and a can of tuna, seasoned with some basil and salt. A few spoonfuls are fine, but again, would probably be much better warmed up. I've spent the afternoon gathering wood on the off chance that I'll build a fire, though Liz is worried I'll burn down the deck. I'm more worried I won't be able to get a fire going. About a month prior, I took a Fire by Friction workshop at the Sorauren Park fieldhouse with an outfit called the PINE Project (Primitive Integrated Naturalist Education). The group was founded in 2008 by a thirty-year-old wilderness guide and educator named Andrew McMartin. McMartin is compact, with a trim red beard and perpetual ball cap, and he has both the patience and entertainment instincts of a magician used to performing for pre-teens. He's also a big believer in teaching environmental awareness by showing how useful the natural environment is; he and his instructors offer classes in everything from wild edible plant identification to tanning animal hides. "They're really cool skills," he says. "And it's a sneaky way to learn about nature." PINE's motto is "Be more, need less."

My classmates included a dozen members of the Toronto Survivalism Group, an informal club of catastrophists and tree huggers that has seen its membership double in the past six months to almost 400. The group gathers regularly—in parks and pubs, community centres and private homes—in order to learn and perfect survival skills, discuss emergency preparedness and watch movies predicting the end of the world as we know it (TEOTWAWKI, another popular acronym). I anticipated a macho group, but the members that turned up this night skewed geekier—it's easier to picture them huddled around a Dungeons and Dragons table than at the Sportsmen's Show.

After a quick intro and the ceremonial burning of sweetgrass, McMartin squatted on the linoleum floor to show us how to start a fire with a bow drill. The device essentially includes a bow made of a stick the length of your arm and some kind of string or rope, a spindle, and a board for the spindle to grind into, creating enough friction to ignite some flammable material. McMartin did this in less than five minutes, his drilling effortless and precise. The smell of the scorching wood and the small ember that finally appeared sweetly perfumed the classroom. But, of course, it was much more difficult than it looked, and we struggled mightily to get even the smallest spark. A few survivalists stayed past midnight—more than six hours—to get their fires going, and eventually everyone ended up with some kind of flame. Everyone except me—in utter frustration, sweaty and sheepish, I left around nine to go home and watch *30 Rock*. Flee more, bleed less.

Laurie Varga, a thirty-one-year-old graphic designer and self-defence teacher, is the founder of the TSG. Her rhetoric, like Dávila's, seems less inspired by *The Road* than "The Road Not Taken." She is simultaneously athletic and bookish, a rangy stunner who could pass for a Mountain Equipment Co-op catalogue model. She was born and raised in Alberta, the daughter of a retired firefighter who also served as the Disaster Services Officer in Calgary. Varga moved to Toronto a decade ago to pursue her design career and, under the influence of her computer scientist boyfriend (now fiancé), began dipping into pessimism porn like James Howard Kunstler's *The Long Emergency* and Thomas Homer-Dixon's *The Upside of Down*. Dismal, depressing stuff. She found it harder and harder to get out of her pyjamas each morning. After about a year of this, and the concomitant discovery of more optimistic, even joyful, end times writing by people like the eco-philosopher Joanna Macy, she battened down the hatches and set out, through the TSG, to build a like-minded community. She's intrigued by the increasingly voguish prophecy that the earth will undergo a cataclysmic transformation in the year 2012, the same year the Mayan calendar comes to an end.

"As a kid, I was really fascinated by the pioneer lifestyle," she says brightly, "and I found out a lot of people want to play pioneer." To her surprise, the TSG, which she started last August, attracted all kinds of weekend warriors, from retirees to vermicomposting condonistas (but few, to Varga's relief, members of the guns-and-ammo crowd). Varga hopes to one day turn her eccentric hobby into some kind of business and, to that end, started Seed and Stone, a website that she's slowly populating with information and educational resources for "people who want to develop a closer relationship with nature and live a modern self-sufficient lifestyle." Right now, the site is sleek but skimpy—Varga has just uploaded her first free e-book, *The Top 5 Simple Things You Can Do to Be Ready for Anything*—but it promises much more. My favourite: a set of materials called "The " 'I'm Not Crazy' Conversation" that promises to facilitate communication with freaked-out loved ones. "I find tumultuous times exciting," Varga says, "and I want to help people get over their fear, to build up their internal resilience."

A few weeks after the PINE workshop, she led another group of us on a hike in Rouge Park. The ragtag company that overcast Saturday included a mechanical engineer, a raw foodie, a bio-chemist, an artist who makes sculpture out of animal bones and computer chips, and a middle-aged woman in capris and flimsy Reeboks who lives in a Whitby trailer park. (She joined the group, she told me, "because of Katrina.") The average age was probably thirty-eight. It was a warm-hearted crew, and during the hike everyone slowed down for and helped out the pokier members. I'm in decent shape, but the only one of us who really looked like he could take care of himself was an outdoorsman from Richmond Hill named Doug Getgood, a gentle, generous fellow and an old pro at this survival stuff. A buddy of Survivorman Les Stroud, Getgood has put in a ton of time at both the gruelling Boulder

Outdoor Survival School and Tom Brown Jr.'s Tracker School in
New Jersey. (Picture a shorter, *Unforgiven*-era Clint Eastwood in
a Tilley hat.) He spent a year living alone in a remote northern
cabin a ten-day canoe trip from civilization. "It was just always
something I wanted to do," he said, with typical humility. When
we divided into three small groups, for navigation, fire-making,
and shelter-building, I selected the last group and was quietly de-
lighted that Getgood was also on my team; the last time I had to
build any kind of shelter, it was a pillow fort for my niece.

Our hike took several hours, mainly because our navigators,
only one of whom had a compass, kept getting confused. We never made it to our designated campsite, but the clouds grew dark,
and we broke for lunch in a clearing. Getgood dug several tarps
and lengths of rope from his immense rucksack. He was totally
prepared, packing a homemade saw crafted from a hockey stick,
at least three different knives (on his belt, slung around his torso,
etc.), and an ornate walking staff with arcane notches carved in
it that I believe he used for measuring things. He demonstrated
complex knots that he had devised himself, and how to make a
perfectly secure A-frame tent with just one tarp, rope, a tree, and
some tent pegs. His quiet competence was dazzling.

As we ate, Varga led us through a discussion of the "survival
mindset," that is, how the body and mind respond in an emergency situation. She kicked things off with a true-false quiz. ("Generally, our brains aren't good at probability and risk analysis. We
tend to respond more to stories than to data." True.) Everyone was
then instructed to write down, without paper or pen, a trait they
thought would be advantageous for survival. We scrounged for
scraps of birchbark and fashioned makeshift pencils by charring
twig tips in the fire. Varga read each unsurprising choice aloud—
calm, humility, compassion (Getgood scrawled this on a stone),

perseverance, a sense of humour—and then each of us expound-
ed upon our particular word. After each trait was discussed, the
person's bark was flung theatrically into the flames. When a dog
walker stalked through our camp, sneering at our illegal campfire,
we must have looked to her like a terrorist cell composed of especially militant Wiccans.

I like to think that I possess all of the above traits, but the word
I came up with—patience—is the one thing, I joked, referencing
my earlier fire-making failure, that I needed to seriously work on.
A bit later, as it began to rain and we all stood underneath one of
Getgood's tarps, Varga launched into a prepared disquisition on
how the most important quality in a survival situation is feeling
that you deserve to survive. "One of the hallmark traits of a survi-
vor," she said, "is the drive to never give up. It's well documented
that those who give up usually fail shortly thereafter."

THE APOCALYPSE IS BORING. The toilet's backed up (thankfully,
Liz flushes it when I'm not looking), and I'm down to my last two
PowerBars. Novels have lost their novelty. I'm increasingly tempted
to turn on the laptop—what gossipy tidbits might I be missing on
Gawker?—and I've abandoned my plan to make pesto from the
garlic mustard that's taken over our backyard. (No olive oil in the
survival rations.)

I remember the one urban survivalist rule of thumb: if you're in
a city when disaster strikes, get the hell out. Get somewhere rural,
where, theoretically, there will be animals to hunt, fresh water,
edible plants, and fewer people around competing for resources.
(Liz and I have a tentative emergency plan that includes getting
to the country home of a lesbian couple we know—a professional
beekeeper and a GP. They're capable and tough and know how to
make a stiff drink.) So, feeling the need to kick it up a notch, I

figure I'll try a dress rehearsal. Abandon the cave and head to the hills. Or, in my case, High Park. It has a fish-stocked freshwater pond, abundant plant life, tons of potential shelter.

The morning I decide to go, my hand-cranked radio tells me that the forecast is for rain—"heavy at times"—and thunderstorms. All I'm allowing myself to take is the bug-out bag—no tent or sleeping bag. The only useful thing in the knapsack is a bright red-and-silver emergency blanket that could serve as either a tarp or groundsheet. I've read up on making shelters and figure that even I can easily slap together a debris hut from deadfall, leaves, and grass. Doug Getgood said he slept in one for three months one winter, staying completely warm and dry.

It takes a while to find the perfect camping spot. I want to be hidden from the police and park staff, curious homeless folk (some of whom I assume live in the park), and marauding, drunken teenagers. But I also want to find a location that's dry, with a tree whose branches fork out at about waist height. I settle on a spot in the West Ravine. It feels secluded enough, heavily wooded and, while close to a couple of trails, fairly invisible from them. There's a good amount of fallen wood, too, and though it's largely rotted, it'll do for my purposes. I don't notice until later the numerous signs warning of coyotes and poison ivy.

I locate a nice thick branch a bit longer than my body that I rest in the Y-shaped nook of the tree—it'll serve as the ridge pole—and set out to gather more branches to rest on a forty-five-degree angle against this pole. Many more branches. With practise, some people can build these huts in about two hours, but it takes me close to five to gather enough wood—and then enough armloads of wet leaves to pile on top of the wood—to finish the thing. Even then, with darkness descending and the rain growing more torrential, I end up leaving the last top sec-

tion relatively uninsulated; I figure my waterproof boots, which
will be poking out the end, will be fine. Despite the boots and
a decent slicker, I'm soaked from the inside from sweat, and my
shirt and khakis are completely waterlogged from the rain.

The shelter looks impressively authentic when I'm done, and
well camouflaged. Inside, it's dark and claustrophobic—I can lie
down but not turn over. But it doesn't leak and, lying on the relatively dry space blanket I've tucked inside, I manage to nod off
while it's still slightly light outside. Exhausted and sort of pleased
with myself, I sleep like a big, wet baby.

For about two hours. When I wake up, it's completely dark.
I'm trembling from the cold—though it's around twelve degrees
outside, the sweat and rainwater have cooled my body, severely
lowering my temperature. My hands and right eye are suddenly
absurdly itchy. I've never experienced poison ivy before, and at
first I assume I've been feasted on by mosquitoes. But the itch is
also somehow on my penis. (FYI: I did have to pee a couple of
times.) It's still raining, and while it's difficult to separate sounds,
I'm certain the patter of rainfall is a hungry coyote pawing around
the hut. Or maybe it's the homeless dude I saw earlier, walking his
bike up one of the trails, a boom box on his handlebars playing
Mariah Carey. I quickly switch on my headlamp and see nothing
but a series of tiny black worms crawling along the ridge pole that
sits about half a foot above my face—miniature leeches, maybe,
that I can picture creeping up my nose, *Slither* style, if I ever do
fall asleep again.

I'm no celebrity, but get me out of here, please. It's around
midnight. If this were a real emergency situation, I'd duck under
an existing manmade shelter made by a man other than myself. So
I grab my bug-out bag and head back into the rain. After wandering around the park for an hour or so, I dart past the zoo and find

myself in the Jamie Bell Adventure Playground. And though it reeks of fresh urine and I can see, not too far off, glowing cigarettes that probably belong to a pack of teen rapists, I climb in and curl up inside the fairy tale-style wooden castle. The rattle and hum of nearby streetcars, the whine of police sirens and the unremitting glare of streetlights are strangely comforting.

A few hours later, I stumble home. Liz is groggy but relieved that I've survived and, better yet, come home early. It's 3 a.m., and she hasn't slept at all. She hugs my frozen, mud-caked body as though I were her husband just back from the war, oblivious to the stench and the possible poison ivy. Screw apocalypse week—I decide to avail myself of indoor plumbing and take a long, hot bath. I'm done playing survivalist for now. The next time I have to build a fire from scratch or live off canned beans, it'll be out of necessity. My clothes are ruined, but the bug-out bag is largely intact, and I tuck it back into its safe spot under the bed. Then I get under the covers, where the only thing that might threaten me is a particularly gassy cat.

THE ILLEGALS

CAROLYN MORRIS
Toronto Life

ALEJANDRA AND GERARDO NEVER thought they would leave
Mexico City behind forever. In the late 1990s, she worked as
the director's assistant at an affiliate of Pittsburgh Paints, and he
had a position in the credit department at a national newspaper,
travelling across Mexico investigating outstanding advertising accounts. They made enough money to be comfortable and had a
close-knit extended family and three young kids, Alberto, Pablo,
and Gloria.

Then, in the spring of 2000, Gerardo and his employers
began to receive anonymous death threats. Gerardo didn't know
why, but guessed that he must have been exposed to something

incriminating during one of his meetings with a rich and powerful advertiser. The threats against his life escalated, until one day his boss called to say he shouldn't come in to work—he should go on an extended holiday.

At the time, Canada didn't require Mexicans to have visas to enter the country, so the family decided to fly to Toronto until things cooled down. A couple weeks into their trip, Gerardo phoned his boss at the newspaper, who said people had come to the office looking for him. Gerardo and Alejandra decided returning any time soon would be too risky, even though Alejandra's father was seriously ill. After three months in Toronto, they filed a refugee claim with the help of an immigrant centre near Oakwood Avenue and St. Clair.

Soon after making their claim, Alejandra and Gerardo found a bachelor apartment for the five of them near Kensington Market. While waiting for the decision on their case, they had access to federal health insurance, work permits, temporary social insurance numbers, career counselling, public schools, provincially subsidized language training, and social services. Both were eager to work again, and took English classes. They started doing odd jobs, and within a year they were off welfare. Alejandra was making minimum wage cleaning hotel rooms, and Gerardo earned $12 an hour removing asbestos and performing other tasks for a demolition company. The jobs weren't ideal, but they felt like decent stepping stones.

As their income increased, they were able to upgrade to a one-bedroom unit in the same building. Over the next few years, they found progressively higher paying jobs—Alejandra worked her way up from housekeeping to serving at banquet halls and cooking lunch at an elementary school. They moved into a larger apartment in midtown Toronto, and after taking a child care course through a settlement office, Alejandra opened a licensed home daycare. She cared for five children, which brought in $3,000 a month.

Gerardo graduated from tearing buildings down to erecting them. His boss owned a small residential construction company and taught him the trade. Though he sometimes longed for a desk job, he was happy to see his salary climb gradually from $12 to $25 an hour. "I learned everything from building foundations to painting," Gerardo tells me. When I ask if he knew any of that in Mexico, he shakes his head and he and his wife laugh.

"I didn't even know how to hold a hammer," he says.

Alejandra points at the calluses and scars on his hands and declares, "They used to look like a lady's hands." His left middle finger bends forward awkwardly—the result of a hammer blow.

He often spent winter months out of work and collecting employment insurance, but they never went back on welfare. They bought a sixty-one-inch TV, a stereo, a dining room set, and a used minivan they paid off in instalments.

While the family's status in Canada was still in limbo, they were comfortable in their new country. Four years after moving, the kids spoke better English than Spanish. They fit in at school. Gloria begged her mother—unsuccessfully—for a dog just like the Yorkshire terrier owned by a classmate. Alberto was obsessed with cars; with his dad's help, he built up a collection of over 100 die-cast model cars. Alberto and Pablo joined air cadets and played football in the summer.

To the kids, Toronto was home and Mexico was the faraway place where their aunts and uncles lived. They didn't expect to be told they didn't belong.

"ALEJANDRA" AND "GERARDO" ARE not their real names. They agreed to tell me their story, but only on the condition of anonymity. They were among 1,317 Mexicans to file refugee claims in 2000. Since then, the number of Mexican claimants has soared, with 8,103 filing in 2008. At the same time, the acceptance rate for Mexican refugees has dropped from 26 to 11 percent.

In 2004, the family was finally granted its refugee hearing. Alejandra and Gerardo would have to convince the adjudicators at the Immigration and Refugee Board that their lives would be in danger if they returned home. Their four-year wait culminated in a single meeting by videoconference. With the help of a translator, Gerardo answered questions the adjudicators in Vancouver had about his job in Mexico and the threats he had received. Because he had lost contact with his employers (he suspected his boss was also in hiding), he didn't have anyone to corroborate his story. The decision came in a letter a few weeks after the hearing, and it was devastating: Canada didn't consider them refugees.

Alejandra and Gerardo's lawyer asked for a judicial review of their case, where the Federal Court examines the decision to make sure no legal errors were made. The review took place a year later and confirmed the adjudicators' ruling.

Alejandra and Gerardo were willing to do anything to avoid uprooting their family once more. They had been gaining momentum, despite the odds against them. They were happy with their jobs and had made their last payment on the van. At sixteen, Alberto landed his first job, working in the sporting goods department at Canadian Tire. He had a girlfriend. He was saving up to buy a car for himself and talked about becoming a lawyer; seeing all the money his parents were spending on legal help, he figured it would be a good career choice.

By April 2008, eight years after they had arrived in Canada, the family was running out of time and options. They were told they'd be deported within twenty-one days. They had to hand over their social insurance cards, work permits, and driver's licences immediately. Alejandra pleaded with immigration officials to let her kids finish the school year, and they agreed, provided she buy five tickets for a flight to Mexico that departed less than a week after the end of classes. The next day, the family spent $2,700 on Air Canada tickets and handed them over to immigration officials.

But they didn't give up. They consulted another lawyer, who suggested they make a claim on humanitarian and compassionate grounds; they could argue that, after so much time spent living and working here, uprooting the children would cause undue hardship. For many people without status, this is the last resort. In 2008, more than 10,000 applicants were granted permanent residency through this type of claim. An immigration officer considers whether the person or family should be allowed to stay by looking at how long they've been in Canada, how well established they are, how successfully they've integrated into society, and what is in the best interests of the children involved. A decision about their claim could take another three years. Their new lawyer said he would try to stop the deportation while awaiting the decision. He would do it all for $10,000. They scrambled to find the money—borrowing from friends and from Alberto's savings—and were able to pay in full.

The day before their flight, Alejandra delivered the family's passports to immigration, even though they had no intention of taking the trip. They didn't say anything to their landlord about their situation, hoping that the lawyer would be able to stop the deportation. Alejandra had given her daycare clients and the home child care agency notice that she'd be on vacation and they would

have to make other arrangements. Gerardo had rented a storage
locker for some of their things—just in case.

On the day of their deportation, the family sat in their living room, praying the rosary. Alejandra tried calling the lawyer
a couple of times, but his secretary said he wasn't available. Immigration officials would be expecting them at Pearson at five
o'clock. At around three, the phone rang and Alejandra answered.
The others watched her worried expression turn to despair as the
lawyer told her he wasn't able to stop the deportation. They would
have to show up at the airport or a warrant would be issued for
their arrest. Alejandra hung up and let loose a deluge of Spanish
curses. Gerardo, normally calm, barked to his wife to pack up the
kids and their coats and call their close friend Diana, a refugee
from Colombia whose girls were in Alejandra's daycare. Alberto,
Pablo, and Gloria frantically gathered as much as they could—
cameras, clothes, model cars. Diana picked Alejandra and the two
younger kids up, while Gerardo and Alberto loaded some of their
furniture and belongings into the family's minivan and drove it to
their storage locker.

"From that moment on," says Alejandra, "we were fugitives,
criminals, thieves—that's how we felt."

LAST YEAR, THE AUDITOR General announced that the Canadian Border Services Agency no longer knew the whereabouts
of 41,000 illegal immigrants—people who were supposed to be
deported but had fallen off the agency's radar, most of them failed
refugee claimants. Warrants were issued, but the immigrants
hadn't been caught. Even though Border Services follows initial
leads to catch people who go underground, it prioritizes cases of
national security and organized crime. Aside from the occasional
workplace raids and crackdowns on temp agencies, there's not

much active searching for non-status immigrants who aren't considered dangerous.

In the months after going into hiding, Alejandra, Gerardo, and Alberto scraped by with money earned from odd jobs. They'd become three of the roughly 100,000 non-status immigrants who work underground in Toronto—an estimate that includes students, temporary workers, and visitors who decide not to leave. Many take jobs as security guards, cleaners, servers, and parking lot attendants—industries in which employers don't always demand work permits.

Alejandra and Gerardo knew that steady work is key for their humanitarian and compassionate grounds application—having gone into hiding will hurt their case, but it doesn't disqualify them. For their hearing, they will need employment letters, bank account documentation, a copy of their lease, and proof that their children are enrolled in school. As non-status immigrants, one of their only paths to legality in Canada is through illegal work. To get status, Alejandra and Gerardo must perfect the art of living underground.

There are tricks to surviving without status. First, community health centres usually have small budgets for uninsured patients, so becoming a patient at a CHC means regular health care. Second, paying income tax can help establish status through a humanitarian and compassionate grounds application, even if the claimant is using an expired social insurance number to file. It's unlikely filing taxes will tip off the government: just because one arm is searching for someone who's gone underground doesn't mean another arm will report that person. Refugee claimants are issued temporary social insurance numbers by Service Canada—with expiry dates that correspond to their work permits issued by Citizenship and Immigration Canada. The Canada Revenue Agency will still accept the number, even after it's expired, and it's not within that agency's mandate to alert immigration officials.

While most non-status immigrants try to avoid paying income tax, working for cash and without a contract, others find more formal methods of arranging secure employment. It's possible to register a business name through Service Ontario without proof of citizenship or landed residency—just pay the standard $60 fee—and work as a subcontractor without a social insurance number. (After the family was ordered deported, Alejandra registered a business that could provide serving staff for banquet halls.) Some non-status immigrants keep bank accounts and deposit paycheques, knowing it's unlikely they'll be tracked down by the government.

Finding a place to live can be the biggest challenge when you don't have status. For the first five months that they were in hiding, the family lived with their friend Diana, who freed up a room in the three-bedroom apartment she shared with her teenage niece and two young daughters. Alejandra and Gerardo searched for an apartment in north Toronto, but every landlord asked for identification, proof of salary, references and post-dated cheques. They started lying and saying they had only one child, trying unsuccessfully to convince someone to rent them a place. While they lived at Diana's, they slept on second-hand beds: a bunk bed for the kids and a mattress on the floor for the parents. Gloria, then nine years old, eased the family's tension by taking unflattering photos of her dad. "She only takes pictures when I'm sleeping," says Gerardo as his daughter grins mischievously, "or when my hair's a mess."

When other kids across the city went back to school in September 2008, Alberto, Pablo, and Gloria stayed home. At first their parents were nervous; they had read about a Costa Rican family who were deported in the summer of 2006 after immigration officials apprehended their children at school. (The following year, the Toronto District School Board adopted a don't ask, don't tell policy, which meant schools would not report non-status students to immigration officials, and officials could not look for students on school grounds.) Finally, weeks after classes had started, Alejandra and Gerardo decided the kids could continue their studies. They found a new school for the younger two. Alberto didn't want to change high schools, so despite the risk he went back to join his puzzled classmates. His grades have suffered. "I don't pay attention. I don't care anymore," Alberto tells me when I ask how school's going. "I'm just trying to pass my courses. But I don't say, 'I'm going to get good grades so that they'll open up doors for me later on, to go to university, and really do something.' Now I'm just trying to finish high school and that's it." All this seventeen-year-old can see are doors closing. He is also terrified of the police officer who hangs out in the hallways of his school. The officer is there as part of a program to build positive relationships between police and youth and to curb violence in high schools. "He sees me and I try not to go near him," Alberto says. "When I leave the school, there's sometimes a police car outside. I try to go out another way because I think the don't ask, don't tell rule is only inside—they can still catch you outside the school." Technically, he's right.

Soon after arriving at Diana's, Gerardo got a parking ticket and, fearing he could be tracked down, sold his minivan for $1,000. The family avoided most of their friends because they thought immigration officials might be asking about them, and they didn't know whom they could trust. They changed their cellphone numbers and, to avoid being traced, often used an Internet line that gave them free outgoing calls with an American number. When Alejandra called her home child care agency and the community centre where she had been employed to run a support group for Latina immigrants, they informed her that immigration officials had been asking about them. Officials had also visited the Canadian Tire where Alberto had been working. Alejandra heard from a former neighbour that officials had been to the apartment as well. She wonders who among their old neighbours and colleagues would have snitched had they known their whereabouts. There are rumours among refugee claimants and immigrants of financial rewards for outing illegals.

THROUGH THE FALL OF 2008, Gerardo found some temporary jobs working for cash in construction and demolition. Alejandra and Alberto found jobs helping out during the back-to-school rush at one of the clothing outlets along Orfus Road, near the Yorkdale Shopping Centre. Alberto unloaded boxes of new merchandise, and Alejandra moved stacks of trendy blue jeans and T-shirts to the front of the store and arranged them on shelves and display tables. They worked nine-hour days along with five or six others. During their half-hour lunch break, they sat at a spare table in the back room and devoured the ham sandwiches Alejandra had made that morning, before going back to folding, arranging, carrying, and tidying. For all this, the temp agency responsible for subcontracting the store's workers paid them $7 an hour—less than minimum wage—and disregarded their lack of work permits. The agency paid the workers by cheque; Alejandra and Alberto cashed theirs at one of the many small stores that take a 2.5 percent cut for the service.

Near the end of her first week at the clothing outlet, Alejandra had dropped off a pile of folded clothes at the front of the store and was heading to the back room when someone grabbed her arm. "Ale! What are you doing here?" She looked up and recognized a woman who worked at her old community centre.

"Oh, hi," she answered apprehensively, then grabbed her cell-phone from her pocket and lifted it to her ear, pretending to get a call. "Just a second," she told the ex-colleague as she darted into the back room and rushed to tell her son, at this point in a panic. She worried that the woman would alert immigration officials but convinced herself to keep working, trying to stay at the back of the store for the rest of the day. She didn't show up to work there again.

Alejandra started volunteering at food banks and community centres in exchange for groceries. After the Sunrise Propane explosion rattled North York in August 2008, she, Gerardo, and Alberto took an $18-an-hour job scouring the neighbourhood in protective gear and masks, looking for asbestos and cleaning up debris. Over Christmas, Alejandra found work for them and a few of their friends, most of them Mexican refugee claimants, as servers at a banquet hall in Vaughan: Alejandra made $15 an hour and was paid $12 an hour for each of her staff of four or five, whom she paid $10 an hour.

The family managed to save some money and were finally able to rent a place of their own in North York. The small house had four bedrooms, more than they needed. And the rent was more than $1,000 a month, well beyond their means. But the landlord never asked for references or papers, so they took it.

ALEJANDRA SERVES TEA AND a homemade Mexican *tres leches* cake to Gerardo, the boys, and me at the family's dining room table. Days after they fled their old apartment, the table was retrieved by a friend. Brightly coloured cloth placemats sit in front of us—red, orange, green, and pink.

Now thirteen years old, Pablo is slender and has his mother's olive complexion. Wearing a dark T-shirt and loose jeans, he tells me in a quiet voice about his friends from his previous school, some of whom he still chats with online. "They hardly know anything about me—why I moved, why I'm not there anymore. I just disappeared." Alejandra hushes him gently and closes the kitchen door to keep his voice from trailing through to the other rooms. She explains with a smile that they're subletting two of their rooms to three other immigrants they met during the Sunrise Propane cleanup. Everyone shares the kitchen and a bathroom. "They don't know about our situation," she whispers to me.

The kids sleep in a small room with a bunk bed, a twin bed, and a mound of clothes and school bags on the floor. Their parents are next door, finally in their own room. The living room is tidy, with weathered curtains that are too big for the window, a donated couch and chairs, and the family's big-screen TV, which, like the dining room table, was salvaged from their previous life.

A week and a half later, I call Alejandra, but a recording tells me that the customer is unavailable. I keep trying for a few days and finally drop by their place on a Tuesday evening. Gerardo greets me warmly and invites me to a bible study and prayer session they're hosting. He jokes that their cellphone had been cut off because they had "overpaid" the bill again—in other words, they hadn't paid it. They've got another phone, though, which they buy cards for. Alejandra is in the kitchen washing some mugs for the guests who start appearing. We sit around the dining room table, drinking tea, munching on imitation Oreos, and talking about God.

After the meeting, I sit in the kitchen as Alejandra cleans the rest of the dishes. "These are all from the weekend," she says. Alejandra, Gerardo, and Alberto had been busy working at the Pride festival, hired by private contractors to clean the streets because garbage collectors were off the job due to the municipal strike.

They worked until the early hours of the morning three days in a row for $10 an hour, on strict instructions to tell anyone who asked that they were volunteering. She laughs, visibly delighted that they had finally earned some cash—around $900.

When we realize it's getting late, Alejandra and Gerardo walk me to the bus stop, sharing a cigarette. They keep balancing debts and odd jobs, struggling to master the delicate art of living underground—working illegally in the hope of one day becoming legal again. They can't predict when their humanitarian and compassionate case will be heard.

"For eight years," Gerardo says, "we had dreams but we couldn't build a future. And now, we're worse off. It's not only, 'What are we going to do tomorrow?' but, 'What's going to happen to us tomorrow?' "

THE WILD QUEST

KATHARINE SANDIFORD
Up Here

I HAVE SEEN DOG-HAIR-COVERED bushmen being swarmed like Hollywood superstars. I have learned the words *gee* and *ha* and the critical difference between a trot and a lope. I have smelled the fresh feces of 300 huskies, heaped in a pile in a snowy field. I have risen at 4:45 a.m. to watch icy-bearded mushers and their steaming dogs emerge silently from the dark woods to file through spotlighted checkpoints. I have eaten twenty cheeseburgers in two weeks. I have touched Lance Mackey's shoulder and considered (briefly) never to wash my hand again. I have curled up to nap on the never-vacuumed carpet in the storeroom of a backwoods roadhouse in Alaska. I have thumbed rides in bush planes. I have called my mother, collect, weeping, from the corner of a rowdy bar. I have felt my jaw literally drop at the sight of dog-teams crawling, paw after paw, up a wind-ravaged mountain. I have fled an icy airstrip, afraid for my life. I have finally figured out why someone would want to race a dog team 1,600 gruelling kilometres through some of the worst weather and wildest wilderness on the planet.

When my editor suggested I follow the 2009 Yukon Quest from its start in Whitehorse, leapfrogging from checkpoint to checkpoint all the way to its completion in Fairbanks, Alaska, two weeks later, I thought it would be a grand adventure: 16 checkpoints, 29 teams, 100 journalists, one big sports drama. It's touted as the "toughest sled-dog race in the world," and, except for a few resupply stations, mushers receive no assistance, covering the whole distance carrying their own food, kibble, and camping gear. The trail is notoriously difficult, with teams facing hundreds of kilometres of jagged "jumble ice" on the Yukon River, four cruel climbs up kilometre-high peaks, extreme cold and blizzards, hallucinations from fatigue, and sometimes hypothermia. They do it for adventure, for glory, maybe for fame, but certainly not for cash. The first prize of US$30,000 barely covers dog food for a year, and compared to the flashy, FOX News-broadcast, arguably-less-arduous Iditarod, with its prize of US$70,000 and a pickup truck, the Quest is more an exercise in debt, masochism, and intense devotion.

FOR ME, THE STORY begins in Whitehorse. Hundreds of spectators pack together for warmth at the start chute on First and Main, where a block of downtown roadway has been infilled with snow, creating a trail down to the Yukon River. It's minus-thirty degrees and everyone's in their winter best: embroidered parkas, artful fur hats, oven-mitt-sized hand protection. There are even toddlers wrapped in sleeping bags and scarves, cooing at the dog-teams preparing to sprint the first 100 meters of the race.

I'm dashing about, trying to cover the countdown to the start, but am distracted by my own dog concerns. Wilbur, my beloved husky-mutt, my fur-child, who gives me a bad rep as the crazy girl who goes everywhere with her dog, is locked inside my car, along with my keys. My car, in turn, is parked illegally near the start line. My worst fears come true when I go to check on the vehicle and see a tow-truck backing toward it. "Wait! There's a dog in there. He'll freeze to death," I yell, knowing full-well Wilbur has the same cold-tolerant genes as the tough-as-nails Quest dogs. The driver yells back, "If you don't move it, I'm taking it, dog or no dog." So I do the unthinkable and smash a side window with my four-pound Sorel boot.

CAR RELOCATED, WILBUR RESCUED, crisis averted, I make it back to the start. Megaphones blare as local favourite Sebastian Schnuelle tears out of the chute. He's got an infectious smile and a wild mat of hair that rivals the coif of a seasoned street bum—all topped with a stuffed animal husky hat. Next up is twinkly-eyed Quebecois racer Normand Cassavant, jumping, waving his arms, getting the crowd screaming like Italian football fans before he and his grinning dogs sprint for the river. Young Jamaican Newton Marshall then sets off, gracefully enduring the MC's lame banter ("You stay warm out there now—keep a reggae tune in your head for us."). And then there's Brent Sass, the hipster heartthrob, with grungy good looks, Buddy Holly glasses, a University of Alaska cross-country ski scholarship, and a growing fan club. He whispers elaborate race strategies into the ear of his lead-dog, Madonna, then leaps athletically onto his sled and charges for the river.

ONCE THE TEAMS ARE gone I patch my window with a garbage bag and duct tape and boot thirty kilometres north to catch the racers as they come around a long bend of the river and under a bridge on the Klondike Highway. The sun is bright and glares off the vast expanse of river snow. Without sunglasses, I can barely tell one musher from another. They slip by in quick and silent succession—a radical difference from the yelping, whimpering, howling cacophony of the start line. The only sounds are the fitful claps of a cluster of spectators, plus the drone of two media heli-copters hovering above.

Did I mention the 2009 race has a record number of journalists following it? Over 100 badges were handed out, mostly to news-paper, TV, and radio reporters, plus a handful of film crews. As far as I can tell, I'm the Quest trail's only magazine writer.

This fact becomes ever more apparent late that night, when, after dropping Wilbur off with friends, I make the icy drive north to Braeburn, the first official checkpoint and a mandatory two-hour layover for all teams. Just before midnight, and moments before the first mushers arrive, I pull up to the small roadhouse—a lonely gas station, restaurant, cluster of cabins, and airstrip 100 kilometres from Whitehorse. A thick, back-lit cloud of diesel ex-haust has accumulated from the two-dozen musher trucks idling in the parking lot. The restaurant is jam-packed with media crews, race officials and a few dog handlers (the mushing equivalent of farm-hands, and the unspoken heroes of the race), and everyone but me is with a friend, partner, or colleague. I find a place to stand by the washrooms, where I can people-watch under the guise of lining up to go whiz. There's chatter in four languages, clanking cutlery, and sticky fistfuls of Braeburn's super-sized cinnamon buns stuffed into bearded maws. When someone pokes their head in to announce that the first musher is drawing near, the room is filled by the raw sound of fifty parkas being zipped. Outside, beneath the dance of headlamps, the leading racers materialize and are quickly assaulted with questions about race strategy. I stand at the back. My deadline is in six months.

A FEW DAYS LATER, I arrive with the rest of the Quest Trail caravan in Dawson City, the halfway point in the race. Here, mushers will take a mandatory two-day layover—to rest, eat, sleep in a bed, launder booties and harnesses, and massage their dogs. The weather has been excellent—not too hot and not too cold—and the trail has been fast and smooth. First into town is William Kleedehn, a German-born Quest veteran with a peg-leg, whose ranch south of Whitehorse he calls "Limp-Along Kennels." Kleedehn snags the prize for being first to the midway mark: four ounces of placer-mined gold. "I'm mushing to win the race," he says to the media. An open Beck's beer can in his hand, he glides off towards his campsite.

MORE MUSHERS PULL IN, and after they attend to their duties, many head to the Pit, Dawson's most debauched bar. Jason Mackey of Kasilof, Alaska, is there, slumped over a pile of beer bottles and ordering another. Although he's a Quest rookie, he's got a world of expectations on his shoulders. Mackey is the little brother of Lance Mackey, the superstar of dog mushing. In 2008, *Sports Illustrated* ranked Lance as the world's second-toughest athlete. After bouncing back from near-fatal cancer, he'd won four consecutive Quests, plus first-place finishes at the Iditarod in 2007 and 2008. But this year, he decided not to run the Quest—so his brother Jason was thought by many to be his heir-apparent. Jason even looks like Lance, which is to say, like a heavy-metal rocker. They've got the same flame-licked baseball cap, tight jeans, curly hair, mischievous grin, slightly crossed eyes, and backwoods good looks. Jason is even sitting at the bar with Lance's kennel-pretty wife, Tonya, who's acting as his handler. But poor Jason pulled into Dawson in twenty-first position—so he bedded down his dogs and headed straight for a drink. "I just wonder what people are thinking of me," he says. He feels he's having bad luck and his dogs just aren't running. "I need lopers, not trotters," he tells me, and drops more beer down his throat. "Oh, and some of them have diarrhea."

Across the room is dreamy Brent Sass. He arrived in Dawson yesterday, just after 2 a.m., in sixth place, music blasting out of his earphones so loud he couldn't hear reporters' questions. I sidle up to him and ask him about his dogs. He says he adores them. Unlike the other mushers, who will sleep in Dawson's provided hotel rooms, Sass will climb under his giant ten-metre-long tarp— painted with huge, block letters that name his kennel, WILD AND FREE—so he can sleep on the straw with his pooches. He lets me in on what he considers the new-age secret to dog-mushing. "Dogs read our energy. You can't mush them if you're feeling negative. They won't run. If you're in a bad mood, you're screwed." That's why he prefers canine company. My heart double-thumps, but it's because I miss Wilbur.

BACK AT THE TERRITORIAL campground on the banks of the frozen Yukon, the air is rich with the stench of dog crap, horsemeat, and woodsmoke. Handlers keep busy massaging and walking dogs to keep their muscles loose. Media buzzards swarm them, outnumbering mushers four to one, circling around frenetically to catch the latest news. When former champion Hans Gatt announces his withdrawal from the race, newsies scramble into a scrum around him, jostling for position in the slush and straw. I join a different mob—the one running to catch Sebastian Schnuelle's departure in fourth place. "For me, this feels like a camping trip," he says in his nasal German accent. "I don't like feeling like it's a race."

With Schnuelle and the rest of the speedy front pack back on the trail, it's time for me to get to the next stop, Eagle, Alaska, a fly-in community 236 kilometres down the river. After Dawson, the race goes roadless until Circle City, Alaska, 500 clicks later. The daily-deadlines group—when they have a free moment between filing stories—offer a space in one of their planes. I ride shotgun with a pilot who looks like he's barely hit puberty and has been smoking weed. It's a sunny day but we're flying low, following the course along the river. I spot a dog team, a tiny beast creeping forward, alone in a universe of wilderness.

EAGLE IS A GRID of hand-built shacks and gravel roads on a sharp outside bend of the Yukon River. The 100 people who live there embody contradiction. They're socialist conservatives, back-to-the-land industrialists, redneck hippies. As if in a commune, everyone, all the time, is glazed-eyed and smiling. During dinner in the school's library, a little group wields violins, guitars, a piano, and a flute to play songs like *This Land is Our Land* and *This Little Light of Mine*. I see one woman with a braid going across her head from one ear to the other. This is America, for sure—there are flags everywhere. But the border? Two days after arriving in Eagle, I'm approached by Rosado, a timid Latino customs agent who softly asks me to come to his motel room with my passport. When I do, we chat for twenty minutes, smile and shake hands. It's like having tea with a friend: a lovely

way to cross a border that in most other places is hostile and
threatening. I, too, am staying in this inn, and although it's
laid out like any other, it's made entirely of squared logs and
overlooks the winding Yukon River and its fields of shark-teeth
jumble ice.

WHEN THE MUSHERS STOP in Eagle, they sleep in bunk beds
at the back of the one-room schoolhouse that serves as a checkpoint. But before they collapse, most sit down for a compliment-
ary hot meal. Scarlett Hall, wife of veteran musher Wayne Hall,
who's racing in the middle of this year's pack, gracefully runs the
checkpoint. I hear the same menu options repeated in her soft
American twang. "Chicken and rice. Chicken, potato, and gravy.
Chicken alfredo. Pancakes and ham. Biscuits and gravy." They're
all pre-prepared homecooked dishes she'll heat up on a paper plate
in the microwave. One year, Lance Mackey pulled up and, like
Monty Python's Mr. Creosote, ordered the whole menu, but instead of exploding all over the room after finishing the last bite, he
crashed in the backroom for four hours, rose and finished the race
in record time. He likely ate 10,000 calories in that one sitting,
the same amount a Yukon Quest dog will eat each day in kibble,
meat, and lard.

Jamaican Newton Marshall chews one bite of the chicken and
rice and asks, "Have you got any hot sauce?" Hall passes him pack-
ets of salt and pepper. His eyes are bloodshot from lack of sleep
and exposure. Frostbite has left a white stamp on the tip of his
nose. "What goes through your head while you're out there?" I
ask. "I won't say it," he says, chuckling. "A lot of Jamaican swearing. *Bumboclot, scunt, rassclat*, you know." Marshall's been suffering
from hallucinations, seeing palm trees and falling asleep on the
sled. He's twenty-five, uneducated, poor, and grew up orphaned,

but is bright, energetic and strong-willed. His employers, tour operators whom he works for as a guide, recognized those qualities and chose him for their Jamaican Dog Sled Team. Funded by musician Jimmy Buffet and sent to train with Yukon champion Hans Gatt for two years, he's now running dogs near the Arctic Circle—a destiny he never could have predicted for himself, and isn't even sure he likes.

Volunteers sit around a bonfire outside the schoolhouse feeding the flame with branches from a stockpile. I start up conservation with the twelve-year-old next to me. His name is Jonathan and his job is to check the mushers in when they arrive. "We count their dogs and look through their stuff," he explains, speaking with the authority of a police officer. "You have to see for yourself and not just take their word that they have everything—a cooker, pair of snowshoes, eight booties per dog." Almost everyone in Eagle has sled dogs, mostly small backyard teams for sport or utility. "We have nine dogs but it's pretty much eight-and-a-half now, because one of them's half dead," Jonathan says. "He's got a big hole in his leg right here. He's never going to run again. That's why my dad needs to take the .45 outside, and not just to do fun shooting."

I CAN HEAR THE howling of the neighbourhood huskies heralding the arrival of Normand Cassavant. His dogs are just short of sprinting as they bound into the checkpoint. Even after Cassavant kicks in the brake, they continue pulling, wagging their tails, even barking. No other team rivals their enthusiasm. Cassavant, too, is spritely, singing, grinning, vibrating. "Why are your dogs so happy?" one of the reporters asks. He replies, "I sing to them constantly. I sing them French folk songs." He launches into a performance for the gathering crowd. "Ta-ta-tee! Ta-ta-ta!" If you've ever doubted sled dogs love to run, Cassavant's team will prove you wrong.

A GRUMPY OLD PILOT flies me and an injured dog (its head sticking out of a burlap travel-bag) from Eagle to Circle. "Nice view, eh?" I say through the headset, as I look down over an undisturbed sprawl of high-mountain plateaus and valleys. But either he's blinded by his own eyebrow hair or just doesn't care, because his only response is to shrug his shoulders. On the tarmac, I realize I'm out of money. I tell him this, even showing him my empty wallet. The idling single-engine Cessna is deafening, so when he shouts, "Who's gonna pay me for your flight?" and I say "*Up Here*," thinking he can invoice the magazine, he probably hears, "Up yours." He throws up his arms, yells "You won't get away with this." I take a stroll around Circle, where bullet holes riddle almost every permeable surface: street signs, boarded-up buildings, even one of the Yukon Quest banners. Deciding I need to escape the possibility of bush-pilot vigilante justice, I grab a muffin at the checkpoint and stick out my thumb.

I'm picked up by the world's authority on sled-dog physiology, Dr. Michael Davis, a professor at Oklahoma State University's Center for Veterinary Health. On the labyrinthine, bumpy drive west, he tells me huskies are physiologically built for endurance: that they can run twelve hours a day, seven days straight, and not experience fatigue like humans do. In fact, after three or four days of racing, they actually start getting faster. By taking blood and muscle-tissue samples of dogs that run both the Quest and Iditarod, Davis is figuring out how long this power can last. Based on what he's seen, "Once they find that extra gear, they can keep going for at least a week or two more."

DAVIS DROPS ME OFF in Central and within a few minutes I'm calling my mom collect from the payphone in the corner of the bar, sobbing. The place is packed with gruff men, loud, big, and drunk. There are no available hotel rooms. There are also no seats at the restaurant, and only one familiar face: Brent Sass's young, pink-haired punk handler, Kyla. I sit across from her, order a cheeseburger with my credit card, and eat it in silence. Later, a Whitehorse reporter tells me there's a room in the back where I can sleep on the floor. I curl up beside a towering stack of double-caffeine Red Bulls in a room littered with cameras, laptops, and journalists. I wake around 3 a.m. to watch Brent Sass eat a steak the size of a textbook.

The next day, I catch a ride with a guy in a pimped out, double-wide, double-long pickup that's pulling a flatbed trailer loaded with six high-performance snowmobiles. In other words, I've caught a ride with an Alaskan Rolls Royce. We're on our way to the checkpoint at Mile 101, a tiny off-grid shack at the bottom of a mountain-pass surrounded by moonscape wilderness. We pull over to look up Eagle Summit, the toughest, steepest, and stormiest peak of the race. On its naked flanks we spot a musher and his team creeping up the glaring white pitch.

A FEW MINUTES LATER, talking with race officials at the checkpoint, I learn there's been a serious reversal. William Kleedehn, who had an eight-hour lead, and who many believed was this year's deserving winner (he's come so close so many times before), got snagged on Eagle Summit. It wasn't the weather, exhaustion, a broken sled, or a malfunction with his prosthetic leg. No, it was sex. His lead dog went into "full-blown leaky heat," driving his male dogs crazy. Four mushers passed Kleedehn on the mountain. Although some tried to help, it was Brent Sass who parked his team at the top, hiked back down 200 metres, and manually pulled the horny team from the front as Kleedehn pushed from the back. Sass, in the end, would win the award for sportsmanship

for this effort. Once they were at the summit, gravity gave Kleedehn an easy run into Mile 101. But he wasn't pleased. As he lay
out a snack for his dogs in the shade behind the shack, he railed at
the frenzied media crew around him. "Look at you guys," he said.
"Everybody gets their photos, their stories. That's the thing that
drives me crazy. Everyone gets paid except the dog mushers."

"Well then, why are you out here?" I shout from the back.

"Not so my dogs can have an orgy, that's for sure," he replies.

I SQUEEZE INTO THE rear of an eight-passenger van and ride on
top of suitcases to get to Two Rivers, the last checkpoint before
Fairbanks and only fifty-three kilometres from the downtown finish line. With four sled-dogs to every human, Two Rivers is called
the dog-mushing capital of the world, a community of ranches
and kennels tied together by a web of well-used sledding trails.
Home to recognized mushers like Aliy Zirkle, the only woman to
win the Quest, the residents are all gathered here to watch, hang
out, and have coffee.

Sebastian Schnuelle has found himself in first place and is celebrating by changing his socks for the first time in the race. If he
wins, Schnuelle says he's going to have to retire. "I can't run on
$30,000," he says, cramming a handful of barbecue chips down
his bearded gullet. He's forty-five minutes ahead of Hugh Neff,
whose heart is stinging after being given a draconian two-hour
penalty for missing the trail in Central—an error that lost him his
lead and likely the whole race. "I saw poo on the road; I thought
that's where the trail went," he pleads, fruitlessly.

IT'S LATE MORNING AT the sunny finish line, and with my media
pass I can stand right inside the chute gates, behind the ribbon.
Schnuelle and his team of huskies come down the Chena River

and through the gates. Only four minutes later is Neff. Both have broken Quest records by completing the course in just over nine days and twenty-three hours—a full three hours faster than Lance Mackey's record. Mackey is there behind the line, sporting his usual fur hat over a baseball cap. I elbow my way up to him with my voice recorder. "Perfect trail, perfect weather—it's no surprise they're breaking records," he says, smugly. "I should be out there battling these boys." His brother Jason scratched in Central.

Schnuelle and Neff stand on a stack of shipping crates fashioned into a podium and answer questions for the hundreds of spectators. "You know how I approached this?" says Schnuelle. "I stuck to a schedule, ignored people around me and focused on the dogs. It wasn't stressful at all. I enjoyed myself the whole way."

I'm madly jealous. And utterly resolved: my days as a Quest groupie are over. It's time to go home. And next time I do this thing, I'll race it with fourteen dogs to keep me company, Wilbur in the lead.

THE BROTHERS KRAMM

ANDREW STEINMETZ
Queen's Quarterly

Who, on his own, has ever really known who gave him life?
—Homer

NOT ALL OF WHAT I know about my family history is rooted in fact. Lots of it I invented as a child growing up in Canada. For years, when I played army in the yard surrounding our house with neighbourhood boys, I saw myself as Abelard Kramm fighting in a trench on the Russian Front. Then, in my early adolescence, after reading about the Battle of Stalingrad, I transported Abelard in my mind to this battle, famous for its number of casualties. It became part of my own private legend where Abelard had died fighting in Stalingrad, when in reality, as I know today, he died thirty kilometres south of Luga. *"Dorfes etwa 30 km sudlich Luga,"* stipulated the letter from his field officer.

Stalingrad seemed important, though. The place name struck a chord in me. Saying Stalingrad provoked an eerie sense of the inevitable meeting the systematic; to my ears, the battle was engineered to end as many human lives as possible. And so it was in Stalingrad that I placed Abelard at dusk: first lighting a cigarette—hands cupped around the orange flame: stupid, stupid—then standing to remove his wool sweater.

The sniper aims. He fires and the bullet passes into my heart.

This is how I died for Abelard, when I was in my early teens.

Later, in my twenties, I wrote a song in which my grandmother living in South America receives the bad news about her brother Abelard.

> *Young man digging on the Russian front*
> *He took his sweater off for the fight*
> *One thing he had never been told*
> *Is love, is hard, and bright.*

I roundly romanticized this Abelard. Why? To this day, I cannot remove my sweater in winter without getting trapped in the weave of obscure emotions. In the middle of the afternoon, alone, anywhere, I'll think directly of Abelard. He cannot see out when he is shot. He falls face down in mud, wet clothes soon swollen. Sometimes, I let myself go a little longer; I kneel beside him and take his hand in my own and slide his gold ring with the family emblem off his finger.

At such moments I feel very alive and grateful, I feel full of thanks not to be a soldier; especially, not one of *their* soldiers, buried kilometres south of Luga.

Wherever Luga is.

* * *

MARIANNE KRAMM, MY PATERNAL grandmother, and her siblings were born and raised Catholic in Upper Silesia, a province in the east of Germany on the border with Poland. While she fled Germany to South America in 1936, her two brothers served in the Third Reich. Abelard died in 1941, of sniper fire, on the Eastern Front; Hrolf Kramm, not until 2003, in Switzerland of septicaemia—or blood poisoning.

I began thinking about them again after a visit to the old-age residence in Kronberg-im-Taunus, outside Frankfurt where I went to see my grandmother in the fall of 2005. She had recently vacated her semi-private room for a bed on the nursing ward, and it was my job, during a three-day visit, to sort through the things she'd taken a lifetime to collect. I would spend my fortieth birthday away from home—Canada—but close, here in Germany, to where so much began and ended for my family generations ago.

After spending many hours of the day with her, I would go walking in the old town, in search of a comfortable restaurant. Untouched by the Allied Air Campaign that levelled neighbouring Frankfurt, Old Kronberg—with its half-timbered houses and its thirteenth-century *Schloss*—remains something of a relic. Church bells sound at even intervals. Cobblestone is omnipresent. The narrow streets run randomly. The little shops sparkle with quaint merchandise. Walking in Old Kronberg, evening after evening, I would eventually succumb to the curious sensation that I really was walking *inside it*.

My grandmother had returned to Germany from the United States, a widow, in 1988. Her timing was excellent: one year before re-unification, national spirits were high. Yet Oma had caused dismay when she declared to the family her intention to move back "home" so soon after the death of my grandfather. Her children—citizens of Canada and the USA—tried in vain to dissuade her. Historical agency may have led her into exile, but something like biological imperative was driving her back to the country she'd never forgotten, and had certainly forgiven.

* * *

NEWS OF ABELARD'S DEATH reached my grandmother in Bogotá, Colombia, early in 1942. The original dispatch from the office of the Oberkommando der Wehrmacht, contained a private letter from Abelard's field officer to his next of kin.

> *Your son died in a tragic manner. A shot that struck his ammunition pouch caused the bullets to explode without injuring him. He sought cover to see if everything was in order. As he took off his pullover, he stood up too straight, and a shot to his heart killed him. He was the only loss that the company had suffered on that day.*

DURING MY VISIT TO Kronberg-im-Taunus, I came across a photocopy of this (odd to say) rather touching letter; and along with it, I discovered a diagram of the battlefield, hand-drawn by the same field officer. The diagram—rudimentary, but carefully composed—shows roads and a bending river, and it pinpoints the battalion's position on the day Abelard died.

The story of Abelard standing, absurdly "too straight," to

remove his pullover is one I heard repeated many times growing up; but never, until now had I been privy to such authentic detail. Abelard's death story—dark, unsung, dangerous—was the kind that might excite a young boy, and it did me. Except for the geographic certainty of the Russian Front and some basic history, I'd not been given any tools—no moral compass—to guide me through my feelings about my family's involvement in the war. That great uncle Abelard was killed fighting for *them,* definitely was ominous. This fact seemed wrong, plain backwards. But I was never ashamed of him. Maybe because the judgemental perspective *of him fighting for them* is too simplistic and I sensed this already, as a boy of ten, eleven, twelve. But anyway what was there to fuss about since Abelard was deceased. In the natural history of my feelings toward him, the latter fact was key, I'm at least sure of that. Abelard was good and dead before I'd even heard his name mentioned in family conversation: killed on a day when no one else in Battalion 48 had lost his life. There was a rightness for sure to this last detail, another element of the story I already knew. It was as if on December 11, 1941, Abelard had paid a price. He was chosen to die; and to die young; he for his company of men. All the more reason I had to whisk my naïve boyhood image of him away, from the battlefield into my imagination, for polishing, possibly for safekeeping.

The photograph I remember best of Abelard—the same one I discovered again in Kronberg in one of my grandmother's photo albums—shows him in his Wehrmacht uniform. Abelard is striking: clear-eyes, full lips, strong jaw, but he is hardly masculine. Instead, he gives a feline impression. The photograph betrays the very subtype of androgynous beauty and athleticism that Leni Riefenstahl catalogued in *Olympia,* her documentary about the 1936 Olympic Games in Berlin.

The first time I saw it, I thought of David Bowie from *Heroes*.

* * *

WHEN MY GRANDMOTHER PREPARED her return to Germany, her brother Hrolf secured for her a sizeable war reparations payment from the West German government. Then, once she'd arrived back on home soil, he let it be known that, in his opinion, it was entirely her fault that she was in need of money and in transit, still, at age seventy-six. Things would have been different, he admonished her, if she had listened to the family and had not married that Jew.

"That Jew" is my grandfather. In 1935, my grandmother had met her future in Herman Hans Feldman, a hawkish medical student. The son of a leather merchant, he, my grandfather, was raised Lutheran, but a Hereditary Health Court had determined that he was *Vierteljuden*, or quarter Jewish. Marianne and her Herman Hans were determined to get married even if this was against the wish of both households. More urgently, their desire flouted the newly hatched Nuremberg Laws.

One afternoon in Breslau, Anne Kramm answered the front door only to find a group of Hitler Youth waiting on the steps. The Nazi brats asked the old lady to please fetch her vile and unclean daughter. They wanted words. Anne Kramm closed the door and sent Marianne's brother Hrolf—on leave from his military posting—back out to confront them, while Marianne and Hermann Hans waited inside. Hrolf told the little shits to get lost. They hesitated before clearing out, but what was to keep them from calling again? And what about this surprising figure who came to the door: was he not wearing the very uniform they aspired to? Was it then some kind of illusion, some kind of trick played on them? What colour uniform was it? Are such things black and white?

I have some of the same questions today.

* * *

I WAS RAISED IN A sprawling house in the suburbs of Montreal, in a close-knit family, which made no room for religion. Still, if religion had no part in my upbringing, over the years I was apt to create tension between my Jewish roots and German past. We were not Jewish, but we had the name. Steinmetz was a Jewish name, didn't everyone know that? Everyone except us? We didn't speak German at home, but visiting relatives did (with my parents). Sometimes I think my not-German and not-Jewish identity manifests itself in negative capability, and fostered the conscience that compels me to keep telling the story of my family until I get at least some of it right.

For this I need to return to 1935.

After marrying in Breslau, my grandparents escaped to South America. Meanwhile, Marianne's family—her father John Maria, mother Anne, and brothers Abelard and Hrolf—had remained in Germany. In 1939, John Maria Kramm sent a jubilant letter to Marianne (now in Bogotá), describing how he'd seen with his own eyes the Luftwaffe flying overhead toward the enemy. The September Campaign and the invasion of Poland, which began one week after the signing of the Molotov-Ribbentrop Pact, would mark the beginning of the Second World War in Europe.

Early on, neither Abelard nor Hrolf saw fighting action. In addition to being soldiers, they were trained at professions that were usefully applied inside the homeland. Hrolf, the doctor, was stationed in Southern Germany. Abelard, an engineer, stayed in Breslau.

So all was quiet for the brothers Kramm.

However, their father—agitated by patriotic fervour—was not at peace. For him, historical fate had not been active enough. So the old man intervened and exercising his social connections, he arranged to have at least one son dispatched to the front lines. It had taken some effort, but he did get the ball rolling for Abelard, steadily in the direction of the Russian Front.

Allegedly, Abelard initially refused his military posting. He was subsequently informed by the authorities that, in this case, if he did not report for duty, they could not vouch for the safety of his mother. Abelard went east. Nothing could have made John Maria Kramm more proud. His boy spearheading the attack and crossing into Poland, fighting the Communists, making his way through the snow to Moscow. Hurrah! Herr Kramm was elated, and carried away by history in the making.

* * *

HROLF SPENT THE WAR inside Germany. He was posted in Konstanz on the border with Switzerland—not a terrifically active front—nonetheless, he lost an eye.

After the war, Hrolf was given the glass eye, which, in my childhood and adolescence, weighed so heavy in my imagination. On the few occasions I met him, I spent my time trying to guess into which socket his glass eye had been inserted, the left, or the right? Each time he came into the room I might wonder which eye was good, and which was bad. I was secretly scared of him even though in Hrolf I immediately recognized my grandmother: sister and brother shared the same Kramm facial architecture, which easily could convert a neutral expression into an impressively sour and disapproving countenance. But I must say, the Kramm family signature is found in their eyes, more Asiatic than Occidental, as if the dominant genes for this almond had rolled down the Steppes, long ago dropping to the floor of Silesia from Mongolia.

What strikes me today is how Hrolf's ocular prosthetic altered how I saw him. As a boy, I poorly understood the mechanics of a glass eye: I believed for some time that his prosthetic "worked," and therefore in my estimation Hrolf was at least part machine. Or else if his eye didn't have powers—if there were no levers or springs inside—I imagined that it lay there like a marble in a hole and blocked his sight; and, therefore, if you plucked it, great uncle Hrolf would be able to see again out of that eye. Correct? But then why didn't anyone go ahead and take it out for him? What was keeping one of the adults from doing so immediately? Obviously, he wouldn't let them!

There was so much boyhood attention given to the foreignness of the thing itself—Might it crack over time? Was it breakable?—that it took me years to realize that, really, it wasn't the glass eye that bothered me so much, no, it was his *absent* eye. The missing one. Beneath surging anxieties, I must have made a pretty basic assumption: missing an eye was his punishment or penalty for being a Nazi. Was he a Nazi? I wasn't sure. But this line of thinking was strengthened when I caught on that great uncle Hrolf let his eyebrows grow (even his eyelashes were very long) to camouflage his prosthetic. He wanted to hide it to stop the questions.

* * *

WHEN MY NUCLEAR FAMILY left Canada to live for two years in East Africa, in the late 1970s, we stopped off in Germany on the way over to visit relatives. One afternoon, my parents took me and my brothers and sister to Dachau, outside Munich. *Arbeit macht Frei* from the gate of the concentration camp might be the first sentence in German I can remember reading. The literal translation, Work Makes Freedom, did not come close to conveying the cruelty of the Nazi policy of extermination through work, nor was such sinister irony fathomable to the ten-year-old tourist I was.

After Munich, we travelled to see uncle Hrolf, still in Constanz. My parents never had anything good to say about him, but we visited anyway. Like him or not, he was family, seemed to be the message.

The central family myth about Hrolf Kramm is that he used his rank and position on the border with Switzerland to help Jewish families escape Germany. Competing myths or the apocrypha suggest that Hrolf's motivation was not solely to "to help the Jews." The fact is after the war he was set up for life, as far as money goes. It is speculated that Hrolf took bribes in return for safe passage to Switzerland. The truth as always is difficult to establish. But when set beside the more recent story about Hrolf Kramm greeting his widowed sister upon her return to Germany and straight away calling her out for marrying a Jew, I have to believe that this was not a man who ever would have acted altruistically during wartime when so much gold was there, literally, for the taking.

Abelard's moral status, in comparison, remains relatively uncomplicated. Abelard paid the full price for being a soldier: he was killed in action. And he died young before age could rot his image in tandem with history. In my twenties, I heard from a great aunt and contemporary of Abelard that Abelard was an "effeminate type." Abelard was gay? Nothing would have disturbed his militaristic father John Maria more than this, surely, in which case the Eastern Front was probably the least embarrassing destination for the youngest Kramm.

* * *

IT OCCURS TO ME that what pushes people to lie and falsify is precisely the pressure to tell the truth. This is something I understood implicitly when I insisted that all there was to know about my great uncle Hrolf was contained in his glass eye. It was impossible to know with certainty what the solution to his character was. And forcing the discovery of facts, pushing too hard, would deaden the chance for illumination.

I'm aware today that at some point during the years of informal inquiry, my ideas about the nature of Hrolf's prosthetic eye turned one variation. I'd already arrived unconsciously at the belief that his disability was some form of penalty. It was the human stain of metaphysical punishment. But then, might it be that I'd been the one all along who was half blind?

What if his wound was self-inflicted? Had Hrolf, during the war and because of it, suffered the guilt of Oedipus? I wished for us all—for all the related Steinmetzs and Kramms—that I was right about this.

But no. It had been an accident. Shrapnel from a grenade explosion. I'd heard, friendly fire.

WALKING THE WAY

TIMOTHY TAYLOR
The Walrus

1.

I CAN'T EXPLAIN THE feeling I'm having here, standing on the beach in Comillas, a little seaside resort on the Cantabrian coast of Spain. I'm wading in the water, actually, because my feet are aching, and as I stare out to sea, my mind drifting, it suddenly occurs to me—ten days and 250 kilometres into a planned twenty-three-day walk across Spain, west from Irun along the centuries-old Catholic pilgrimage route to the famous cathedral town of Santiago de Compostela—that my journey has really, finally begun.

Which doesn't make sense, given that my body is telling me this pilgrimage (or whatever it is I'm doing here; the question remains open) began long ago. Call it another "long-walk paradox." I've been making a list. I scrawled the first one into the margin of my Los Caminos del Norte guidebook back on day two. My trail mate, Dave, and I were climbing around the lighthouse south of Pasajes San Pedro, having just parted company with Heidi from Michigan, who'd pressed a Spanish-English dictionary into my hands after our lunch of calamari *bocadillo* on the quays. (*I'm just, like, really worried about you guys walking all the way across Spain not speaking any Spanish.*) Then she disappeared up the trail, walking at a speed neither of us could have quite matched jogging. We climbed on up the hill, past the graveyard and around to the lighthouse, gasping in the heat. Somewhere out there, we stopped and I wrote "Long-walk paradox #1: pain/beauty" in an unsteady hand, standing on that wild shoulder of Basque greenery above the heaving, Windex-coloured sea.

I'm not even sure what I meant by that now. Pain/beauty. Perhaps I was imagining a hypothetical third quality that encompassed both. But now the day is collapsing around me. Spanish families are packing their coolers and rolling up their beach towels, heading for their cars, heading home. The sun is dipping toward the western ridge, the sky growing long, deepening from blue to grey. Dave is back in the pension, reading Beevor's *The Battle for Spain*. Our conversation has been getting thin at the edges, with hundreds of kilometres still to go. I'm out here soaking my feet, remembering that I was in Bilbao a couple of days ago and didn't see the Guggenheim because I was so tired that lying in my hotel watching Gran Torino seemed like a better idea. Eastwood riddled with bullets at the end, stretched out on the lawn like a crucifix. Eastwood rebranded as Christ—shoulda seen that coming.

And here one of the beach kids boots a soccer ball past his friend, and it rolls all the way down to the waves where I pick it up and throw it back, and he stares at me, curiosity edged with suspicion. Me standing there in the waves with my iPhone, pecking in notes. I guess I don't look like I'm from around here, even if I'm doing what people have been doing along this coast since the remains of the apostle James, the brother of Jesus, were first discovered in Galicia in the ninth century. That is: walking west, wondering why.

I thumb-type the words. "Long walk paradox #2: the walk really starts when you feel like you've already been walking forever."

2.

> *If you came this way,*
> *Taking any route, starting from anywhere,*
> *At any time or at any season,*
> *It would always be the same: you would have to put off*
> *Sense and notion.*
> —T.S. Eliot, "Little Gidding," from *The Four Quartets*

PEOPLE TELL YOU ALL kinds of stories about why they're doing it, taking weeks to come this way. Down the Basque Hills and across the sands of the Playa de la Arena, up to El Haya, down the blaring Cantabrian motorways, the misty back lanes, through the shaking pines and fragrant eucalyptus, the red dirt, the gossiping donkeys, the halting breeze. They tell you they're heading to the festival at Santiago, or they're meeting friends in Finisterre. They tell you they're travelling on the cheap before finishing school. But most commonly they talk of freedom, which is a jarring answer if you associate the word with autonomy, self-definition, individual routes through the maze of life. On the north coast, there is only one way to Santiago de Compostela, and you are reminded of your surrender to that path every kilometre or so by a yellow sign or a scallop shell indicating the way forward. This way. Up that hill. Turn left past the churchyard. The markers make rudimentary the human day, collapsing all options, all routes, all avenues to one. Freedom. Really?

But that's what they say. To be free. To feel free. A political science student from Germany. A nursing instructor from Norway. A bookie from the UK, same story. He says, "I just like the freedom. Just walking. No hassles, right?"

I'm more in sympathy with a theatrical agent from Germany who stops to watch me photographing flowers outside a café. I'm killing time while Dave works his BlackBerry inside, handling emails from a job that never stops. She says, "That should be a nice shot." And when we get to the point in the conversation where we talk about *why*, she says, "Well, I guess to change my mind about a few things."

Nobody talks about religion, faith, metaphysics. None of that. Nobody says, because my mother died three years ago and I haven't been the same since. Nobody says, because not long ago at a party I got into a drunken argument about philosophical materialism— the belief that the only thing that exists is physical matter—and found myself yelling at a woman, "Then why are we here? Why are *you* here?"

Nobody would admit to that. To losing it. To getting belligerent over the possibility of transcendence. Nobody would admit that, because it would indicate that you somehow *needed* to walk 800 kilometres across Spain.

I confess. Guilty. I somehow needed to do exactly that.

3.

WE WALK AND WALK. We talk at first, but then much less. On the first day, Dave said, "A friend warned me that you and I would probably be doing top ten movies of all time by the end of this thing. Because by day twenty, dude, we're going to have talked about *everything else*."

Dave's friend was wrong. Make no mistake. I'm here because our friendship is an old one. We've been pals since college, and have stayed in touch ever since, even after he set off on an international life that has taken him from Geneva to South Africa to London and beyond. We've stayed in touch for a reason, and when he suggested this trip over dinner in London, where I last saw him, I didn't hesitate. For me, Dave may be the only person on earth from whom the suggestion to walk 800 kilometres together would not seem insane. So there's talking to be done. And in the morning, with a coffee *con leche* and a wedge of tortilla inside us, with fresh legs, breathing light, cool air and smelling the farms, the soil, the botanical plenitude, words are free and our discussion is as wide as the horizon, as curious as the world. Politics, money, books, kids, family. What's up with mutual friends. Religion once, nothing too personal.

But on tired legs, with the sun high as we climb a long slope toward a final ridgeline, our destination a smudge of buildings some stubborn distance ahead of us, our progress imperceptible—during those stretches we're prisoners to what we're doing. Marooned in the flow. Paradox # 3. You take somewhere around 25,000 steps a day. Each one of these depends on all the others. Each is mission critical. So each one—each single footfall, crunch of broken stone, scuff of dust, kicked pebble skipping ahead—is both a tiny non-event and one occupying a space as large as the universe. Each footstep, in the moment you take it, is all you have. And there comes a point each day, sometimes as early as mid-morning, when words simply fail. If there's a conversation after noon, it's generally about food.

We eat like teenagers. The Trek might be worth it for this alone, the metabolism roaring like a blast furnace. We eat slow-roasted lamb shoulders, platters of octopus and smoked ham, anchovies, and green olives, *patatas con chorizo*, oxtails, *bocadillos* with thick slices of cheese or rings of fried calamari. Once, *escalope jamon*, which turned out to be ham cold cuts breaded and deep fried, perhaps our only culinary disappointment. In Castro-Urdiales we found ourselves looking out over the boats in the harbour, eating a whole monkfish cooked in oil with slivers of garlic and served with bread. And in El Haya, a slab of beef *churleton* between us, grilled an inch and a half thick and served with crisp fries and tangy salad. The owner kept pouring us more brandy, pleased to see us devouring the local specialty, reminding us all the while that he normally ate a whole *churleton* himself, sometimes two. After dinner, we talked with Horst, a German economist who worked on contract for BMW and spent long months walking in between.

Then we slept. We crashed, we went deep. And we awoke huge spirited, talkative, filled with the energy of our plan.

"Get to the Primitivo," Horst had told us, speaking of the mountain route from Oviedo over the remote inner hills of Asturias and Galicia and down to the walled city of Lugo. "Hurry through Cantabria if you have to, but take your time in the mountains." Horst had already covered 4,000 kilometres when we met him, and would cover 4,000 more by the time he returned home late in the year. Lost fifteen kilos so far. He showed us notches on his belt.

So that's where we're going. That's where the whole trip is

now heading. To the Primitivo. To the Original Way of the medieval pilgrims.

I say to Dave: gonna party like it's 1399.

He says: let's go, let's go, let's go.

4.

If you came at night like a broken king,
If you came by day not knowing what you came for,
It would be the same, when you leave the rough road
And turn behind the pig sty to the dull façade
And the tombstone.

MY MOTHER DIED OF cancer in March 2006, a few days after her seventy-sixth birthday. She'd been diagnosed in August 2004 and given two to four months to live, but was obviously tougher than the doctors first guessed. Lots of people say this about their parents, I realize. Mothers in particular. *Man, but she was tough.* And perhaps we say this because we need them to be strong, like anybody else. Knowing there is heartache for our toughest moms.

You could say she was born in the wrong place at the wrong time. Ursula Kuppenheim, in Munster, in 1930; gentle mother, father's aide, all Jews. These weren't great coordinates to land on just a few months before 6.4 million Germans voted Hitler into the Reichstag. So my mother became a *"Mischling* of the first degree," as the taxonomically minded Nazis called people with exactly two Jewish grandparents. There was no comfort in the designation. The Nazis were regressive taxonomists, even before 1942, when Eichmann determined that *"Mischlinge* of the first degree will, as regards the final solution of the Jewish question, be treated as Jews." Already by 1940, my mother's paternal grandparents had died as the SS cleared Jews out of the town of Pforzheim. Two months later, her father fled Germany using the single visa he was able to get for passage to Ecuador. My mother, my aunt, and my grand-mother rode out the war in Münster, and later, after receiving news that *Mischlinge* were to be arrested there, in hiding places in and around Aberslow. The family wasn't reunited until 1948, when the International Refugee Organization arranged transit for the three women from Germany, through Paris and Genoa, then by boat across the Atlantic to a reunion with my grandfather in Ecuador.

Where life began again, in what my mother once described to me as a drifting, dreamlike state: out of place and distant from all the futures she might once have considered likely. Certainly, she couldn't have imagined meeting my father. In the late 1940s, she was managing a bookstore, the Librería Cientifica, in Guayaquil. My father was working in the Philippine jungle, rebuilding an electrical generating plant. As a kid, I once plotted these locations on a globe and determined them to be almost precisely on oppos-ite sides of the planet. Here was a vector intersect you'd call a long shot, in the geo-statistical sense of it.

BUT IT HAPPENED. ALL that way across the world to end up at the same house party. In she walked. There he was. How do these things happen? We know the rational answer. It's called a random event, albeit a happy one in this case. All human story is after all, in the eyes of science, the product of quanto-chaotic material unfolding. There is a new canon of rationalist literature devoted to debunking other interpretations, other ways of imagining the fab-ric of your own life. Fate, destiny, divine will, even luck. All these are romantic or worse: intellectual dummy sucking, as Richard Dawkins memorably put it.

Nonsense, my mother would have said. Stories care nothing for

statistics, in either our telling or our living of them. As for philosophical materialism, well, one man's rationalism is another man's
eugenics program. The Nazis had a material view of my mother:
she was a biogenetic phenomenon. She didn't accept their definition of her any more than she accepted their final solution to the
problem she represented to them. It's to that brutal early schooling
that I trace her later tendencies, which coalesced around a single
governing principle: you could not allow yourself to be defined
solely by your physical properties. There had to be another dimension of the self. Your survival depended on deeper resolution.
And while she personally sought that resolution in Christianity,
the more practical way in which I experienced her worldview as
a child during the '70s was through her committed resistance to
consumerism, a material value system very much in ascendancy.

Brand promises were always broken. I don't remember ever not
knowing she felt this way, even if she rarely said so. She lived the
message. No television in the house. No junk food or soda in the
diet. Homemade clothes, at least until we were teenagers and insisted otherwise. Holidays on the West Coast Trail and in other
back-to-nature settings. Once a year, following a successful piano
recital, we were allowed to choose a brand-name breakfast cereal
(for me, always Captain Crunch). Otherwise, it was homemade
granola and tiger's milk, an orange juice and brewer's yeast con-
coction we downed in a series of grimacing gulps.

In *The Brady Bunch* '70s, in shag-carpeted, then groovy West
Vancouver, these practices made us nonconformist freaks. It wasn't
a matter of self-denial. I understand this now. On my mother's
part, it was self-affirmation. Specifically, a removal of the self from
the governing ambit of commerce and fashion, a wilful conviction
that connected her to the beyond.

And here is where I believe she sourced that conviction: *she* didn't believe that her birth happened in the wrong place at the wrong time, nor that it was a chance occurrence. She believed it happened as intended. Of course life's material phenomena were real, notably Hitler's existence and much later the fact of her me-tastasized colon cancer. But the cause and effect at play in the world and in her body were not the essential story. The essential story was that because they were *intended,* her life and all lives had intrinsic, ineffable value derived and defined not by organic materials or physical properties or consumer goods, but by their meanings. In other words, derived and defined in a way inaccess-ible to either markets or science. Derived and defined spiritually.

"Religious" was never quite the right word for her, though. Her faith had no overarching ritual. She was antipodal to religious ceremony, it now seems to me, to codes and rites either Cath-olic or Protestant, including this very pilgrimage. She was instead a product of personal belief and reformation. Charles Taylor's "disembedded" individual, unplugged from the hierarchies that would define and destroy her. Yet choosing to live her life as if the spiritual were bound up in the physical, the musical soundtrack playing endlessly behind the toy-strewn family room scenes of her mother-of-five life.

Mischling *of the first degree.* If my mother had had a coat of arms, the motto might have read: *Says you.*

5.

WE CROSS CANTABRIA INTO its forested western reaches, past the sprawling estuaries of the Tina Menor and Tina Mayor, past the flat expanse of inland water reflecting the sky, past the blue-green hills, past the clouds shooting in to gather at the foot of the Cantabrian mountain range paralleling our path from the Basque country behind us all the way to the Galician border. Climbing the long slope into Asturias, we get lost in a hillside eucalyptus forest short of Unquera. We end up following a narrow track kilometres past a marked turnoff, swatting bugs in the heat, running gauntlets of thorns, while below us through the fragrant trees we can see the road we're supposed to meet dropping farther and farther away. We stop and retrace our steps, trying different trails that all fringe out to nothing in the brush. It takes several hours before we make our way down and across the valley—overheated, scratched, sweating, irritable—and climb the final steep stone path to Colombres, where we're planning to stay.

It's approaching that summit that I get my first taste of pilgrim euphoria. Endorphin flows, runner's high—it belongs in that group of phenomena. The sudden head-rush sense of your own movement and power, like the thrill of lift-off in an airplane, only writ down to human scale and speed. As I climb the hill, I feel that chain of thousands of steps, hundreds of thousands now, carrying me upward and upward. I feel the earth roll under my feet as if propelled by my very motion.

I take my own picture at the crest of the hill, camera held out at arm's length. There's a *capilla de animas* here, a little chapel set up for recitation of the angelus. I don't know the prayer, but I'm gripped by a feeling, an exhilarating sense of *lessening,* the world briefly rendered inconsequential. A summit feeling. The photo later reveals me to be grinning a bit madly, seized by the moment and out of breath.

I have no pictures of the moment just following, however, maybe fifteen minutes later, when Dave and I discover that both hotels in Colombres are closed. That we must carry on to El Peral, a series of gas stations and truck stops on the highway to Villaviciosa, where tankers and big rigs howl by, and none of the

restaurants are open, and the bartender who handles room keys at
the motel ignores our presence, clearly willing us to carry on out
of his jurisdiction. Dave and I with our packs at the bar, ready to
crumple from fatigue. Twenty minutes spent wondering if we're
sleeping under a hedge or hailing a taxi to the next town or what.

So that summit feeling of immunity does not last. The world
returns. But with the world also comes a young woman, who
intervenes and talks to the man in Spanish. I can tell, from hand
gestures, facial expressions, what this is all about. She's saying,
Come on, they'd like a room. One room with two beds. Peregrinos.
Yes, they're peregrinos. *Just give them a room.*

6.

UP AND DOWN. THIS is the inner and outer topography when
you walk for weeks on end. Once you're locked into it, the trek
becomes an endless cycle of arrivals and departures. Always entering or leaving some fold in the land, climbing or dropping off
a ridgeline, a valley behind or in front, the roll of a hill stretching
upward or downward ahead of you. After 300 or 400 kilometres
of walking, it seems I've been coming forever on some new set
of views and possibilities. Another paradox for my list. That the
real constant of the trail should be this ever-changing sameness
of the landscape. That and the sounds of sheep and cowbells, the
hovering cries of birds.

On the train to Oviedo, where we will begin the original medieval way, the Primitivo, we retreat to our respective playlists and
books. We turn inland, the hills rushing past, burnt orange in the
morning sun. The ocean slips behind. Last glimpse of it is a mir-
rored flash, the entire coastline obscured in a fizz of light shards,
prisming and refracting.

I brought two books with me on this trip, Eliot's *Four Quartets,* and *Don Quixote*. Spanish pilgrims chuckle to see me lugging around the Cervantes, a book they remember not quite finishing in high school. I'm dragging it through Spain nevertheless, reading passages in hotel rooms and bars. I spill wine on it. Fortuna ashes. Bits of *bocadillo* and tortilla. It gets burnt, then rained on. Some of the pages fall out.

But I want this book with me. The great Spanish masterpiece. Also the first modern novel. The ancestor document that branches out to all my literary heroes. This book is, in a sense, the mother of all reasons why I decided that being a writer was worth a life's effort. And when you've just finished a novel yourself and it's out to your publisher . . . when the atmosphere in the book business is as dark as it has been since the fall of 2008 . . . when you're on the road walking miles in silence and thinking about the future and your own place in it . . . well, then it makes a certain amount of pilgrim-sense to clutch the lodestone, hold tight the talisman, hang the juju from a cord around your neck.

Miguel de Cervantes, all two kilos and 940 pages of you, I pray to you now in my hour of . . .

Although: my hour of what, exactly? I can't say *need*. Food and shelter are needs—the things we seek spontaneously, without encouragement or guidance. Even vagabonding across Spain, I have plenty of both. My hour relates to the world I left behind. I doubt I'm alone in feeling a little exposed by the events of 2008, in feeling especially anxious about what the future holds. We never truly know the answer to this question, of course, but some circumstances, such as a history-making market crash, make it distinctly more pressing.

So, too, though, does our contemporary vulnerability to that market. Beyond the numbers and beyond our bank accounts, the market has come to intersect with our very sense of self. Having

lost the definitions once provided by family, church, and civil society, who among us doesn't self-identify significantly in terms of
what we do for a living? And who among us, then, didn't feel a
tremor as markets around the globe wiped out billions of dollars
of value? Who didn't entertain the question: what am I going to be
when this is all over? Or even: *who* am I going to be?

I read "The Tale of Foolish Curiosity" that night, lying in our
hotel in Oviedo, with its high northern view overlooking the busy
Calle de Jovellanos. In the story, I find a strange and surprising re-
verberation of our current vulnerability. Anselmo marries Camilla,
then convinces his best friend, Lothario, to try to seduce her in
order to test her faithfulness. Anselmo's plan works too well. Lothario and Camilla become lovers. So: "From that time on Anselmo was the most deliciously deluded man in the whole world.
He himself led home by the hand the man who had completely
destroyed his good name, in the firm belief that he had brought
him nothing but glory."

Not everyone likes this story. J. M. Cohen, the translator of the
edition I'm reading, goes so far as to say in his introduction that
neither the story's "morality nor its psychology bears a moment's
examination," then suggests that impatient readers "skip it." But
with respect to the late Mr. Cohen—translator of Pasternak, Rous-
seau, Christopher Columbus, and many others—I disagree in the
strongest terms. "The Tale of Foolish Curiosity" might well be the
very heart of *Don Quixote*, because it lays bare what Cervantes sees
at the heart of human aspiration. Just as Don Quixote is inspired
by tales of the knight errant Amadis of Gaul, and suffers mightily
for the desires he inherits from his fictional model, so, too, are
Anselmo and Lothario inspired by what the other desires. What
Anselmo has, he needs Lothario to crave in order for it to have
value. What Lothario did not previously desire, he discovers—

through the modelling example of his friend Anselmo—is the one possession without which he cannot live.

I'm influenced by René Girard in my reading of this passage, specifically his theory of "mimetic desire." According to Girard, we don't desire anything we wish to possess based on its objective merits. Nor do we choose what to desire based on innate preference. In such matters—in acquiring the repertoire of objects and experiences and relationships that illustrate what we think of as our taste—we are wholly lacking in spontaneity, and rely instead on the inspiration of a model. These models, which Girard refers to as "mediators," can be either internal (people close to us with whom we consider ourselves equal) or external (people distant from us whose authority we acknowledge). Amadis of Gaul is safely external to Don Quixote in this analysis, a mediator whose example the hero might do best to avoid, but to whom Quixote bears no grudge, despite his dents and bruises. Lothario and Anselmo, on the other hand, are internal mediators for each other. And because they see themselves as equal, their relationship is necessarily rivalrous and unstable. Indeed, it can be sustained only by Anselmo's delusion.

People sometimes react poorly to Girard's interpretation of desire, and it's easy enough to see why. Our highest admiration is reserved for those whom we imagine to have emotional autonomy, those of whom it might be said that they are steadfastly self-directed. This is our working definition of integrity: personal, artistic, professional. And if I am truthful, I'll admit to holding that exact view of my mother. She betrayed no worldly influence. When I was eight years old and wanted North Star runners, her failure to endorse the relationship between those shoes and my potential social status was a source of great irritation for me.

As an adult, however, I am filled with awe by thoughts of her independence. One of the last things I remember her saying was spoken not to me but to my brother, yet it lives in my memory as if I had heard the words myself, because it is so true to my sense of who she was. She told him, with real urgency, real intensity: "You must believe in your *self*."

So, to recognize that our self is beholden to external models, then, is to admit real weakness. Which is why we don't like to be told that the reason we're checking our cellphones for messages is because we subconsciously register the guy sitting opposite us on the bus checking his. Why we don't like to contemplate that our satisfaction with the apartment we own rises and falls depending on which guest is visiting: our pal who still rents, or the friends with a big house. Why we resist the notion that the cars we drive, or the cuisine we fancy, or the style of dress we adopt is anything less than a personal aesthetic, definitively ours. And why we certainly don't like to think that our self-image really does fluctuate with our Facebook friend count or the number of people following us on Twitter.

We don't like to think these things because they make us feel contingent, provisional, caught in the gulf between being and appearing. These considerations—sadly alienating us from our heroes—make us feel *vulnerable*.

"Oh, hell," Hermia says to Lysander, "to choose love by another's eyes."

Which is interesting to consider in light of the great mimetic hurricane that was the financial collapse of 2008. Interesting to consider particularly that economists are now referring to this collapse as a "Minsky moment," after Hyman Minsky (1919–1996), who theorized that human nature leads to market instability, as people are fundamentally momentum, not value, investors. That is, people enact their desires in the market mimetically, based entirely on the desires enacted by others.

Of course, even as I read the Cervantes and consider these matters, I can't help but see myself ensnared in the phenomenon. Call
it the final paradox of this trail: that I hoped to alleviate my sense
of vulnerability, to escape the mimetic funhouse, by doing a pilgrimage, of all things. By following a centuries-old path across a
centuries-old country, placing my feet into the faded prints of a
million million million feet that have fallen before mine.

7.

And what the dead had no speech for, when living,
They can tell you, being dead: the communication
Of the dead is tongued with fire beyond the language of the living.
The trail dwindles to a point.

IT NARROWS AND TURNS; like a nautilus shell, it directs you toward some inner part of itself. After passing through Oviedo and
hiking three days to Tineo, we turn into the heart of the Primitivo.
Four long, mountainous days lie ahead. About 120 kilometres in
total. Tineo to Polla Allende, then to Grandas de Salime. From
there to A Fonsagrada, and finally to O Cádavo. And as we leave
Tineo in the pre-dawn blue, rose light colouring the clouds to the
east, I sense us arriving at the heart of matters. Turning with the
inner spiral.

We cross the hillside, travelling west into the valley south of
the Sierra de Obona. The trail is full of pilgrims this morning,
Spanish kids and older couples. People nod and greet. They say,
bon camino. Past the glowing green summit over Piedratecha, we
descend down a long, straight forest path through a stand of
red pines and walk for a few kilometres with Mary, an Irish

schoolteacher from Galway. This isn't her first pilgrimage. She does them, she says, for the freedom of it.

Onward and onward. The days compress and stretch simultaneously. In Berducedo, where there are no other pilgrims around, we ask the old woman running the corner store if she can make us a *bocadillo*, and she nods and shrugs, and retreats into her own kitchen through a doorway past the shelf of plumbing supplies, returning in a few minutes with sandwiches cut roughly from a loaf of brown bread, thick wedges of cheese, and folded layers of *jamon serrano*. In a roadside café just past the Alto de Lavadoire, where the washroom has a wasp's nest in it and a crew of red chickens runs riot out front between the legs of the table, the lady who owns the place has laid out a bowl of hazelnuts for pilgrims, with a small hammer provided for cracking. On the ridgeline near Buspol, wind turbines churn the sky, emitting a steady, low roar and "wielding more arms than the giant Briareus," as Cervantes would have it. And just past the turbines, right where the path leads behind a farmhouse and onto the open hillside above the lake, we come across a guy and his girlfriend. He's sitting in front of a small grotto with a statue of the Virgin, sitting with his head in his hands, his girlfriend hovering nervously nearby.

What's wrong? I ask her.

She tells me that the gate at the end of the lane is closed and there's a bull in the paddock beyond. And since there's no other way around, they're considering the fact that they'll have to go back down that long, steep hill we all just climbed, all the way back to La Mesa, where she thinks the *refugio* is already full.

We go ahead anyway, too exhausted to consider turning back. When we reach the end of the lane, we find the gate closed, just as the woman said. And we see the bull beyond. But at kilometre twenty-five of our longest day, the thirty-six-kilometre leg to

Grandas de Salime, neither of us sees the bull as I see him now in my memory—this magnificent and terrifying creature with his curling horns and rippling flanks. We see a cow. So we push open the gate and stump wearily through the paddock to the far end while the bull gazes up into the darkening clouds and never stops chewing his cud for even a moment to consider us.

Spiralling and spiralling. An inchoate sense of something building. Some shape or sensation from which I might judge my reasons for being here. My own answer to the question *why*. It comes close, descending into Polla Allende along a rocky path, my knees in agony. I'm as tired as I've been on the entire hike, and I think suddenly of my mother. A sharp and penetrating thought. Not a *presence*, I stress. There is no sense of proximity, no breath of a ghostly nearness. The dust is rising, and I can see the spire of the church in the town below. And something shifts in me. I'm seeing myself in motion, doing something that would have pleased her enormously. Not the pilgrimage per se, not the ritual in which I join many others. What would have pleased her about me humping across Spain with an old friend and *Don Quixote* in my knapsack is the continuance it demands. She would have been pleased to see me take each of these steps without knowing entirely what I was doing, knowing only enough to take that step. Continuing, continuing. She did that, I think to myself. She did continue. And I am inspired by the memory.

The following morning, we climb the pass at Puerto Palo to the roofline of Spain, where the bare hills roll away in all directions. West of the pass, we come to Montefurado, a seemingly abandoned hamlet of six or eight stone buildings and a chapel, daisy-chained along the narrow ridge. On the hillside beyond the town, past the Saint Bernard keeping silent watch over our progress, the path narrows and twists down toward Lastra through the spiny

gorse and flowering broom, the ferns and low thorns. We're walking far apart now, as much as half a kilometre. And here it comes
again, like Google Maps set to satellite view. I see my movement
across the world.

And again I find myself thinking about my mother, but with
something added. Something new, singing in on the hot, high
winds of the Sierra del Palo. It takes me a moment to register it.
And then I get it. By following her example of continuance, by
taking that one step after the other, by doing only what I know I
have to do and thinking no further ahead, I come to appreciate my
arrival somewhere entirely fresh. A place of complete sufficiency,
in which I know I have everything I need for the moment, in the
moment. Wind and the smell of cows. Bells in the distance. I'm
stopped in my tracks, standing alone on a Spanish hill where I will
never stand again. I'm light as air. I desire nothing.

The moment is fleeting, of course. Our days continue. Life
continues. Feet get sore, and hamstrings act up. Moods worsen.
Words are exchanged. In A Fonsagrada, I write in my notebook:
"We're grinding it out now." Which is true for me, certainly. All
thoughts of continuance and sufficiency gone from my head. I
catch myself finally, a full day and a half after the high of Montefurado, standing outside a café just through the pass at Acebo,
where we've stopped for a quick rest and a coffee. Dave's answering
emails inside. It's been fifteen minutes, twenty. I'm impatient. I'm
irritable. Standing in a garbage bag coat because I've left my rain
slicker somewhere along the route, waiting, waiting, while a black
bank of clouds vaults up out of the west toward us. Twenty-four
hours from euphoric to miserable.

I resolve to get it back. Dave comes out of the café. We walk
on. We arrive in A Fonsagrada. Eat, sleep. Walk on again. And
late on that last day of the Primitivo, heading into O Cádavo, we

drop down off the green flanks of the Sierra do Hospital and past
the town of Paradavella. Here the trail dips down below the road,
winding behind the small stone church at Degolada and past the
hamlet of Couto, stacked stone buildings with leaning, lichen-
covered walls, slate roofs, wild cats, wind in the high pines. We
trudge into the forest along a steep embankment to a part of the
trail that seems to cut almost vertically through the forest toward
the road, now far above us.

This is brutal. We're exhausted. It's hot. It's late. If we'd stayed
on the road and forgone the scenery, we'd be 400 metres up the
hillside now, not facing down this bank of loose stone and broken
rocks, tilted stumps and tortured switchbacks.

What can you do but keep going. So we take that first step,
and so it begins again. This time with one more thing added. I
sing myself to the top. (Silently.) I sing to myself. *Keep going. Keep
going.* Tuneless, chanty. Like a work song, that's what it is. I'm a
prisoner of this damn trail, and here is my work song. *Keep going.
Keep going.* Fifty metres up, and we're pouring with sweat, which
shakes loose from my forehead and darkens the stones at my feet.
Up and up. And I'm thinking of her, of course I am. Another fifty
metres. Another hundred. No end in sight. The wind dies. *Keep
going. Keep going.* Another hundred. And then it comes on. I realize the chant is working. I'm either driving myself insane, or this
damn song is *working.* Some kind of reverse energy loop. About
halfway up, I realize I'm not expending energy anymore. I'm
somehow gaining it. I'm actually recharging. Of course it's nuts,
but that's what I'm feeling. I'm not tiring, I'm getting stronger. I'm
going faster. I'm floating up this hill. I'm not even breathing hard
anymore. It's a miracle! Call the Vatican! And when I arrive at the
pavement at the top, I let out a huge whoop and throw my hat
in the air, and it spirals up and up, and for a second it blocks the

sun. My hat winks out the entire sun. And then it falls back down, onto the road, just in time for Dave to emerge from the woods and stare at me with all due alarm and personal concern.

Which is understandable, if not strictly necessary. I'm grinning like a fool, but something else, too. I feel the feeling. And now I know its name, too. She lived with this feeling. And its name is *freedom*.

8.

AFTER TWENTY-THREE DAYS, THE destination seems unlikely to live up to the route. Santiago is rain soaked and clogged with pilgrims. They walk singing down the flagstones next to the cathedral. They gossip in the square. We watch. We eat brilliant tapas at Taverno do Bispo. It's my birthday. We have a few, get a little drunk. I say, "I'm old." Dave says, "Yeah, but you look great." We're old friends, and now, for all the silence we have invested in each other, I think we are better friends than before.

We go to bed in the nicest hotel room we've had. Top-floor room looking out across the wet city toward the cathedral. I can't sleep. I surf the news and check email. No word from the publisher about my novel. Dave is snoring.

I get up and go to the window. Across the blackness, they've turned on the cathedral lights, the whole Gothic structure now glowing silver, mercury, gold, blue. The clouds wreathing around it, underlit and vaulting, as if to extend the structure high into the swirling sky. And I know then that I've walked all this way just to see this sight. This garish, amazing, crazy sight. To see it with my mother's eyes. Touching the beyond.

I text my wife, thumbing in the words. I write: *Santiago is shining*.

PRODIGAL BAND

CHRIS TURNER
Alberta Views

WHEN NILS EDENLOFF WAS a high school student in Fort Mc-
Murray, there was a minor scandal one summer involving a gaggle
of teens who decided to ride their bicycles to Edmonton. It was
received truth somehow that it was a four-day journey by bike,
and who could blame a kid stuck in Fort Mac for daydreaming
of escape? Only the one real road out of town—who wouldn't
get to wondering how far a hardpedalling crew could get before
someone's parents figured it out and jumped in the pickup to give
chase? Not hard at all to imagine the fanciful conversation becoming a solid notion and then a plan. Flashlights and non-perishable
food stuffed secretively in packs. A date set, a clear morning of

a certain kind of inviting blue. An innocent bike ride into the woods that never looped back.

It's the kind of quiet small-town tale that you only ever hear if it goes gothic. If you know Fort Mac at all, you can already picture the churning wheels of the tar sands-bound rig, the driver who would never expect to find kids on bikes out on Highway 63. In this case, though, the story's final act simply went banal—the kids chased down, groundings administered, the details soon fading, and only the yearning goofball gall remaining as it passed into schoolyard legend.

For some reason, though, the story came back to Edenloff a decade later, as he tried to write his way through a lonely spell in Toronto. He was a couple years out of the University of Alberta, in a self-imposed exile from an Edmonton that felt like a rut. He'd left, or so he told himself, because all the great bands that never came to Edmonton inevitably played Toronto. Some old Fort Mac friends were around town as well, and there'd been idle chitchat about getting their high school band back together, but of course nothing had come of it. Edenloff had instead taken to strumming his guitar as the co-host of an open-mic night at a Cabbagetown dive called The Winchester—he and a new friend named Paul on the drums, a rotating cast of other regulars and, often as not, barely any audience. Eventually a young woman named Amy joined them with some regularity, singing background harmonies and tinkling the keys of a keyboard or xylophone or pounding a second drum of her own.

It felt right, the three of them together, or as right as anything happening at some afterthought open-mic night in a soon-to-be-condemned tavern ever could, and Edenloff started working out some lyrics. He still wondered where he belonged in the Big Smoke—wondered if he ever *would* belong, really, as Toronto's uninvited foster kids inevitably do—and when he tried to write, he was haunted by memories of his Alberta youth. Stuff he hadn't thought of in years. Like the quixotic tale of some pipe-dreaming kids who tried to bike to Edmonton one summer.

In Edenloff's version, the kids have become teenage lovers. The weather's gone frigid, an icy wind *freezing each of the lymph nodes* as they sneak past a slumbering grandfather and peel their clothes off, finding solace in their mingling body heat and an impossible yearning for transcendence. Paul Banwatt's drums beat out the urgent fumbling double-time rhythm of teen sex and punk rock, Amy Cole's voice comes in high and piercing on the last chorus, and Edenloff finds the top of his narrow vocal range, the very limitation of it amplifying the desperate, doomed passion of the plan. *And I love you and you know / You love me and it shows / Edmonton's just a four night / Bike ride out of town.*

This is "Four Night Rider," the eleventh of thirteen songs on *Hometowns*, the debut album by Edenloff's three-piece band, the Rural Alberta Advantage, and there is much that is startling about it all. In particular, *Hometowns* is as intimate and tender a portrait of Alberta as any in the annals of Canadian popular music, tinged with fond memory and regret but never offhanded or syrupy in its nostalgia. And because it is so specific about its subjects, and because such specificity is such a rarity in Canadian pop, it kind of unintentionally points to the empty expanses around it where the rest of our mythology should reside. A place—any place—is made important by its stories, and we Albertans are impoverished by our dearth of pop myth-making. For this alone—were *Hometowns* not also a fantastic collection of beautifully crafted songs, I mean—it would be a landmark record.

FIRST THOUGH, LET'S ADDRESS the stuff of standard pop criticism. If this were a straight-and-narrow music review, I'd first want to note that the RAA has taken the best possible lessons from the short-lived, cult-inspiring indie band Neutral Milk Hotel and its mercurial singer-songwriter Jeff Mangum—in particular that passionate honesty and reckless abandon trump a three-octave vocal range every time when it comes to rock 'n' roll. I'd want to mention as well that Edenloff and his bandmates have cribbed only the best parts of the oeuvre of current indie darlings Arcade Fire—a delicate dynamism, a taste for epic themes, unconventional instruments, and semi-orchestral arrangements. And I'd definitely point out that *Hometowns* expands impressively on the thematic work of Winnipeg's Weakerthans, thoroughly inhabiting the prairie in every song. In the aggregate, the album is a jangling pop tour de force that is either punk streaked with folk or folk infected with punk and is melodic and catchy as all get out.

And even though I'm aiming for more than a standard music review—because I think *Hometowns* deserves more care than that—there are some other details I should probably get out of the way. The name comes from a defunct provincial government marketing slogan, by way of an e-mail from Edenloff's brother in which he half-seriously told Nils he was "off to explore the Rural Alberta Advantage"—by which he meant that he was headed to their family cabin near Donalda to hang out with some girls he'd come to know. Edenloff went to Toronto around 2002 and the band coalesced as a three-piece around 2006 or so. They started writing songs and paid their dues up and down Queen West, and by early 2008 the RAA had a self-produced, self-released debut. So did every other half-talented assemblage of indie-rockers in the free world. That and three bucks will, at best, get you a latte on Queen West, dig?

Anything could've happened next. But what did happen next—this being 2008—was that the songs skipped from hard-drive to hard-drive and they developed a bit of an Internet following (which inexplicably included a handful of very influential American entertainment lawyers and venture capitalists). Thus did the RAA came to the attention of the overseers of a subscription music downloading service called eMusic.com, a sort of hipster iTunes whose influence was just then hitting the meaty part of a steep upward curve. *Hometowns* was named eMusic's unsigned pick of the month for November 2008, and because the RAA are in the aggregate more mathematically inclined than many aspiring rock 'n' roll bands (Edenloff is a software engineer by training), they can verifiably attest that their fan base saw literally exponential growth, more or less overnight. Then came a spotlight gig at the career-making SXSW music festival in Austin, Texas, after which Saddle Creek Records, a highly influential indie label best known as the home of A-list singer-songwriter Conor Oberst, picked up the album and rereleased it to an even larger audience in early July. Pitchfork Media—the *Rolling Stone* of online pop music geekery—gave it an eight out of ten, which in that forum is a hair's breadth from instant-classic status. The RAA embarked on their first real tour, played New York, Chicago, Seattle, LA. Also Calgary and Edmonton, for the first time ever, which I'll also come back to.

None of this matters much to me, though, except the eMusic thing, because I'm a subscriber and the moment I saw the band name I had basically no choice but to download it. I don't know what I was expecting, but I wasn't ready for possibly the best Canadian pop debut I've ever heard.[1] And I was wholly unprepared for a series of musical sketches of Alberta so powerful it made me stop to realize there's never really been any other pop-music picture of the place this specific and compelling maybe ever. Which, finally, is the reason we're even talking about all this.

The thirteen songs on *Hometowns* are fully saturated with Alberta. The landscapes that are too often harsh but just as often transcendent in their quiet beauty, the cities and towns that both attract and repulse and are never entirely left behind. And most of all, yes, the abiding, authentic love Alberta can inspire, usually hard-won and sometimes bittersweet but all the more potent for it.

I fell in love with *Hometowns* through the speakers of my car stereo as I drove back roads in late winter—Edmonton to Camrose, Calgary to Taber and back again—and by the time I was done I knew my perception of my home had been fundamentally altered. Maybe the most striking thing about *Hometowns* is the way the sound (I'm told unconsciously) mimics the landscape. The RAA's sound is lush and forceful but never cluttered. Smatterings of keyboard or strings slide in and then fade off, bits of skronking horn or ringing xylophone erupt and then disappear like summer rain. There are a great many empty spaces in the songs, places that draw your ear the way the wide snowy expanses between the golden tips of dead grass catch your eye. Just when you think you're listening to a lulling ballad, the drums emerge with the sudden drama of a Badlands canyon and are just as quickly gone. In much the same way it's impossible to watch the moon rise gently over the Ontario countryside in summer without thinking of Neil Young's blue, blue windows behind the stars, I doubt I'll ever again watch the snow-blanketed prairie unfold through a frosted windshield without hearing echoes of the haunting horns that fill the final section of the RAA's "Luciana."

A WARM JUNE EVENING in Calgary now, and the RAA are on-stage at Broken City on the second night of the Sled Island Festival. They'd played a gig earlier in the evening at Central United Church, but this is truly their Alberta homecoming—they fit the venue as seamlessly as the Wild Rose on tap behind the bar. The album's still weeks away from official release, but it's clear they've got an expectant audience here, and you can tell it's kind of overwhelming the band. They're still in that modest, thanks-for-coming phase of a thing they can barely believe is becoming a career, and they're almost embarrassed by it.

Nils Edenloff likes to explain his stories a little before launching into them. "Normally at this point," he's saying, "I'll tell the audience there's this town in Alberta where the mountain collapsed and . . ." He's interrupted by cheers and whoops. He shrugs and mumbles something like *guess I don't need to do that here*, and the RAA launch into "Frank, AB"—a retelling of the great gothic tragedy of the Frank Slide from the point of view of a stalwart couple buried beneath the rubble in an eternal embrace. It's one of the stronger tracks on the album, but here at Broken City on the first night it's ever been played for an Alberta audience, it finds its own mythic level. There have to be at least a dozen people singing along: *And I'll hold, I'll hold on to your touch / Until there's nothing left of us / To save you from this life.*

There are probably a thousand ways to mess up a dirge about the Frank Slide, a thousand different missteps that lead down the path to Stompin' Tom kitsch.[2] The only way seemingly imaginable to avoid that trap—and never is it more apparent than it is in this room on this night—is to close it with an essentially acapella coda so naked and earnest it convinces you this is a century-old folk song the RAA must've unearthed from the provincial archives. The barest scrape of strings, a fading heartbeat thump of drum, and Edenloff's taut voice finding the bloodied human face of the Slide: *And under the rubble of the mountain that tumbled / I will hold you forever / I will hold you forever.* In the stunned moment of silence before the crowd erupts, you can hear the song click snugly into some permanent place on the landscape, filling a particularly conspicuous hole in the pockmarked stone face of Canadian myth.

CANADA SELDOM GETS TO be itself in the broader globalized mythos of pop. The Beatles will forever be as Liverpudlian as Penny Lane itself, Lou Reed and the Strokes inconceivable as anything other than New Yorkers, the Grateful Dead as San Franciscan as a cable car. But the goal of Canadian pop hopefuls has until very recently been to vanish into generic Americanness, often denaturing themselves into bland pap (viz. Nickelback of Hanna, AB, and Avril Lavigne of Napanee, ON) and leading to that cloying Canadian pastime of pointing out all the disguised Canadiana out there to bemused foreigners. "Hey, did you know 'The Night They Drove Old Dixie Down' was written by a kid from Toronto named Robbie Robertson? That k.d. lang picked up her twang not in Texas but in Consort, AB?"[3]

The trend has mostly continued even as Canada has become, in recent years, a wellspring of indie music so bountiful it's become a kind of in-joke—there's a Georgia-based band called Of Montreal and an influential Indiana based record label named Secretly Canadian. Canadian pop is generally either, well, secretly Canadian or so pointedly Canuckified it never raises a tremor outside our borders (viz. the Tragically Hip, the Rheostatics, and, yes, ol' Stompin' Tom). There are world-conquering pop songs about particular London neighbourhoods and certain Manhattan intersections, but try to think of a single one that contains a Canadian place name.

Which is why there's something not just refreshing but almost post-colonially validating about the RAA. The first words enunciated on *Hometowns* are these ones from "The Ballad of the RAA": *We unbearably / Left the prairies / And my heart, since / Well it never moved an inch*. A few lines later, Edenloff is on about trading Garneau (the Edmonton neighbourhood) for Dundas (the Toronto thoroughfare) and the Rockies for the Great Lakes. These are the recollections of a particular homesick Alberta kid on the streets of Toronto, an ambitious Canadian hinterlander's bewilderment at life in the Big Smoke—a phenomenon nearly as common as the tale of the small-town boy's arrival in the Big Apple but never properly mythologized until Edenloff came along. Visions of escape and lamentations for what's left behind permeate nearly every song on the album—dead roads haunted by terrible ghosts, a redemptive dethbridge (sic) that leads only out of Lethbridge, a heart turned to petrified wood and a dark, empty apartment at the other end. And then, on the second-last track, the album reaches its thematic crescendo on a mini-epic pointedly entitled "Edmonton."

What'll I do if you never want to come back? / Sitting in a city that's always on the attack—so Edenloff's homage to his former hometown begins, though the city on the attack is not Edmonton but Toronto. Here's Edenloff on the song's inspiration: "I guess at the time I moved to Toronto, it just seemed like, 'Aw, I'm never going to figure this place out. Why does it always suck here?' Not the city itself—it just seemed like I wasn't the right person for the place. I was always losing. When I first moved there, I got all my stuff stolen, and I got robbed, like, my first hour in Toronto and spent nine months finding a job and thinking, 'God, I suck!' "

The song changes tone midway through. A bittersweet chord progression tinged with hope overtakes Edenloff's frustrated guitar riff and a lovely little buoyant two-step erupts from the drums.[4] When Edenloff starts singing again his voice is soaring, almost

ecstatic, and he is lost in a memory so delicate and perfect and
almost parodically specific that in a sense it tells the whole album's
story in a few lines. When Edenloff was in school in Edmonton,
there was an apparently well-known sort of pastime in which you
and your friends—or, as appears to be the case in the song, a special someone—would go in the evening to the sloping field beneath the Alberta Legislature. You'd position yourselves between
the building itself and the blinding purple floodlights illuminating
it, and you would stare out through the lights to the city beyond.

All of it turned electric purple, luminous, a dreamscape for a
thrumming city. In the final lines of the RAA's "Edmonton," the
quirky pastime takes on the weight of transcendent myth. Like
this: *Meet me there again under the lights at the "Leg" / And we will
burn out our eyes seeking out these purple nights.*

ROYAL CANADIAN LEGION HALL No. 1, downtown Calgary. The
Friday night of Sled Island, and whatever the original plans for the
festival may have been, it feels like it's found its *raison d'être* here
on 7th Ave. The streets outside are uncharacteristically dense with
evening strollers headed from venue to venue, and later tonight
the staid Legion Hall with its Old Style Pilsner on tap will play
host to bizarre and wildly hip bands from Seattle and Brooklyn.
Right now, though, the RAA's final Sled Island set is hitting its
stride, filling the old hall with a collection of stories worthy of this
historic space.

Every time Nils Edenloff introduces "Edmonton" at the festival, he makes a sheepish kind of apology about it being about
Edmonton, as if expecting the province's notorious bipolar urban
rivalry to break out in response. It never does. This is not an Oil-
ers/Flames game or a debate about government spending imbal-
ances. It's a song about living in a city in Alberta and sometimes

sort of resenting it but making your own fun there, and Calgarians can relate to that as easily as Edmontonians can.

It's a great performance, but for whatever reason, "Edmonton" is not the peak of this set. The RAA really brings the house down a few songs later with "Luciana," a careening punk song about doomed love. The lyrics are half-buried in growling guitar and a ferociously unhinged drumbeat that somehow also seems to keep 4/4 time. You can tell, because there's a joyous stomp shaking the dance floor in time with it. The room feels as one, deliriously lost in the roar of a newly minted Alberta myth.

ENDNOTES:

1. Superlatives like this are all too common in pop criticism, but I've gone back through my record collection and scrolled through my iTunes library and think this one's legit. Four of the tracks on *The Songs of Leonard Cohen* are full-on masterpieces, but I couldn't hum a bar from a single one of the others. I'm not sure which record you'd call Neil Young's debut, but in any case it was recorded in LA, and what's more he didn't make one that I consider a masterpiece until his second solo album (*Everybody Knows This Is Nowhere*). The Tragically Hip didn't hit full stride until their fourth album (*Fully Completely*), and Blue Rodeo is more of a singles band. Sloan's *Smeared* will always have an exquisite first-year-of-undergrad magic for me, but there are only four or five of the twelve tracks I've bothered to import into iTunes. There's an argument to be made that either the Arcade Fire or Broken Social Scene debuts (or both) are maybe more polished than *Hometowns*, more fully formed, but there's also a preciousness to both that eventually starts to grate on me. The New Pornographers' *Mass Romantic* is a real contender, and I know I haven't spent as much time as I should with all the songs on Wolf Parade's *Apologies to the Queen Mary* that aren't "Shine a Light" or "Dinner Bells." Still.

2. I mean no offence here. Hell, ol' Stompin' Tom earned his place in the Hall of Fame solely on the merits of rhyming *plinko, stinko,* and *Inco* on "Sudbury Saturday Night." But it's no accident that the best possible way to read, say, "Bud the Spud" is as an illustrated children's story (which version my daughter could not get enough of at the age of about 2¾).

3. It's even worse when it comes to film; where Alberta's badlands are made to impersonate Wyoming, Vancouver stands in for some generic X-Filed postindustrial America, and—in a particularly highly visible (if banal) example—the Tim Hortons of Mike Myers's real-life Scarborough youth is forced to become the entirely fictitious Stan Mikita Donuts of suburban Chicago in the *Wayne's World* movies.

4. Because my focus has been largely thematic, I've neglected to mention until now that Paul Banwatt is some kind of inspired percussionist. At the risk of dancing about architecture, I'll just say there's a kind of offhand precision and completely disarming phrasing to the drums on *Hometowns,* which repeatedly sets the tone for an entire song in a single rhythm change. This is particularly true of the marching cadence that pops up at 2:06 of "Edmonton," which is one of the few such percussion moments I'd put in the same class as the bit in the Rolling Stones' "Rocks Off" when Charlie Watts brings the song back from the murk of the bridge in a single staccato six-beat burst and ushers in maybe the best single line in rock 'n' roll history (i.e., *the sunshine bores the daylights outta me*). But I digress.

THE FUTURE HAS BEGUN

NORA UNDERWOOD
The Walrus

BRYAN GILVESY DOESN'T APPRECIATE being asked first how much his beef costs. In fact, if you ask him the price before anything else, he might just refuse to sell it to you. It's not that he's a particularly grouchy guy; he simply knows what's involved in producing tender, lean, clean beef—and that level of knowledge and care isn't without cost.

Gilvesy is a fifty-one-year-old farmer in southwestern Ontario who has worked the land since he was nineteen and has, quite possibly, seen the future. For the past fifteen years, he has been raising Texas longhorn cattle, a genetically diverse breed, which roam as they would in the wild through relatively disease-free lives, eating a wide variety of plants, and calving without human interference. For the former tobacco grower, the longhorns were the first in a long chain of dominoes.

His farm—100 hectares of arable land and 45 hectares of reforested woodlot—is almost entirely sustainable now. He maintains a pure coldwater stream for trout, using a solar pump to deliver the water to his cattle in the field; thirty birdhouses for the bluebirds that eat the flies off his cows' backs; and a place for native bees to proliferate. Gilvesy says the tipping point came four years ago, when he planted three hectares of drought-resistant tall-grass prairie, a deep-rooting ecosystem that provides nesting habitat for several bird species but has been in decline in Ontario. He doesn't disturb the grassland until late July, when it's mature and has served its purpose; then he allows his cattle to feed on the top growth. "We've developed a new way of doing business," he says. "Grocers have spent careers making you think beef is beef is beef—Australian, New Zealand, Canadian, grass fed, corn fed. But beef isn't beef. My beef costs more because of what goes into it."

Gilvesy's timing couldn't be better. He sells his hormone-free meat directly to his customers, rather than going through meat packers and distributors, and the feedback he's receiving from these farmgate transactions tells him that food quality and the environment are becoming big issues. It's a no-brainer for him: "We believe we've made the environment better, we've produced a healthier food supply, and we're getting more rewards from the marketplace. There are a lot of wins in farming this way."

MAYBE WE DIDN'T GIVE it too much thought when eating a medium-rare hamburger stopped being an option; after all, no one would think twice about passing on underdone chicken. But in recent years, it seems caution lights are flashing over pretty much everything in North America: carrot juice in Florida and Georgia tainted with botulism, bagged spinach from central California found to contain E. coli, raspberries imported from Guatemala infected with a parasite, cases of E. coli and salmonella traced to alfalfa sprouts in Michigan and Virginia. This past summer, jalapeno and serrano peppers from Mexico were contaminated with salmonella—an outbreak that, according to the US Centers for Disease Control, affected almost 1,500 people in 43 states and Canada. Then there was polluted cantaloupe from Honduras, and adulterated milk products from China. Of course, last summer belonged to Maple Leaf Foods, whose Toronto plant was infected with the listeria bacterium, subsequently linked to the deaths of at least twenty people across the country.

A bad few years? Maybe. But more likely the tip of the iceberg. "The infrastructure on which our present food system is based is unsustainable at every level, from the seed to the table," says Herb Barbolet, a food policy researcher at Simon Fraser University and one of North America's leading food activists. "The premises it's built on, at least in North America—corporate concentration, export marketing, globalization, heavy reliance on energy—they're all susceptible to collapse."

While the threats to global industrialized agriculture are diverse, from the potential of bioterrorism to the reality of extreme weather wiping out crops in a flash, nothing gets people really thinking about the food supply quite as effectively as the topic of food and waterborne diseases. According to a survey comparing seventeen industrialized countries, released earlier this year by the University of Regina, Canada ranks fifth for food safety, behind the UK, Japan, Denmark, and Australia. Nevertheless, we're hearing more about tainted food today precisely because more cases are showing up; according to the CDC, one in four Americans a year now gets food poisoning, commonly caused by E. coli, a bacillus found in the intestines of humans and animals and transmitted primarily through fecal matter. When crops and livestock are raised together in tight quarters on an industrial scale, food easily becomes contaminated through direct contact with animals or manure, or as a result of poor hygiene by workers. Then E. coli ends up on your dinner plate.

Globalization amplifies the problem.

Last June, scientists gathered in Boston for a general meeting of the American Society for Microbiology to discuss how cheaper labour costs outside North America will lead to more imports— and more foodborne diseases. In 2004, for the first time, they said, the US imported more than it exported. Two years later, 80 percent of the fish and seafood sold there was shipped in, much of it from Asia, where raw sewage and livestock manure are often used as fertilizer in fish farming.

Government food inspectors cannot keep up. In 2001, for example, the US Food and Drug Administration reported that more than a quarter of the tainted seafood imports it identified were contaminated with salmonella, and more than half of those were shrimp. But the volume of imports is so high that the FDA cannot inspect even 1 percent of what comes into the country.

"Salmonella is conventionally an animal organism, in birds or mammals," says veterinarian and epidemiologist David Waltner-Toews, author of the book *Food, Sex and Salmonella.* "So what's this about it showing up in plants? " He tells of a friend who investigated a place where almonds—whose popularity has grown exponentially in recent years—were being grown. He found that farmers had planted the trees so densely, and the level of organic matter under the trees was so thick, that salmonella was actually growing in the soil.

"Suddenly, we're all inside the animal," says the vet in his characteristically vivid manner of speaking. "It's no longer simply a matter of having the chicken and tomatoes on the counter and there's cross-contamination; that's the more conventional stuff. But when it becomes systemic and gets into the soil, and the produce itself, then it's more problematic. You don't know where it's lurking anymore."

While the problems in the system are certainly grand, the common "solutions" tend to focus narrowly, as Waltner Toews notes, on "these tomatoes, in these fields." Technology for identifying the source of contaminants has improved dramatically: particular strains of a disease, for example, can be traced by their DNA fingerprints. But that doesn't mean much if a contaminated crop is distributed across North America. "By the time it gets to the grocery store, you don't know where it came from," he says. In fact, your food may well travel thousands of kilometres before it reaches your table.

That frustrates Laura Young, a food advocate raised on a farm her family still owns in the Holland Marsh, a flat, fertile tract of land north of Toronto that produces $50 million worth of produce a year. Grocery stores in the area sell imported vegetables when the same ones are growing literally steps away. This past spring, Young and another food advocate started the Holland Marsh Greenbelt Association, which included establishing a farmers' market. Now they are focusing on the idea of a national food preparedness program. "Our government asks us to be prepared to feed ourselves for seventy-two hours in case of a disaster," explains Young. "So why shouldn't we expect our government to preserve, secure, and organize our food resources to feed us now and in the future?"

Young believes farmers involved in such a program should be treated as emergency personnel. If outside food supplies were suddenly cut off, they would know what was available and what could be set aside for people in their area, including, in this case, Toronto. An emergency transportation plan would also have to be in place. "It would actually be a blueprint or a template for a community to value its food resources and know how to protect them and access them in times of emergency."

To achieve true security, however, the food system must undergo a massive change, experts say. That means reducing its dependence on cheap fuel, which is fast disappearing anyway, and getting rid of redundancies—the importing of what we export, for example. Most important, it means elevating food to a loftier place on the priority list, and expecting to pay more for something better.

"Cheap food is the problem nobody wants to name," says Wayne Roberts, acting manager of the Toronto Food Policy Council. "It's forcing everyone to drive prices down, and it's totally irrational." Waltner Toews agrees: "Rich people want protein, and they don't want to pay high prices for it. The only way you can really do that is through economies of scale: instead of 500 or 1,000 chickens on a farm, you have 50,000 or 100,000; if you can make these birds grow faster, that also helps the price. You're just creating epidemic conditions."

Much of the food in grocery stores, schools, even hospitals, is distributed by just four or five global food service companies. It is cheap because it is bought in mass quantities from as few places as possible—imported from countries where labour costs are low. "Tell me how much Maple Leaf saved by having a centralized system," says Roberts. "The system has no stability to it, because it violates every principle of nature and economics."

The solution is painfully obvious and simple, most agree, but not so easy to implement. Many of the food issues of concern in the developed world boil down to the same things: not only do we want food to be cheap, we want it year round, whether it's in season or not. So, again, we rely on a handful of global sources to bring us food from other countries, often at the expense of the content (the longer the wait between picking and eating a fruit or vegetable, for example, the lower its nutritional value), and often from places where farming practices are riskier. These methods force local, small-scale growers and processors out of business, which only perpetuates the problem.

HERB BARBOLET, LIKE MANY others, believes the necessary re-invention of the food system involves, in a sense, taking several steps backward—localizing, relocalizing, and/or creating from scratch. He farmed organically for a decade and cofounded Farm-Folk/CityFolk, a nonprofit society based in Vancouver dedicated to creating local, sustainable food systems. "There's a lot of work going into creating demand for local produce," he says, "but very little done on creating supply." The latter is extremely complex and requires a sea change in respect for farmers, for farmland, and for water. "It challenges the ideology of the metaphysicists who call themselves economists that the market is what rules."

Nonetheless, there are encouraging signs. Across North America, individuals and groups—food policy councils, community economic development centres, academics, health and nutrition experts—are working to improve the food system. Shoppers are starting to pay more attention to agricultural policy and, through local farmers' markets, are spending more of their food dollars closer to home. At the moment, most of these efforts are disconnected; what is needed now, experts say, is collaboration at all levels. "We need a lot more entrepreneurs, a lot more skilled people, a lot more farmers and fishers and ranchers," says Barbolet. "And to make it viable for them to stay in or to get in, we have to change the economic system we're operating under."

More than a year ago, Barbolet helped create a network of networks called Local Food First in BC, which facilitates collaboration and cooperation among everyone from restaurateurs and food purveyors to government representatives and private consultants. "It's about linking up and trying to increase the efficiency of the various members—about reinforcing and supporting each of the separate initiatives," he explains.

If you ask Barbolet what kind of model he has in mind, he names Emilia Romagna, a fertile region of northern Italy known for its food industry. There, he says, the market is simultaneously cooperative and competitive. "They don't understand Americans—they can't imagine why you'd try to kill your competition." Instead, they peacefully coexist, "and then compete like hell to have the best product possible." In terms of food policies, Barbolet says Cuba has the most elegant in the world. Since 1989, when the country was suddenly plunged into a crisis after the collapse of the Soviet Union (which had until then supplied food and provisions), Cuba has become one of the most outstanding examples of urban agriculture. Bearing in mind that much of its land is state owned and therefore not subject to competition, farming is managed by city residents on tiny plots, and provides fresh local produce for much of the country, as well as some 350,000 jobs.

On a smaller scale, similar supply systems are cropping up in Canada and the US. Nevin Cohen, an expert in environmental planning and an assistant professor of urban studies at the New School for Liberal Arts in New York, documents some of the many communities incorporating residential housing and working farms in the December 3, 2007, issue of *The Nation*. One of the most successful, he writes, is Prairie Crossing, a self-described conservation community about sixty-five kilometres northwest of Chicago. Connected to the city by two rail stations, its 359 single-family homes and 36 condominiums coexist with prairie grass-lands, wetlands, and 62 hectares of organic farmland. "Carving out farmland and farmers' markets in the midst of homes," Cohen writes, "these communities offer unusually inclusive spaces where residents can bond with their neighbours and with the people growing and selling food. They enable residents to know, quite intimately, the sources and attributes of the food they buy, en-couraging producers in turn to adopt more transparent produc-tion methods."

LORI STAHLBRAND HAS BEEN thinking about food for a long time. The former CBC broadcaster and co-author of the book *Real Food for a Change* was working for the World Wildlife Fund Canada in 2000, trying to reduce pesticide use in Ontario agricultural oper-ations, when she decided to start a program dedicated to establish-ing a sustainable food system. For the past three years, Stahlbrand has been president of Local Food Plus, an award-winning Toronto organization that links institutions with local food. "A lot of people out there wanted to support a new way of doing agriculture," she says, "but the only way they could was through smallscale pro-jects, like buying at a farmers' market, or buying certified organics, which were increasingly coming from California or farther afield. If we wanted to give people a chance to support local sustainable food systems, we had to give them a way to identify them."

Stahlbrand's first target was universities. Like most large in-stitutions, universities contract out to one of three major food service companies. Influencing how those companies did business,

Stahlbrand figured, was the key. "Universities can have a really enormous impact," she says. "They have buying power, they have clout, and they can start playing a role in changing the system." In 2005, she found a willing partner in New College at the University of Toronto. The college was renewing contracts for food services, and Stahlbrand and her team helped write new requirements that 10 percent of the food budget be supplied from local sources, with a 5 five percent annual increase. The changes went into effect in September 2006, enabling her to raise more money and approach farmers. In the meantime, other colleges at U of T have come on board, and Stahlbrand is now deluged by calls from schools wanting to set up similar programs. Last year, Local Food Plus moved about a million dollars' worth of local, sustainable food to schools, and about two dozen restaurants and small retailers. Last fall, they added half a dozen medium-sized retailers to their stable.

Local Food Plus certifies farmers as local, sustainable growers; they are rated, using a point system, on their production systems—crop or animal—as well as on energy efficiency, labour conditions, biodiversity, and animal welfare. Those who earn the requisite points are actively linked to supply chains, and get a 10 percent premium on their food.

Rebuilding actual relationships among suppliers, distributors, and buyers, and encouraging them to work in new ways, is essential. "Toronto Public Health did a study a while ago and found that Toronto would have three days' worth of food if the borders were to close," says Stahlbrand. "Meanwhile, we're paving over our best agricultural land in southern Ontario. Can you blame farmers for selling out? It's taken fifty years to dismantle the local food distribution system." She is confident things will improve once this new way of business is established. "But we're now working against the flow."

Stahlbrand's husband is coming at the whole issue of food from a different angle. Wayne Roberts's food policy council, the first of its kind in Canada, is appointed by the Toronto Board of Health and made up of city councillors and volunteers from various backgrounds. Roberts and his group are trying to change the way government thinks about food. "You could read a lot of stuff and not read about food," he says. "It would be nutrition or a compost department or a safety department, but it would never be food as a whole thing that goes from seed to farm, fork to plate, fork to compost. If you look at a city, or any government, it's organized around the premise that there is no food. There is a waste program." Roberts's group reminds the municipal government that there are many aspects to the food issue. "And that enables us to come up with solutions that benefit many groups."

Politically and socially, Toronto is ahead of the curve, with forward-thinking organizations, community gardening, and a community food security board. "We helped put green roofs on the North American agenda in the early 1990s," says Roberts. The Toronto Official Plan of 2002, which just took effect last year, was one of the first in North America to deal with food. "Now the position is that city planners must respond to food issues." Other food policy councils are on their way: one is operating in Vancouver now, and councils are forming in Montreal and Victoria and across the US.

And a growing number of consumers are clearly ready for change. "This is not a crisis-driven movement," says Roberts. "It's about authenticity and the concern that we don't know where food is coming from. It's part of a genuine reevaluation." He also credits the fact that there is increased disposable income for food and a large group prepared to pay. In addition, immigration growth has made an impact. "Most cultures in the world have not been

so alienated from nature and from their own bodies," he adds.
"However low their income, they've come here with a reasonably
high level of skill around cooking and a preference for fresh food
and whole food."

BY FAR ONE OF the most fantastical and massive concepts for the
future of food came out of a medical ecology course at Columbia
University in New York nine years ago. It began with the premise
that if you damage the environment there will be health risks, and
with the desire to do something locally that would have global implications. The idea has now been refined and reworked by eighty-
two students, the first class focused on the possibilities of rooftop
gardening in Manhattan.

Initial results were disappointing: the study identified thirteen
acres of suitable rooftop in the city, with rice as the crop most
likely to succeed—but that yield would feed a mere 2 percent of
Manhattan residents. Dickson Despommier, a professor of public
health, urged his students to move their operations inside, to re-
imagine abandoned apartment buildings, air force bases, empty
lots. He coined the term "vertical farming" to help them visualize
indoor spaces that could be converted to hydroponics, or aero-
ponics, a growing method that entails the constant spraying of
suspended plants with nutrient rich water.

While the idea of growing fruits and vegetables indoors on
a massive scale may seem absurd, NASA scientists had already
begun to research the potential of hydroponic vegetables, and
Despommier's students were able to use some of the information
collected by the US space agency. As he says, it turns out there
isn't anything you can't grow indoors—including a redwood tree.
"You can control the growth characteristics; you can stack crops
on top of each other. We began to look around and say, who's

doing this? The answer is nobody. Not a single person is growing food in tall buildings."

There are myriad problems to work out in the prototype stage: how much water would be needed, how much and what kind of energy to use, and so on. Waste is an important issue, because if you don't deal with this, Despommier says, then the structure is not viable, and it becomes a burden. In his vision, agricultural runoff doesn't exist; black water (waste water containing biological effluent) and grey water (which contains no food or body waste) are purified by the plants and recycled. Furthermore, energy could potentially be derived from human waste. Each component of this plan exists now. "All are being done in small scales around the world. We have to pull them all together, put them under one roof."

Already, several people have weighed in with fabulous, futuristic building designs, including Despommier, who designed one vertical farm that looks like an extraterrestrial pyramid. In his mind, the prototype might be four or five storeys tall (and would cost $20 million to $30 million to build). Once enough is known, potentially within a couple of years, the first full-scale version could be built: a thirty-storey building that would cost hundreds of millions of dollars and could theoretically feed 50,000 people. He acknowledges the risks associated with such centralization, but an argument could be made for having hospitals and schools— even individual apartment buildings—produce enough food to become self-sufficient.

Naturally, as a growing area is magnified, so is the potential for problems. Chief among them, of course, are pests, which in a vertical farm could potentially have a devastating impact. But Despommier thinks if plants are offered the same protection as patients suffering from immunosuppression—that is, workers would go through the same drill as staff in a hospital or high-tech electronics factory—then a building could be made pest and disease-free.

As for the energy needs of vertical farms, Despommier is considering a resource unlikely to be depleted: deriving power from human feces. In an average year, he says, the bodily waste generated by 7.5 million New Yorkers could be converted into 900 million kilowatt hours of electricity. "What's wrong with that?" he says. "Not a goddamn thing." His vision has generated interest among city officials across the US. Manhattan borough president Scott Stringer is putting together a feasibility study on vertical farming for the mayor of New York. Officials in Portland, Oregon, are pondering its potential. And in Seattle, a similar but smaller design for an urban agriculture centre won a green building contest in 2007; the proposal would grow grains, produce, and even chickens to provide a third of the food for the building's 400 residents—all on a fraction of a hectare.

A similarly grand project, albeit on a smaller scale, has been quietly chugging away for a decade, 200 kilometres north of the Arctic Circle. Behind Igloo Church, at the corner of Gwich'in Road and Breynat Street, is the Inuvik Community Greenhouse, the northernmost commercial hothouse on the continent. Since November 1998, the former hockey arena has been home to a variety of crops and flowers over two areas: a 12,000-square-foot community garden, where residents and local groups can tend to their own; and a 4,000-square-foot commercial greenhouse that pays for itself. Despite a relatively short season—mid-May to late September—eight weeks of nonstop sun intensifies the growth. Now residents of Inuvik, whose mean temperature is minus 9.7°C, have access to fresh local produce for as many months of the year as most of the rest of Canada.

DEMAND FOR BRYAN GILVESY'S beef is growing steadily. This year, he will process between forty and fifty animals; last year, he added fourteen heifers to his breeding herd; the year before, nine. He knows his market has room to expand, and he's comfortable raising his prices. "We find our customers are motivated by a lack of trust in the mainstream food distribution system," he explains. "They need to trust the quality of the food and the cleanliness of it [that it is hormone and antibiotic free], and they love to see that we care for the environment." Hundreds of visitors have toured his farm to see how his operation works; other growers in the area are increasingly interested in farming more sustainably.

Slowly, slowly, things are starting to change. But the necessarily massive systemic overhaul is still far from a reality. "For every solution we're trying, we have to battle against all sorts of regulations and impediments," says Barbolet. "But if a transnational wants to bring in a genetically modified product, it gets subsidies. It's ass backwards." Nothing he and others envision will take fewer than twenty or thirty years, at best, to put in place. However, he says, "there's no other choice."

CONTRIBUTOR BIOGRAPHIES

KATHERINE ASHENBURG began her work life as an academic specializing in Dickens. Later she became a CBC Radio producer, an editor at the *Globe and Mail*, and a freelance writer. Her work has appeared in the *New York Times*, *Toronto Life*, the *American Scholar*, among other publications. She is the author of three books, *Going to Town: Architectural Walking Tours in Southern Ontario*, *The Mourner's Dance: What We Do When People Die*, and *The Dirt on Clean: An Unsanitized History*. The last was chosen as one of 25 Books to Remember by the New York Public Library and one of the year's best history books by the *Independent* newspaper in Britain.

IRA BASEN joined CBC Radio in 1984 and was senior producer at *Sunday Morning* and *Quirks and Quarks*. He was involved in the creation of three network programs *The Inside Track* (1985), *This Morning* (1997), and *Workology* (2001), as well as several special series, including *Spin Cycles* (2007) and *News 2.0* (2009). He has also written for *Saturday Night*, *The Walrus*, *Maisonneuve*, and the *Canadian Journal of Communication*. He is a media columnist at cbc.ca, and a contributing editor at J-Source.ca. Ira currently teaches at Ryerson University and the DeGroote School of Business at McMaster University.

WILL BRAUN served as co-editor of *Geez* magazine from its inception in 2005 until 2009. He now devotes his time to parenting, writing, growing vegetables, and advocacy related to impacts of hydroelectric dams in northern Manitoba. Braun lives in Winnipeg with his wife and two young children.

TYEE BRIDGE is a writer and essayist in Vancouver, BC. He's

currently working on a nonfiction book about the end of the world. For excerpts and updates, visit him at tyeebridge.com.

ABOU FARMAN is a writer and artist. His writing has appeared in academic journals, magazines, and newspapers including *Maisonneuve*, *Canadian Ethnic Studies*, *History and Anthropology*, Transition, the *Globe and Mail*, *Books in Canada*, the *Believer*, *The Huffington Post*, *Bidoun*, and *The Utne Review*. He has been nominated for two National Magazine Awards and has twice won the Critics Desk Award from *Arc*. As part of the duo caraballo-farman, he has exhibited installation and video art at the Tate Modern, UK, and PS1/MOMA, NY, amongst others, and has been the recipient of several grants including a Canada Council grant in Media Arts and a 2010 Guggenheim Fellowship.

PAUL GALLANT is a freelance writer/editor who has lived on both coasts of Canada but now calls Toronto home. He has been lead editor of Vancouver's (defunct) *loop* magazine, *Xtra!* Biweekly, and *fab* magazine in Toronto. He writes a regular theatre column for *Eye Weekly*, covers urban innovation for Yonge Street Media, and has written for *Chatelaine*, CBC.ca, *Spacing*, *Maisonneuve*, *This* magazine, *Out* magazine, and the *Toronto Star*, among other publications.

LISA GREGOIRE is a five-foot-two hockey player, Radiohead fan, Air Force brat, Luddite, mother of twins, and teller of stories. Her Nunavut romance bloomed in the early 1990s during a three-year reporting stint at Nunatsiaq News in Iqaluit, the best job she ever had. After a decade with daily newspapers, she quit to pursue a life of righteous poverty as a freelancer. Based in Ottawa, she contributes to local and national magazines including *Canadian Geographic*, the *Walrus*, and *Ottawa Magazine*.

DANIELLE GROEN is a writer and editor in Toronto. Her work has appeared in the *Globe and Mail*, the *Walrus*, *Chatelaine*, and *Toronto Life*, among other publications. She was named Best New Magazine Writer at the 2009 National Magazine Awards for her article "This is Your Brain on Love."

ELIZABETH HAY has written seven books. Her most recent, the novel *Late Nights on Air*, won the Giller Prize. She lives in Ottawa.

JASON MCBRIDE is a freelance writer and editor based in Toronto. He's a regular contributor to *Toronto Life*, the *Globe and Mail*, the *Believer* and other publications.

CAROLYN MORRIS is a freelance journalist based in Toronto. A recent graduate from the Master of Journalism program at Ryerson University, she has written feature articles for *Toronto Life*, *This* magazine, and the *Ryerson Review of Journalism*. She learned Spanish after quitting university to travel and teach English in Latin America at nineteen years old. She has lived in Guatemala, El Salvador, and Mexico. While working on an article about people in Canada without health insurance, she met many non-status immigrants who had originally come to the country as temporary workers, refugee claimants, or visitors.

KATHARINE SANDIFORD is the Yukon-based associate editor of *Up Here* magazine, a pan-territorial culture and travel magazine that won Magazine of the Year at the 2010 National Magazine Awards. Raised in downtown Ottawa, she now lives in a rustic log cabin on the shores of Marsh Lake, seventy kilometres south of Whitehorse, Yukon, where sailing, skijoring (skiing while getting pulled by dogs), and berry-picking occupy her when she's not writing.

ANDREW STEINMETZ has been the fiction editor of Esplanade Books/Véhicule Press since 2002. Steinmetz's last novel, *Eva's Threepenny Theatre* (Gaspereau Press), was a finalist for the 2009 Rogers Writers' Trust Fiction Prize.

TIMOTHY TAYLOR is an award-winning writer, and the author of the novel *Stanley Park* (2001) as well as *Silent Cruise* (short fiction) and a second novel, *Story House*. His nonfiction work has been widely published and recognized, and he is a contributing editor for *enRoute* magazine and *Vancouver* magazine, as well as the Big Ideas columnist for *Report on Business* magazine.

CHRIS TURNER is the author of the 2007 bestseller *The Geography of Hope: A Tour of the World We Need*, a finalist for the Governor General's Award for Nonfiction. He is also the author of *Planet Simpson: How a Cartoon Masterpiece Documented an Era and Defined a Generation*. His reporting on energy, sustainability, and culture appears regularly in the *Walrus*, the *Globe and Mail*, *Canadian Geographic*, and many other publications. He lives in Calgary, where he is at work on a new book about the global sustainability movement, to be published by Random House in 2011.

NORA UNDERWOOD is an award-winning Toronto writer and editor. Her articles have appeared in publications such as the *Walrus*, *Maclean's*, *Elm Street*, the *Globe and Mail*, and the *Report on Business* magazine, among others.

PERMISSION ACKNOWLEDGEMENTS

(February 2009) © 2009 by Danielle Groen. Used with permission of the author.

"Last Poems," originally appeared in *New Quarterly* (Spring 2009) © 2009 by Elizabeth Hay. Used with permission of the author.

"Preparation for the End of the World," originally appeared in *Toronto Life* (September 2009) © 2009 by Jason McBride. Used with permission of the author.

"The Illegals," originally appeared in *Toronto Life* (November 2009) © 2009 by Carolyn Morris. Used with permission of the author.

"The Wild Quest," originally appeared in *Up Here* (Oct/Nov 2009) © 2009 by Katharine Sandiford. Used with permission of the author.

"The Brothers Kramm," originally appeared in *Queen's Quarterly* (Winter 2009) by Andrew Steinmetz. Used with permission of the author.

"Walking the Way," originally appeared in *Walrus* magazine (December 2009) by Timothy Taylor. Used with permission of the author.

"The Prodigal Band," originally appeared in *Alberta Views* (December 2009) © 2009 by Chris Turner. Used with permission of the author.

"The Future Has Begun," originally appeared in *Walrus* magazine (January/February 2009) by Nora Underwood. Used with permission of the author.

EDITOR BIOGRAPHIES

ALEX BOYD writes poems, fiction, reviews, and essays, and has had work published in magazines and newspapers such as *Taddle Creek, Books in Canada,* the *Globe and Mail, Quill & Quire, The Antigonish Review,* and websites such as *Nthposition.* He booked and hosted the I.V. Lounge Reading Series in Toronto for five years and edits the online journal *Northern Poetry Review.* His personal site is alexboyd.com, and his award-winning first book of poems *Making Bones Walk* was published in 2007. Previous to this collection of essays, he co-edited *The Best Canadian Essays 2009.*

KAMAL AL-SOLAYLEE is an assistant professor at Ryerson University's School of Journalism and a former theatre critic for the *Globe and Mail.* He holds a PhD in Victorian Literature from Nottingham University, England, and has taught in the theatre programs of both Waterloo and York universities. His byline has appeared in the *National Post, Report on Business* magazine, *Elle Canada, Canadian Notes and Queries,* and *Eye Weekly.* He's currently editing an anthology of plays from Toronto's Tarragon Theatre for Playwrights Canada Press and writing *Intolerable: A Memoir of Extremes* for HarperCollins Canada.

Alex and Kamal would like to thank everyone at Tightrope Books for taking on this important series, as well as all the contributors for their inspiring work and graciousness in allowing us to republish it.

Made You Think!

www.TightropeBooks.com